SEMEIA 63

CHARACTERIZATION
IN BIBLICAL LITERATURE

Editors:
Elizabeth Struthers Malbon
Adele Berlin

©1993
by the Society of Biblical Literature

SEMEIA 63

Copyright © 1993 by the Society of Biblical Literature

All rights reserved. No part of this work may be reproduced or transmitted in any form or by any means, electronic or mechanical, including photocopying and recording, or by means of any information storage or retrieval system, except as may be expressly permitted by the 1976 Copyright Act or in writing from the publisher. Requests for permission should be addressed in writing to the Rights and Permissions Office, Society of Biblical Literature, 825 Houston Mill Road, Atlanta, GA 30329, USA.

ISSN 0095-571X
ISBN 1-58983-069-5

Printed in the United States of America
on acid-free paper

CONTENTS

Contributors to this Issue v

Preface
    Elizabeth Struthers Malbon
    Adele Berlin VII

I. NARRATORS/CHARACTERS/READERS

1. Characterization and Reader Construction of
   Characters in the Gospels
       Fred W. Burnett.. 1

2. Character in the Boundary: Bakhtin's Interdividuality
   in Biblical Narratives
       David McCracken... 29

3. Narrator as Character: Mapping a Reader-Oriented
   Approach to Narration in Luke-Acts
       John A. Darr 43

4. Signs of the Flesh: Observations on
   Characterization in the Bible
       Alice Bach 61

5. Cyborgs, Ciphers, and Sexuality: Re-Theorizing
   Literary and Biblical Character
       Laura E. Donaldson... 81

Response: Characterizing Character in Biblical Narrative
    Robert M. Fowler... 97

Response: In Our Image We Create Him, Male and Female
We Create Them: The E/Affect of Biblical Characterization
    Ilona N. Rashkow.. 105

II. THE UNNAMED AND THE UNNAMEABLE

6. Anonymity and Character in the Books of Samuel
       Adele Reinhartz 117

7. The Narrative Function of Anonymity in Fourth
   Gospel Characterization
       David R. Beck 143

8. The Character(ization) of God in 2 Samuel 7:1-17
   Kenneth M. Craig, Jr. 159

9. "God's Voice You Have Never Heard, God's Form You Have Never Seen": The Characterization of God in the Gospel of John
   Marianne Meye Thompson 177

   Response: Divine and Anonymous Characterization in Biblical Narrative
   Robert Polzin 205

   Response: Reading Readers Reading Characters
   Evelyn R. Thibeaux 215

CONTRIBUTORS TO THIS ISSUE

Alice Bach
    Department of Religious Studies
    Stanford University
    Stanford, CA 94305-2165

David R. Beck
    Graduate Program in Religion
    Duke University
    Durham, NC 27706

Adele Berlin
    Department of Hebrew and East
    Asian Languages and Literatures
    University of Maryland
    College Park, MD 20742-4831

Fred W. Burnett
    Department of Bible and Religion
    Anderson College
    Anderson, IN 46012-3462

Kenneth M. Craig, Jr.
    Department of Religion and
    Philosophy
    Chowan College
    Murfreesboro, NC 27855

John A. Darr
    Department of Theology
    Boston College
    Chestnut Hill, MA 02167-3806

Laura Donaldson
    Literature and Women's Studies
    Antioch College
    Yellow Springs, OH 45387

Robert M. Fowler
    Department of Religion
    Baldwin-Wallace College
    Berea, OH 44017

Elizabeth Struthers Malbon
    Department of Religion
    Virginia Polytechnic Institute
    and State University
    Blacksburg, VA 24061-0135

David McCracken
    Department of English
    University of Washington
    Seattle, WA 98195

Robert Polzin
    School of Comparative Literary
    Studies
    Carleton University
    Ottawa, Ontario
    Canada K1S 5B6

Ilona N. Rashkow
    Department of Comparative Studies
    State University of New York
    Stony Brook, NY 11794-3355

Adele Reinhartz
    Department of Religious Studies
    McMaster University
    Hamilton, Ontario
    Canada, L8S 4K1

Evelyn R. Thibeaux
    Theology Department
    Georgetown University
    Washington, DC 20057-0998

Marianne Meye Thompson
    School of Theology
    Fuller Theological Seminary
    Pasadena, CA 91182

Preface

Elizabeth Struthers Malbon
Adele Berlin

Frank Kermode has described character as a "source of opacity, of complex, various and never definitive interpretation" (*The Genesis of Secrecy* [Cambridge: Harvard University Press, 1979], 75). This volume does not intend to dispute Kermode's observation by offering a "definitive interpretation." The collection of essays seeks, rather, to exemplify the complex, various, and open-ended interpretation of character and characterization that has been a part of recent literary approaches to Hebrew Bible and New Testament narratives.

This volume grows out of sessions of the Biblical Criticism and Literary Criticism Section at the 1992 Society of Biblical Literature annual meeting. Five of the papers included here (Bach, Beck, Donaldson, McCracken, Reinhartz) were presented there; two sessions focusing on characterization were chaired by the editors of this volume. Two additional papers were presented to related groups at the same meeting: Kenneth Craig's paper to a session of the Reading, Rhetoric, and Hebrew Bible Section concerned with the characterization of God; John Darr's paper to the Literary Aspects of the Gospels and Acts Group. An earlier version of Fred Burnett's paper had been presented to the Literary Aspects Group some years before. Marianne Meye Thompson's paper was specifically written for the present volume. Conversations among the contributors and editors in and around the sessions at the 1992 meeting prepared the way for the conversations within this volume—now broadened to include four respondents and, we hope, to invite the readers in.

The Biblical Criticism and Literary Criticism Section presents both exegetical and theoretical papers and concerns itself with texts from both the Hebrew Bible and the New Testament, and these characteristics are reflected in this volume. While each of the nine papers includes an exegetical component (four from the Hebrew Bible, four from the New Testament, and one with reference to narratives from both), each paper also includes some theoretical discussion. In many of the essays this theoretical discussion is a substantial portion. The Hebrew Bible papers and the New Testament papers are intermixed to highlight common theoretical concerns.

We present the papers in two parts. In Part 1—Narrators/Characters/Readers—five papers (Burnett, McCracken, Darr, Bach, Donaldson) deal with issues of the varied interrelations of narrators, characters, and readers. Two respondents, Ilona Rashkow from Hebrew Bible studies and Robert Fowler from the New Testament area, address theoretical and exegetical issues raised by these five essays. The cumulative effect of essays and responses on our "implied reader" is likely to be a fuller appreciation of the complexity of these interrelations. Can characters be understood individually or only in relation to other characters? Is the narrator a character? Just another character? Or the most powerful character? How does the reader relate to the characters? To the narrator? Do/should readers follow the narrator's lead in interpreting and evaluating characters, or do/should readers resist such narratorial authority in favor of allowing the characters to develop in other ways?

In Part 2—The Unnamed and the Unnameable—four papers (Reinhartz, Beck, Craig, Thompson) discuss two extreme types of characters—anonymous characters and God—in two biblical books, Samuel and the Gospel of John. Two respondents, Robert Polzin from Hebrew Bible and Evelyn Thibeaux from New Testament, comment on aspects of the dialogue that is implicit within and among these juxtaposed essays. How are anonymous characters different from named characters? How is God as a character different from human characters? Do narrators and readers relate differently to anonymous characters? To God as a character? Can investigating these distinctive characters shed light on understanding all types of characters?

This volume, like the Bible itself, is a multi-voiced work. The authors engage with literary theorists, with biblical critics, with literary scholars of the Bible, and with one another. Of course, at the base of all the discussion is an engagement with the biblical text. The respondents provide yet another level—a meta-discussion—weaving together the theoretical underpinnings of the articles, agreeing or disagreeing with the authors, and offering their own readings. The whole is, in the end, not a definitive statement on characterization in the Bible, but an exciting exchange of ideas on where we have been, where we are now, and where we might go in our understanding of this important topic in the literary interpretation of the Bible.

Elizabeth Struthers Malbon
Adele Berlin
Editors

I
NARRATORS/CHARACTERS/ READERS

CHARACTERIZATION AND READER CONSTRUCTION OF CHARACTERS IN THE GOSPELS

Fred W. Burnett
Anderson College

ABSTRACT

A "character" is a construct developed during the reading process out of textual indicators such as proper names. A "character" is also an effect of the reading process. When the reading process is taken into account, it is clear that characterization should be considered as a continuum on which even secondary characters may achieve some degree of "individuality." On the one hand, as a construct of textual indicators and connotations from which readers infer traits, a character can be dissolved into the segments of the textual indicators from which it was constructed. On the other hand, as an effect of the reading process and as a paradigm of attributive propositions, a character may seem to "transcend" the text. In the canonical gospels it is helpful for the reader-critic to think in terms of "degrees of characterization," and to plot textual indicators on a continuum that moves perhaps from "agent" to "type" to "character." The difficulty in seeing a character's textuality will depend largely upon the degree of characterization it has achieved during the reading process. As an example, Peter in the Gospel of Matthew is a "type," but "he" achieves a higher degree of characterization than the disciples do as a group.

Recent work on narrative criticism of the Gospels has emphasized plot and story, but very little has been done with characterization. This is due mostly to the disarray of the theoretical discussion about characterization in current literary criticism. The need for studies of characterization in the Gospels, however, is an urgent one since other areas of inquiry, like christology, may depend partially upon the results (e.g. Keck).

This article will survey the issues that must be resolved before any serious study of characterization in the Gospels can be done. Three areas of debate are most pressing for Gospel critics: the debate in current literary criticism about characterization in fiction, the debate about the most appropriate genre with which to compare the Gospels, and the debate about characterization in both classical and Graeco-Roman literature. It will be argued that any theory of characterization for the Gospels must consider both the textual indicators and the reading process. When the latter is taken into account, it becomes clear that characterization must be considered as a continuum on which even secondary characters may momentarily achieve "individuality." Although this article is primarily a survey of the theoretical issues and of their bearing on characterization in the Gospels, its thesis will be applied summarily to the character of Peter in the Gospel of Matthew.

The Literary-Critical Discussion

The current debate about characterization centers around the question of whether characters in *any* text are persons or words. Are characters individuals or personalities, in any sense of these words, that can transcend the text in which they exist, or, are characters only functions of the text and its plot (Rimmon-Kenan: 31-32)? For example, Robert Scholes warns critics that "the greatest mistake we can make in dealing with characters in fiction is to insist on their 'reality'. *No character in a book is a real person.* Not even if he is in a history book and is called Ulysses S. Grant" (17, emphasis added). Scholes's position represents basically what Marvin Mudrick calls the "purist" argument, as contrasted with the "realist" position.

The "realists" argue that characters do acquire an independence from the plots in which they occur, and that characters can be discussed apart from their literary contexts. Mudrick himself chooses the purist position, but he adds a caveat:

> ... today [in contrast to the nineteenth-century] we know that fictional or dramatic characters are only more or less efficient patterns of words subordinate to larger patterns; but it remains a fact that legends can gather round Hamlet as they gather round historical figures ... (213).

Mudrick contends, then, that both approaches have their problems. The purist critics have trouble reducing characters to plot functionaries in Chaucer, Shakespeare, and other great character writers, but the realists have trouble talking about characters as real persons with most dramatists and writers of allegory (211). Norman Holland states what the impasse has become for critics: "The old critics say we must think of dramatic characters as real people; the new critics say we must not. Logically, we cannot have it both ways, and logic comes down squarely against treating the characters as real" (266). The question for Holland is whether logic or experience is to govern the critic. He points out, for example, that psychoanalytic critics do in fact treat characters as though they are real people. Thus it *can* be done, but *should* it be done (267-71)?

Several critics, however, have decided that they can treat characters as both people and words. Seymour Chatman, for example, questions the Aristotelian primacy of plot over character for every narrative. He argues for an "open structuralist theory" of character as the only viable theory, that is, a theory that would "treat characters as autonomous beings, not as mere plot functions" (1980:119, cf. 117-19, 132). Chatman, then, steers a middle course between those who argue that the critical focus should be on the medium (the words or the plot) and those who argue that it should be on the characters. He contends that both critical acts can be justified; they simply have different focuses. "Both character and event," Chatman says, "are logically necessary to narrative; where chief interest falls is a matter of the changing tastes of authors and their publics" (1980:113, cf. 136-37).

If character and action are interdependent, then subordination of one to the other depends on the type of narrative and the focus of the reader-critic. Because of the critic's focus, the hierarchy of plot/character is fluid and reversible. Shlomith Rimmon-Kenan's conclusion is applicable here:

> The reversibility of hierarchies is characteristic not only of ordinary reading but also of literary criticism and theory. Hence it is legitimate to subordinate character to action when we study action but equally legitimate to subordinate action to character when the latter is the focus of our study (36).

A major implication of the "reversibility of hierarchies" is that "character" is a construct that is developed during the reading process. "Character," that is, is an *effect* of reading (Todorov: 77).

The reading process seems to be a process of naming connotations that are evoked in various ways by the text. As Roland Barthes contends: "the seme (or the signified connotation, strictly speaking) is a connotator of persons, places, objects, of which the signified is a *character*. Character is an adjective, an attribute, a predicate (for example: *unnatural, shadowy, star, composite, excessive, impious*, etc.)" (190; see also Garvey: 63; Chatman 1980: 125). A character, then, is constructed by the reader from indicators that are distributed along the textual continuum. Traits are inferred by the reader from the indicators. The indicators themselves—discourse information (such as the narrator's statements, statements of other characters, setting, and so forth) and the speech and action of the character—are what is meant by "characterization" (cf. Rimmon-Kenan: 59; Berlin: 33-42).

To say that "character" is a construct that is developed during the reading process means, on the one hand, that character can be reduced to textuality. It can be dissolved into the segments of a closed text and/or the motifs from which it was constructed. The process of construction, in other words, can be reversed (Weinsheimer: 195). On the other hand, character as an *effect* of the reading process can "transcend" the text. "Character" as a paradigm of attributive propositions can give the illusion of individuality or even personality to the reader. Whether or not transcendence of the text occurs will depend both on the indicators that the text provides and the reading conventions that the reader assumes for the narrative in question.

It is difficult to know what reading conventions are presupposed by the Gospels. The "death of character" in modern fiction, which is usually dated from D. H. Lawrence (McCarthy: 173; Macauley and Lanning: 61; Mudrick: 212), cannot be assumed as a reading convention for any literature before the nineteenth century. The death of character is usually attributed to the dissolution of the view of the stable Self, but this, of course, cannot be taken as a reading convention of the Gospels (cf. Macauley and Lanning: 94-98). As Rimmon-Kenan poignantly asks: "even if we grant the 'death' of character in contemporary literature, can we also retrospectively 'kill' him in nineteenth-century fiction?" (31). Chatman's caution, though in another context, is also to the point: "It would be a fundamental misconception to assume that there is only a difference of degree and not of kind between the simplest narrative—the folk tale or fairy tale—and modern fiction" (1972:78). In sum, theories of characterization that are drawn from modern narrative poetics can be applied to biblical texts only when the horizon of expectations for what constitutes a character in a particular biblical text has been clarified (cf. Culpepper: 105).

Characterization in Classical Literature

With regard to most literature even remotely related to the time of the Gospels, it is argued generally that characters were types rather than individuals in any sense, and that they seldom diverged from traits that were initially given to them in the narrative. The main difference between ancient biographical literature (that is, literature roughly before the rise of the novel in the eighteenth century) and modern biographical literature is that in the former characterization and reading conventions understood the character to be typical, static, and immutable, while in the latter character is individual, open to change, and developing (Gill: 471; Macauley and Lanning: 61; Mudrick: 211). There is little doubt that in classical writers characters were presented as types, that is, either as an ideal representation or as an example of the characteristics of a species or group (Korfmacher: 85). The implications for reading a text with this understanding of characterization are stated clearly by Scholes and Kellogg:

> In every case, whenever we consider a character as a type, we are moving away from considering him as an individual character and moving toward considering him as part of some larger framework. This framework may be moral, theological, referable to some extra-literary scheme; or it may be referable to part of the narrative situation itself (204).

Although this view of characterization has been extremely influential in biblical studies, especially in Gospel criticism, several issues need to be raised.

First, in studying characters in biblical literature scholars have almost been forced to use understandings of characterization from the classical world. It has been pointed out many times that there is no comparable presentation in any Jewish literature to that of Jesus in the Gospels. The Talmud and midrashim have some biographical fragments about rabbis, but these are within the framework of haggadic stories from the tannaitic and amoraic ages. The stories show little interest in a connected, biographical narrative in which the sayings of the rabbis are to be understood (Vermes: 20; Neusner: 47). The Qumran community produced nothing biographical about the Teacher of Righteousness or any other members of the community. In apocryphal and pseudepigraphal literature there is little biographical writing, and what does exist only has the aim of contemporization of the material. Biography or autobiography in Jewish literature is attested only in Greek. In Philo's *Life of Moses* the interest is in allegorical teaching about virtues, and in Josephus' *Vita* there is little to compare with the interests of the Evangelists. Even in the Hebrew Bible only the stories about David are related at any length, and it is questionable whether or not they are biographical in any sense (Stanton: 126-31; Vermes: 20; cf. Koch: 202-205). This is not to deny that the Hebrew Bible has highly complex narratives, but only to say that the concern does not seem to be primarily with the individual character. It is usually argued, for example, that the patriarchal stories seem to deal with eponymous heroes even if the historicity of the individual patriarchs is affirmed (see McKane: 12, 16; Redford: 66-67; Fokkelman). Any *literary* individuality is usually suppressed by the interpreter on the assumption that real, historical readers would not have individuality in any sense as part of their reconstructive repertoire. Meir Sternberg has rightly questioned this assumption, and much work remains to be done in this regard with narratives in the Hebrew Bible and in Jewish-hellenistic narratives (253-55 passim).

Almost by default, then, biblical scholars have been forced to turn to the classical world for their understanding of characterization (cf. Stanton: 135). At first thought, it seems more plausible for Gospel critics to have studied characterization in hellenistic narratives rather than in classical literature. However, there are several reasons why characterization in classical literature became important for Gospel critics. First, postclassical writings like the Gospels and the hellenistic novel have not been considered "true" literature by literary critics (Hägg: 3-4). Second, there was a revival in the Roman Imperial Period of classicism and Atticism.

Hellenistic writers tried to follow Aristotle and his rules for characterization (Hägg: 114). Third, although the Greek novel originated in the hellenistic period (Hägg: xi), it is not unusual for these writers also to follow Aristotle's understanding of both plot and characterization. If Graham Anderson is right, the temporal gap, though it is wide between hellenistic and classical writers, may be inconsequential for studying plot and character in hellenistic novels, particularly since they were (1) retellings of ancient plots in new contexts and (2) attempts to follow Aristotle (19, 27, 88, 217). In this respect George A. Kennedy shows both the necessity of using classical rhetoric to interpret the Gospels and its relevance in the New Testament period generally, even for "*Kleinliteratur*" like the Gospels (1-33). As Kennedy says, "Classical rhetoric was one of the constraints under which New Testament writers worked" (160). Finally, once form-critics had accepted the conclusions given above, and had taken the Homeric model as the one for understanding the oral development behind biblical literature, the emphasis on the conventional and the typical in biblical characterization, rather than on the individual and the personal, became the dominant view. It was then supported by appeals to typical characterization in classical literature (see Eissfeldt: 3-4; Kümmel: 82-83, 306; Talbert: 1-23; Shuler: 1-23). It is also necessary to turn to the Greeks by default because they were the only ones who structured a system of rhetoric and poetics that is extant. As Kennedy says: "In understanding how their [Jewish or Greek] rhetoric worked we have little choice but to employ the concepts and terms of the Greeks" (10). In spite of the lack of extant rhetorical handbooks, it is now being recognized that the Jewish world had its distinctive rhetorical practices (Katz), though much work remains to be done in identifying Jewish rhetorical practices. This is not to deny that the study of characterization in classical literature can be justified historically and philosophically (Stanton: 118-19; Vermes: 148 n. 28). There are, however, problems with the use of this material, and this brings us to the second point about using typical characterization from classical literature as the norm for understanding characterization in the Gospels.

Classical scholarship has usually made its understanding of types genre-specific. Korfmacher, for example, concludes his study of classical type-characterization with this remark:

> The considerations here advanced will perhaps suffice to indicate that in comedy, tragedy, and epic at least the fixed type characters of rhetorical theory were subjected to modifications in accord with the *genre* in which they chanced to appear (85).

The problem, of course, is that the Gospels, while they are closer to literary forms from the hellenistic world than to anything from Judaism, do not fit precisely any extant genre. If the aims of characterization were different for each genre, then using characterization from one genre (e.g. the encomium) or from several different genres could be misleading when applied to the Gospels. If the aims of biography and history, for example, were carefully separated (Stanton: 123), then even though the personages portrayed may be types, the emphases that the reader should infer from the *same* type could be quite different for each genre (cf. Osley: 20). The debate continues, of course, not only about the genre of each Gospel but also about what constitutes a genre at all, and about just how important knowledge of a genre is to interpretation.[1] Perhaps the study of characterization in the Gospels should be less genre-specific (cf. Stanton: 118-19). In any case, one should proceed with caution before concluding that characterization in any Gospel is like characterization in the so-called "classical or hellenistic world."

Biblical studies has inherited its emphasis upon the typical and the representative from the form-critics who, in turn, took over the emphasis on the typical from classicists. The typical and the conventional were enhanced in the study of biblical characterization by the repression of the individual and the personal. The latter emphases in the Gospels were seen as later and legendary (see n. 10 below; Koch: 11-16; Knierim; Muilenburg). For reading the Gospels this has meant that the Evangelists had little interest in the past of Jesus or any other Gospel personage. Günther Bornkamm, for example, is correct when he says that the Evangelists in relating history were proclaiming "who he is, not who he was. . . . what belongs to the past in the history of Jesus should always be investigated and understood in relation to its significance for the present time today and the coming time of God's future" (17). It does seem to be the case that "the early Church did not allow the life of Jesus to become a thing of the past" (Marxsen: 127-28), but does it follow that the Evangelists had little interest in the *human* character, or even in the "personality" of Jesus? The conclusion that they did not have such interests has been tied to the twin assertions that the Gospels are not biographies in any sense and are to be classified with "folk literature" (*Kleinliteratur*). Probably the statement that is quoted most often in this regard is Bultmann's:

> There is no historical-biographical interest in the Gospels, and that is why they have nothing to say about Jesus' human personality, his appearance and character, his origin, education and development; quite apart from the fact

---

[1] For a review of the debate see Guelich, who concludes: "Thus one looks in vain to the Graeco-roman as to the Jewish literary world for a comparable literary analogy to the Gospels" (194). In terms of genre and interpretation, Stuart Miller has stated the problem that confronts any literary critic: "Genres, as everyone knows, do not really exist. Croce has rightly told us that each work of art is individual. Yet genre terms are inescapable if one is to talk about literature . . . " (3).

that they do not command the cultivated techniques of composition necessary for grand literature, nor let the personalities of their author appear (372; cf. Conzelmann: 15-16).

These conclusions have recently been questioned (e.g. Shuler; Stanton; Talbert), but the emphasis on reading personages in the Gospels as types persists, probably because of the influence of both form criticism and arguments based upon characterization in classical literature.

A third point that must be made about using characterization in classical literature to study the Gospels, however, is made by some classicists themselves. They have argued that it is an oversimplification and a distortion to assert that the main difference between ancient and modern characterization is that the former portrays the character as static and unidimensional (see Pelling). Christopher Gill, for example, points out that although this is one difference between ancient and modern techniques of characterization, this conclusion "exaggerates the degree of difference in this respect" (471). Gill contends that a more accurate way of stating the difference is "that between a character-centered and a personality-centered form of biography" (471).

Gill's concern is to show that ancient historiography and biography, though it does not highlight personality, does allow for and portray character development. In this respect historiographers and biographers within both Greek and Roman philosophical schools recognized that a number of factors working in combination influenced the development and change of an adult character. Gill, then, rejects the dichotomy between "nature" (*physis*) and "character" (*ēthos*). He claims that ancient historiographers, no less than philosophers, saw one's nature (*physis*) as *one* factor among many—upbringing, habitual training, education—in character-formation. What this means, of course, is that one's innate qualities (*physis*) do not necessarily determine the ethical character (*ēthos*) that one eventually develops (470-71).

Several other factors enter the discussion at this point. First, there is little extant evidence of any genre that could be called "biographical" apart from Plutarch's *Lives*. Much of the discussion about characterization, therefore, has concentrated on Plutarch. Gill concludes that Plutarch does allow for development of character (473-480),[2] and it does seem to be an

---

[2] Contrast D. A. Russell who argues that although Plutarch does admit the possibility of change in one's *ēthos*, he seems not to allow for change in one's *physis*. This means, of course, that Plutarch's conception of characterization is probably the progressive revelation of innate qualities. Russell, however, rightly leaves the question open. It is unclear whether or not Plutarch envisioned a change in one's *physis*, or at least in the degeneration of it, and Russell acknowledges that in Plutarch *ēthos* and *physis* are often blurred together (139-54, esp. 147 and n. 2). This semantic ambiguity is precisely one of the points upon which Gill seizes.

overstatement to say that change and development of character were unknown in ancient historiography and biography (cf. Stanton: 121). Does this mean, though, that development of character, without the presentation of a character's inward life or "personality," is primarily a plot formulation rather than a character formulation (cf. Scholes and Kellogg: 168-69)? It does seem clear that the modern understanding that a character is to be understood *primarily* through his or her psychological development is not part of ancient characterization (Dihle, 1956: 81; 1983). However, does it also follow that ancient historiographers had no interest in the character as an *individual* since little of the character's inward life is presented? This remains an open question.

Second, for ancient characterization in general it certainly seems that one's character (*ēthos*) is revealed through one's action (*praxis*; Russell: 144; Stanton: 122; cf. Koester: 253; Robbins: 114). This indirect method of characterization seems to be the main method of the ancient world, and the Gospels are certainly not an exception (Stanton: 167). The key question is: if the reader is to infer traits about a character from that personage's words and actions, do the reading conventions of the particular text under scrutiny allow the reader any room to construct the character's individuality? There are several things that lead to an affirmative answer.

First, it does seem that there was an interest in the individual in the ancient world. It is true that the evidence for interest in the individual is primarily non-literary, but is there any relation between the two, that is, does the developing interest in non-literary portraiture reflect a larger cultural code for the understanding of character in other media? G. Misener, for example, argues that individual portraiture of historical persons was attempted by Ion of Chios in the fifth century BCE. At the same time, fifth-century drama masks began to move from the typical to the individual, showing an interest in facial expressions. Under Euripides' influence the masks became more realistic about the way the character *as an individual* was perceived by the audience. Misener believes that the portraitures and the drama masks of the fifth century reflect a change from the typical to individuality.

Misener also relates her discussion to the plastic arts and concludes: "A similar change from the typical and ideal to the individual begins to appear in plastic art toward the end of this period" (105). Misener extends her discussion to the Peripatetics, who practiced portraiture of legendary heroes, and to Plutarch, whom she considers the best extant representative of Peripatetic biography. She concludes that for Plutarch both physical appearance and acts disclose one's inner character (108 n. 4; cf. Evans). If the move from the typical towards the individual in non-literary portraiture did assume a larger cultural code, and semiotic study would seem to support such a suggestion (e.g. Silverman), this would have far-reaching ramifications for the study of ancient characterization, especially since many of the accepted conclusions have been based upon Plutarch's *Lives*.

What Misener has argued for the Greeks, Hanfmann has argued for the Romans. Roman portraiture was mostly typical, that is, it represented the virtues of a group, through the third and second centuries BCE. Individuation proceeded slowly until "interest in individual personality clearly becomes a paramount concern in the time of the late Republic (100-30 B. C.)." It is important to note that Hanfmann attributes some of this development to the influence of hellenistic portraiture (454-55). Thus the developments in Roman and in Greek portraiture are not isolated and idiosyncratic ones, and they seem to suggest a larger cultural code at work.[3]

A. S. Osley has traced what is known of Greek biography before Plutarch. Although he does not argue for a development from the typical to the individual, Osley does note that the Alexandrian librarians had enough data to compose biographical notes on authors for cataloguing books, that in Greek oratory very personal attacks were made on the private lives of opponents, and that funeral encomia seemed to be personal and individualistic. He also contends that at least two of Aristotle's pupils, Aristoxenus and Phaenias, made personality a prominent part of their biographies. He is concerned with *how* biographies were written, but he concludes:

> With the break-up of Greek political life a unified conception of history was lost; interest was stirred no longer by the underlying meaning of contemporary events, but by the biographies of personalities (16-17).

A second reason for arguing that reading conventions at the time of the Gospels' production may have allowed for readerly construction of a character's individuality concerns Greek tragedy. Greek tragedy has played an important role in the discussion of ancient characterization, especially as it relates to the Gospels (cf. Bilezikan). It is usually argued that tragic characters were for the most part typical and undeveloping. No less of an authority than H. D. F. Kitto can say that "Greek tragedy never interested itself . . . in the development of character" (24). That much seems clear. What does not seem so clear is: does Greek tragedy exclude all interest in the character as an individual?

---

[3] Hanfmann, though, interprets the Greek view of personality as still essentially a typical one. He thus has to deal with the problem of how the influence of the typical portraits could arise at all, not to mention have influence, "in an age which unmistakably indicates the rise of individualism" (456). Perhaps Misener's discussion of the rise of individualism in hellenistic portraiture supplies the key to Hanfmann's dilemma.

Kitto himself apparently does not believe this to be the case. He points out that the structure of the Greek theater itself was a limiting factor on characterization:

> The Greek theatre, normally confined by its Chorus to one time and place, could not trace change or growth in character; what it could do was to reveal more and more of the depths of a character *already existing* (169, emphasis added).

This tells one how tragedy presented character, but it does not tell how the audience "read" the character presented in any particular tragedy. Was the character in a particular tragedy to be read in light of prior tragedies about the same character so that the audience could perceive development or regression in the character? Or, if a character was being presented for the first time, would audience expectations include an intertextual expectation for subsequent tragedies about the same character? Kitto does not raise these questions, but he does imply answers to them.

Kitto points out that the confines of time and space on characterization were accidental, not fundamental, in Greek tragedy. That is, it was physically very difficult to move the Chorus around the stage (169 n. 1). Kitto also acknowledges that in some tragedies the situation and plot were subservient to character, for example, in Sophocles' *Electra* (71-72, 337). Most importantly, Kitto confirms the point Misener makes about the individuation of tragic masks in Euripidean tragedies. In Euripides' later plays, especially in the stories about Electra and Orestes, Kitto sees characters "who are regarded purely as individuals, not in any degree as types, or tragic and exemplary embodiments of some universal passion" (258).

From modern views of characterization, which are interested in psychological description and change, indirect characterization in tragedy or in ancient biography and historiography appears to be simplistic. It appears to be minimal characterization, and thus it is easy to argue from a modern point of view that characters were only types and symbols. How audiences and readers inferred characters from the words, deeds, and relationships, and by what larger codes, however, still seems to be an open question. The discussions of the interest in the individual in portraiture and in tragedy, and the limited number of extant sources for both tragedies and biographical writing, should make Gospel critics reconsider the possibility from a narrative-critical viewpoint that ancient audiences and readers constructed much fuller characters than is usually thought.

It is, for example, very difficult to transfer characters from one tragedy to another. Creon appears in Sophocles' *Antigone, Oedipus Tyrannus,* and *Oedipus at Colonus*. It seems impossible to imagine the docile and passive Creon of the *Antigone* as the same Creon who is active and tyrannical in

Oedipus Tyrannus or the brazen liar in *Oedipus at Colonus*. There appears to us to be no consistent conception of Creon's character. However, does this mean that Creon must be confined to each particular play and that a "common critical error is the tendency to take these plays as some kind of trilogy" (Beye: 269, cf. 270-71)? The lack of other sources about Creon, and the modern distaste for minimal and indirect characterization, may cause one to read these characters solely as types when for ancient audiences oral traditions, discussions at home and at work about Creon, and so forth, may have contributed to Creon's change of character between plays (cf. Griffin).

Concerning the lack of sources (and the lack of knowledge of the larger codes), it is usually argued that both legendary and historical characters in tragedy had been "fixed" long before tragic poetry began. The poets had to deal with the fact that heroic personages were fixed and perhaps stereotyped in the audience's mind. At the same time, the evidence indicates that "if the persons of the heroic world are fixed, they are fluid as well, and their stories, in variants, can vary them" (Lattimore: 58-59; cf. Brereton: 26). Thus there can be several Creons or Helens who may appear conflicting to us, but to an ancient audience they may be read as a change in the character of the individual.[4]

The indirect, minimal method of characterization seems to be the problem for modern critics in allowing for individuality in ancient characterization. Beye recognizes the problem and leans towards interpreting the characters solely as types. He has to acknowledge, however, that it could also be argued that "neither playwright nor audience needed extensive characterization, that the actions were natural and complex individual extensions of fully realized characters that peopled the minds of every member of the culture" (269).[5] Thus, what appears to modern

---

[4] P. E. Easterling takes issue with the dictum of G. H. Gellie about characters in Greek tragedies, namely, "These people are different only because their stories are different" (209, quoted in Easterling, 1983:141). Easterling argues that the impression of individuality for even minor characters who function as types in Sophocles' plays comes not only from the rhetoric of the situation and characterization by style but also from the image that Sophocles had about his characters, from pre-existing mythological identities for even minor characters, and from audience-reader imagination at work, particularly at ambiguous points, or what reader-response critics call "gaps," in the narrative (Easterling, 1983:138-45; 1990:88-89).

[5] This view, of course, contrasts with the usual interpretation of Aristotle that subordinates character to plot in tragedy and contends that names only indicate types (*Poetics* §9). For critiques of Aristotle's view of tragedy and its value for interpreting tragedy, see Bilezikan and the literature cited there. D. D. Raphael concludes his study of tragedy with a typical critique of Aristotle: "I have delayed too long over Aristotle, longer than his theory of tragedy deserves. Little did he dream, poor man, that his scrappy remarks would be taken so seriously by later dramatists and critics. His fate at their hands is indeed unmerited, a fit object for our pity" (23 cf. 16-24).

critics as a minimum of characterization may have been read in maximal terms by contemporary auditors and readers. Stanton capitalizes on this uncertainty for his discussion of Jesus in the Gospels:

> If the gospel traditions did intend to sketch out the character of Jesus of Nazareth, to show what sort of person he was, how would this have been accomplished? . . . the techniques of modern biographical writing were not those of the ancient world, where simple accounts of the actions, words and relationships of the subject were considered to provide at least as satisfactory a portrait as any character analysis or comment by the author. Hence there is no need to conclude that an investigation of the gospel traditions which finds somewhat similar "unsophisticated" methods in them, and which emphasizes the degree to which they reflect the character of Jesus is based on presuppositions drawn from the modern world with its intense interest in personality and biography. The gospel traditions employ techniques of character portrayal which seem almost naive to the modern reader and which can be and have been overlooked by scholarly eyes. A very simple and brief account of a person's relationships with others can reveal a good deal about the person concerned; the synoptic traditions need not be eliminated on account of their brevity. As long as such accounts referring to the same person cohere with one another, a few words can reveal a good deal about the character of the person concerned (167-68).

I have not discussed the Jewish traditions because they have usually been ignored in any comparison with the presentation of Jesus in the Gospels. Robert Alter, however, has raised the same question for Jewish literature. He asks: "In short, all the indicators of nuanced individuality to which the Western literary tradition has accustomed us . . . would appear to be absent from the Bible. In what way, then, is one to explain how, from these laconic texts, figures like Rebekah . . . emerge [as] characters who, *beyond any archetypal role they may play as bearers of a divine mandate*, have been etched as indelibly vivid individuals in the imagination of a hundred generations?" (114, emphasis added; cf. Sternberg, chs. 9-10). Form-critics have minimized legendary material in the Gospels, and its role in characterization now needs to be explored, particularly in relation to haggadic materials.

To return to the question with which this discussion began, it does seem plausible that reading conventions that demanded that the reader infer character indirectly from words, deeds, and relationships could allow even for the typical character to fluctuate between type and individuality. If so, then it would seem wise to understand characterization, for any biblical text at least, on a continuum. This would imply for narratives like the Gospels that the focus should be on the *degree* of characterization rather than on characterization as primarily typical. Adele Berlin's suggestion is very helpful in this respect:

> One might think of them [degrees of characters] as points on a continuum: 1) the agent, about whom nothing is known except what is necessary for the plot; the agent is a function of the plot or part of the setting; 2) the type, who has a limited and stereotyped range of traits, and who represents the class of people with these traits; 3) the character, who has a broader range of traits (not all belonging to the same class of people), and about whom we know more than is necessary for the plot (32).

Sternberg has argued a similar case for characterization in biblical narrative (253-54, chs. 9-10), as has Bar-Efrat (91). Before these suggestions are applied to the example of Peter in Matthew, there are two other brief points that should be considered.

"Character" was defined above as a paradigm of attributive propositions constructed during the reading process from indicators along the textual continuum. It was also argued that character, as an effect of reading, may "transcend" the text at times and seem to possess individuality. The reading process itself, as an imaginative process of filling gaps in the narrative, encourages the reader to develop individual images of textual indicators (Iser: 282-83; Cixous: 384-85; Holland: 273-74). The indirect method of characterization encourages the illusion of individuality by demanding that the reader infer traits from words, deeds, relationships, and attributive propositions given in the text.

Chatman's discussion is helpful here. He defines a "trait" in terms of narrative criticism as "a narrative adjective out of the vernacular labeling a personal quality of a character, as it persists over part or whole of the story (its 'domain')" (1980: 125). Inference of such traits is crucial for reading classical narrative, Chatman says, because traits "contribute to that sense of the verisimilar consistency of characters" that is the cornerstone of classical narrative (1980: 122). The reader, of course, infers traits from the contemporary trait-code of the real world. The traits may not exist in the text as actual verbal adjectives, but "clearly we must infer these traits to understand the narrative, and comprehending readers do so. Thus the traits exist at the story level: indeed, the whole discourse is expressly designed to prompt their emergence in the reader's consciousness" (1980: 125).

Chatman's argument suggests that a trait is a convenient, but necessary, grouping by the reader of a plurality of unrelated textual indicators. A trait, then, is often not "veridical," or "really there" in the text, but it is a reader's construct. Gordon Allport, speaking of persons rather than texts, has estimated that in English there are approximately eighteen thousand words designating traits, excluding hyphenated words and longer descriptive phrases. The mathematical possibilities for inferring traits from one's actions, words, or relationships seem almost infinite. If one infers from traits that a personage is a certain "type," then the type, for Allport, exists only nominally, that is, in the eye of the beholder.

Allport, then, rejects the notion that clear-cut types exist (334-55). This is so not only because the type may be an idiosyncratic reconstruction that does not reside in the actual person alluded to, but also because "no trait theory can be sound unless it allows for, and accounts for, the variability of a person's conduct" (333). Traits (and types) usually designate what one perceives as the constant portion that allows the designated person to transcend the trait. In other words, whether observing real persons or reconstructing a character from a narrative, indicators (acts or words) at different points in the continuum (a person's life or in a text) may cause the inferred pattern of traits to be restructured, thus giving the notion of variation or "individuality" (cf. 334).

Part of the importance of Allport's conclusions is that Chatman builds his argument about characterization on Allport's discussion of inferring traits. Although Chatman is content to leave to other theorists the understanding of mechanisms about how a reader's inference of traits issues in the notion of personality for fictional characters, he is convinced that it happens (1980: 125-26). The refusal to acknowledge the process of trait construction, along with the consequent refusal to apply the notion of "personality" to characters, is for Chatman "to deny an absolutely fundamental aesthetic experience" (1980: 138, cf. 117; see also Barthes: 6-11, discussed by Silverman: ch. 6).

A character, then, is a paradigm of constructed traits that the reader attaches to a name (cf. Chatman 1980: 137). The proper name, especially in "classical" texts like the Gospels, becomes the crucial factor in the construction of a character, but it also allows the character to transcend the text by helping to create the illusion of individuality or "personality" for the reader (Burnett, 1992: 125-26; cf. Kermode: 77-78). Barthes is very succinct about this point:

> When identical semes traverse the same proper name several times and appear to settle upon it, a character is created. Thus, the character is a product of combinations: the combination is relatively stable (denoted by the recurrence of the semes) and more or less complex (involving more or less congruent, more or less contradictory figures); this complexity determines the character's "personality," which is just as much a combination as the odor of a dish or the bouquet of a wine. The proper name acts as a magnetic field for the semes; referring in fact to a body, it draws the semic configuration into an evolving (biographical) tense (67-68).

Or, even more directly to my point, Barthes says: "What gives the illusion that the sum [of semes] is supplanted by a precious remainder (something like *individuality* . . .) is the Proper Name, the difference completed by what is *proper* to it. *The proper name enables the person to exist outside the semes* [emphasis added], whose sum nonetheless constitutes it entirely" (191; cf. Culler: 235-37; Weinsheimer: 187-88). For biblical narrative Sternberg is straight to the point:

> If for a biblical agent to come on stage nameless is to be declared faceless, then to bear a name is to assume an identity: to become a singular existent, with an assured place in history and a future in the story. It is the naming and dramatization of biblical characters, then, that do duty for the redundant epithets that elsewhere specify character in the interests of realism (331; cf. Burnett, 1992).

One more factor that has not allowed biblical critics to accept the fact that a typical character can at times fluctuate between being typical and yet somehow possess individuality has been Forster's distinction between the flat and the round character. Even in Forster, however, there are hints that flat and round characters should be understood on a continuum rather than as mutually exclusive categories (Rimmon-Kenan: 40-42). The importance of this point for a discussion of types is that Forster understands flat characters virtually as types in ancient literature (Forster: 103-4). That Forster himself understood that "flat" and "round" were not mutually exclusive categories is shown in his discussion of Jane Austen's Lady Bertram. In this text a flat character fluctuates and becomes a round character for Forster because the narrative endows Lady Bertram with opinions. Forster comments that "these are strong words, and they used to worry me because I thought Jane Austen's moral sense was getting out of hand." He then asks of Austen: "has she [Austen] any right to agitate calm, consistent Lady Bertram?" (Forster: 113, cf. 112).

G. C. Jones correctly notes that with this comment Forster acknowledges an important process in construction of characters, namely, that a flat character can be transformed momentarily into a round one. Forster, though, does not pursue this insight, and he chooses instead to explain the change in Lady Bertram in terms of the logic of the scene (Jones: 121-122). The narrator's comments on Lady Bertram were not essential to the plot, and momentarily she was transformed into a round character with an inner life of possibly more than one trait.[6]

The tendency of critics who have used Forster's distinctions on characters in biblical literature has been to say that if a character is flat and typical, then any notion of roundness or individuality is excluded.[7] If

---

[6] Jones prefers to discuss the transformation in terms of narrative point of view (125-27).

[7] It seems that Harvey's notion of ficelles, which is virtually the same as Forster's notion of flat characters, has been used in a similar way. Harvey, however, tends to view ficelles on a continuum between type and individual (58, 62-73, 147-48, 215-17; cf. Culpepper:102-103). The critic should distinguish carefully between the notions of the "idiosyncratic" and the "individual" for biblical characters. "Idiosyncrasy" implies

these categories are seen as degrees of characterization, however, then characters who are typical can become round momentarily during the reading process. In other words, both the strategies of characterization in the text and the process of the reader's construction of character need to be emphasized in biblical characterization, as Docherty has argued for both "readerly" and "writerly" texts. He contends: "It is in the interaction of the writer's language with the positions it affords the reader that the element of the text which we call 'character' is produced" (xiii-xiv).

Summary

The current debate about characterization in narrative fiction recognizes the textuality of "characters," but it also allows the reader-critic to focus on character as textual segments or as an effect, a reading construct, that can, depending upon the textual indicators, allow the reader-critic to speak of characters as "persons." It seems best to speak of degrees of characterization in biblical texts, and to plot textual indicators on a continuum for any particular text, from words at one pole to "persons" at the other pole. In the case of literature like the Gospels the continuum of actant (agent) to type to character is a useful scheme.

Reading conventions for character construction in ancient literature (and drama) preferred indirect characterization, and personages were for the most part typical and flat. There is, however, some indication, especially in portraiture and drama, that personages at times could be read as developing and approaching individuality. When the possibility of such reading conventions in ancient literature is coupled with the contemporary notion of reading as a process of nomination, particularly in readerly texts like the Gospels, it is certainly plausible that textual indicators in certain texts could allow for reader construction of a character as a "person." Even if a personage is a type (flat) in some texts, the indicators could allow for momentary transformation into a rounder character. I am convinced that this happens, for example, in the case of Peter in the Gospel of Matthew.

---

modern notions of a character who responds to events in uniquely singular ways while "individuality" need not carry the same implication. A biblical character may leave the reader with the impression of individuality because of that character's situation or response to events, yet he or she can still be representative of a generic ethos. In other words, one should not expect the *ēthos* of a character to reveal every idiosyncrasy of that character's "person." Although it is not easy to determine exactly what a biblical character's individuality may entail, the notion of individuality allows the critic to avoid proceeding as if there could be no middle ground between modern understandings of the individual and the generalized type in biblical characterization (Pelling:253-56; cf. Goldhill:105-14).

Peter in Matthew

Although this theoretical discussion can only be applied summarily to a reading of Peter in Matthew (for a fuller reading see Burnett, 1987), I agree with those who argue that in Matthew Peter is predominately a type who represents the characteristics of the disciples as a group (e.g. Kingsbury). This is evident primarily in Peter's role as spokesperson for the group. There are, however, several textual indicators, or techniques of characterization, that allow the reader to transform Peter momentarily into an individual who transcends his typical function as a member of the disciples.[8]

A primary technique of characterization that encourages the reader to construct the personage "Peter" as an individual is that Peter has at least two names: Simon (Bar-jona) and "Peter" (*ho Petros*). The proper names, of course, enable the reader to identify the semes as the same character, but having more than one name could be ambiguous and cause the reader to have more gaps to fill. Thus a character like Peter becomes more complex for the reader. This is true particularly when the names (or titles) seem to be interchangeable (4:18; 10:2; 16:16, 17; cf. Weinsheimer: 195).

Furthermore, whether it is a name or a title, there is no closure for the reader concerning Peter. The reader does not know if Peter becomes the "Rock," as *ho Petros* implies, or even what this function means. This indeterminacy creates a gap and requires the reader's imagination to fill it. In this one sense, at least, Peter is an open-ended character. Peter is not limited to actions only within the narrative world, but he is open to possible future actions as the "Rock" of the disciples (cf. Chatman, 1980:133). It is precisely this kind of textual indicator and indeterminacy that helps to create the illusion that names refer to something independent of texts, and it helps to support the illusion of the non-textuality of characters. The text has a beginning and an ending, and is thus closed, but the reader is encouraged to speculate beyond the ending of the text. Unless the reading conventions encourage the reader to keep the text bounded, characters can be extended beyond the text and approach the status of historical persons (see Weinsheimer [187-88], who argues that the reading convention that "so and so is a character in _____ book" did not emerge until the mid-eighteenth century with the rise of the novel).

Another way that the reader is encouraged to construct a character out of Peter is that the reader is given more knowledge about Peter than is necessary for the plot. From Matt 8:14, for example, the reader learns that Peter has a house, is married or is a widower, and probably has relatives

---

[8] It is interesting that some critics can argue that Peter stands out so prominently in Matthew that he is the dominant character, almost overshadowing Jesus (e.g. Kähler).

who live with him or nearby. Peter has a brother who, not incidentally, is always identified as Peter's brother (4:18; 10:2). The reader also knows that Peter is a fisherman (4:18). This is not much knowledge, but it is a higher degree of characterization than the "agent" usually has (cf. Berlin: 32). These touches of privacy are unnecessary to the plot and are indicators, however minute, of "personhood" (cf. Lattimore: 63).

Another textual indicator that may cause readers to construct individuality is whether or not a personage is given emotions and opinions. In Matthew fearlessness is given by Jesus as an important trait for discipleship (10:26, 28, 31), but fear caused by life-threatening circumstances characterizes both Peter and the disciples (14:26). There is little question that the reader is to infer fear as a trait not only for the disciples who flee at Jesus' arrest (26:56), but also for Peter's denial where the reader's focus is solely upon him (26:69-75). Peter also expresses strong opinions. He disagrees not only with Jesus but, by implication, with God as well (16:22; 26:33, 35).

It is true that Peter's emotions and opinions usually represent the whole group of disciples. There are textual indicators, however, that allow the reader momentarily to see Peter as separate from the group. The main ones are where Peter contrasts his fidelity to Jesus with the group's fidelity (26:33), and his denial scene (26:69-75). Peter also has a scene alone with Jesus (17:24-27), and he is the only disciple for whom Jesus works a miracle (14:28-32; cf. 17:27). Even though he is a secondary character, Peter also gets knowledge that only the reader has, thus converging the discourses of reader, narrator, and character (16:16; cf. 1:1, 17, 18; 2:4; 11:2). This knowledge is particularly important at Peter's recognition scene because the character now apparently sees himself as the narrator and reader have seen him all along (26:75).

Although most of the textual indicators mentioned above continue to characterize Peter as a type who is representative of discipleship, Peter's denial/recognition scene is where he is momentarily "rounded" for the reader. Peter's denial is not essential to the plot, and it has nothing to do with Jesus' trial and fate.[9] The recognition of himself/herself by a secondary character *and* a whole scene of dialogue with other secondary characters is something almost unheard of in ancient literature. Auerbach, for example, is intrigued with this scene. He says that "the nature and the

---

[9] This seems to distinguish Peter's recognition scene from that of the *major* characters in tragedies. Recognition in tragedies was integral to the plot (cf. Brereton:35-37; Bilezikan:101). Peter's recognition approximates Aristotle's third type of recognition that is due to memory and issues in a display of feelings (*Poetics* §16.8). There is, however, no reversal of the plot, and the discovery (the change from ignorance to knowledge) is only for Peter as a secondary character, not for the main character (Jesus) or the audience (cf. *Poetics* §10.10-11).

scene of the conflict . . . fall entirely outside the domain of classical antiquity," and the scene "fits into no antique genre." The use of direct discourse among such secondary characters, he feels, proves his point (42, 45-46). This scene encourages the reader to take an interest in the character or "personality" of Peter himself.[10]

Chatman proposes three criteria for distinguishing between mere "walk-ons" (agents) and characters. First, he asks if the existent is "human," that is, does it stand out in any sense as a person? With touches of familial relationships, emotions, and opinions, Peter does seem to meet this criterion. Second, does the existent have a name? The importance of the names *ho Petros* and Simon (Bar-jona) for understanding Peter is quite evident. A related question is: does the existent appear independently in a scene? Peter does. Finally, to what degree does the existent affect the plot, and to what degree does the plot affect the existent? Peter functions mostly as a foil for Jesus' teaching, but there does seem to be an interest in him that is independent of the plot, especially in the denial scene.

Chatman softens his own scheme by saying that "the above fail as criterial marks of character, but they seem relevant as features." He concludes, however, that the features are relevant to the reading process and should be placed on a continuum:

> Characterhood, in this view, would be a question of degree: a human being who is named, present, and important is *more likely* to be a character (be he ever so minor) than an object that is named, present, and important, or a human being who is named, present, but unimportant, or whatever (1980:141, cf. 139-40).

In terms of Chatman's approach, a sequential, diachronic reading of Peter suggests that Peter is a secondary character who functions as a type but who, at certain points on the textual continuum, approaches character-

---

[10] Although this scene may be the most important one for the characterization of Peter in Matthew, it has been summarily dismissed by form-critics because it consists of legendary materials. It is thus removed to the periphery of early Christian proclamation, or in this case the Passion Narrative (e.g. Dibelius:115, 215). The fruition of this approach is seen, for example, in the excellent study by Brown, Donfried, and Reumann. They rightly ask: "If all the authority is meant for the body of the disciples, why is Peter so often the one singled out by Matthew? *A priori*, was he not a somewhat unlikely choice since he denied the master publicly? Or did that very fact give Peter a special place not only as a type but as a person?" (105). The telling thing is that they do not deal with the denial scene at all in their exegesis. Form and redaction critics have not only removed any interest in the personal to the periphery of proclamation, but they have also posed a false dichotomy of either a type or a person. The former is always integral to early Christian proclamation while the latter is always legendary and thus peripheral to proclamation.

hood and even "personality."[11] If this is the case, it may mean that "personal" aspects of characters in the gospel narratives, especially the personality of Jesus, played a more important role in early Christian proclamation than form and redaction critics have been willing to admit.

WORKS CONSULTED

Allport, Gordon
    1967   *Pattern and Growth in Personality.* New York: Holt, Rinehart, and Winston.

Alter, Robert
    1981   *The Art of Biblical Narrative.* New York: Basic.

Anderson, Graham
    1984   *Ancient Fiction: The Novel in the Graeco-Roman World.* London: Croom Helm.

Auerbach, Erich
    1953   *Mimesis: The Representation of Reality in Western Literature.* Princeton: Princeton University Press.

Bar-Efrat, Shimon
    1989   *Narrative Art in the Bible.* Bible and Literature Series, 17. Sheffield: Almond.

Barthes, Roland
    1974   *S/Z.* New York: Hill and Wang.

Berlin, Adele
    1983   *Poetics and Interpretation of Biblical Narrative.* Sheffield: Almond.

Beye, Charles R.
    1975   *Ancient Greek Literature and Society.* Garden City, NY: Anchor.

Bilezikan, Gilbert G.
    1977   *The Liberated Gospel: A Comparison of the Gospel of Mark and Greek Tragedy.* Grand Rapids: Baker.

---

[11] The reader does not just construct a character by reading sequentially. As I have argued, the reader constructs a *paradigm* of traits *at the story level* from indicators that are strewn along the textual continuum. A great deal of work remains to be done with paradigmatic study of character in biblical narratives, though some work is underway (Malbon, 1986; 1989; Darr).

    In another context James Garvey has proposed a model to help determine whether or not characterization has occurred and to what degree (63-78). His model could work in concert with Chatman's view of characterization since Garvey also rejects the dichotomy of either person or textual function in the reading of character.

Bornkamm, Günther
1960   *Jesus of Nazareth*. New York: Harper & Row.

Brereton, Geoffrey
1968   *Principles of Tragedy: A Rational Examination of the Tragic Concept in Life and Literature*. Coral Gables, FL: University of Miami Press.

Brown, Raymond, Karl P. Donfried, and John Reumann
1973   *Peter in the New Testament*. New York: Paulist; Minneapolis: Augsburg.

Bultmann, Rudolf
1968   *The History of the Synoptic Tradition*. Rev. ed. New York: Harper & Row.

Burnett, Fred W.
1987   "Characterization in Matthew: Reader Construction of the Disciple Peter." *Mckendree Pastoral Review* 4:13-44.
1992   "The Undecidability of the Proper Name 'Jesus' in Matthew." *Semeia* 54:123-44.

Chatman, Seymour
1972   "On the Formalist-Structuralist Theory of Character." *Journal of Literary Semantics* 1:57-79.
1980   *Story and Discourse: Narrative Structure in Fiction and Film*. Ithaca: Cornell University Press.

Cixous, Hélène
1973-74   "The Character of 'Character'." *New Literary History* 5:383-402.

Conzelmann, Hans
1973   *Jesus*. Philadelphia: Fortress.

Culler, Jonathan
1978   *Structuralist Poetics: Structuralism, Linguistics, and the Study of Literature*. Ithaca: Cornell University Press.

Culpepper, R. Alan
1983   *Anatomy of the Fourth Gospel: A Study in Literary Design*. Philadelphia: Fortress.

Darr, John
1992   *On Character Building: The Reader and the Rhetoric of Characterization in Luke-Acts*. Louisville: Westminster/John Knox.

Dibelius, Martin
n. d.   *From Tradition to Gospel*. New York: Scribners.

Dihle, Albrecht
1956   *Studien zur Griechischen Biographie*. Göttingen: Vandenhoeck & Ruprecht.
1983   "Die Evangelien und die griechische Biographie." Pp. 383-412 in *Das Evangelium und die Evangelien*. Ed. Peter Stuhlmacher. Tübingen: J. C. B. Mohr.

Docherty, Thomas
 1983 *Reading (Absent) Character: Towards a Theory of Characterization in Fiction.* Oxford: Clarendon.

Easterling, P. E.
 1983 "Character in Sophocles." Pp. 138-45 in *Greek Tragedy: Modern Essays in Criticism.* Ed. Erich Segal. New York: Harper & Row.
 1990 "Constructing Character in Greek Tragedy." Pp. 83- 99 in *Characterization and Individuality in Greek Literature.* Ed. Christopher Pelling. Oxford: Clarendon.

Eissfeldt, Otto
 1965 *The Old Testament: An Introduction.* New York: Harper & Row.

Evans, Elizabeth C.
 1948 "Literary Portraiture in Ancient Epic." *Harvard Studies in Classical Philology* 48-49:189-217.

Fokkelman, J. P.
 1975 *Narrative Art in Genesis.* Assen: Van Gorcum.

Forster, E. M.
 1927 *Aspects of the Novel.* New York: Harcourt & Brace.

Garvey, James
 1978 "Characterization in Narrative." *Poetics* 7:63-78.

Gellie, G. H.
 1972 *Sophocles: A Reading.* Melbourne: n.p.

Gill, Christopher
 1983 "The Question of Character Development: Plutarch and Tacitus." *Classical Quarterly* 33:469-87.

Goldhill, Simon
 1990 "Character and Action, Representation and Reading: Greek Tragedy and Its Critics." Pp. 100-127 in *Characterization and Individuality in Greek Literature.* Ed. Christopher Pelling. Oxford: Clarendon.

Griffin, Jasper
 1990 "Characterization in Euripides: *Hippolytus* and *Iphigeneia in Aulis.*" Pp. 128-49 in *Characterization and Individuality in Greek Literature.* Ed. Christopher Pelling. Oxford: Clarendon.

Guelich, Robert
 1983 "The Gospel Genre." Pp. 183-219 in *Das Evangelium und die Evangelien.* Ed. Peter Stuhlmacher. Tübingen: J. C. B. Mohr.

Hägg, Thomas
 1983 *The Novel in Antiquity.* Berkeley: University of California Press.

Hanfmann, George M. A.
 1952 "Observations on Roman Portraiture." *Latomus* 11:454-65.

Harvey, W. J.
　1966　　Character and the Novel. Ithaca: Cornell University Press.

Holland, Norman
　1975　　The Dynamics of Literary Response. New York: W. W. Norton.

Iser, Wolfgang
　1980　　The Implied Reader: Patterns of Communication in Prose Fiction from Bunyan to Beckett. Baltimore: Johns Hopkins University Press.

Jones, Grahame C.
　1983　　"'Flat' and 'Round' Characters, the Example of Stendhal." Australian Journal of French Studies 20:115-29.

Kähler, Christoph
　1976-77　"Zur Form- und Traditions-geschichte von Matth. XVI.17-19." NTS 23:36-58.

Katz, Ronald C.
　1977　　The Structure of Ancient Arguments: Rhetoric and Its Near Eastern Origin. New York: Shapolsky/Steinmatzky Publishing.

Keck, Leander
　1986　　"Toward the Renewal of New Testament Christology." NTS 32:362-77.

Kennedy, George A.
　1984　　New Testament Interpretation through Rhetorical Criticism. Chapel Hill: University of North Carolina Press.

Kermode, Frank
　1979　　The Genesis of Secrecy: On the Interpretation of Narrative. Cambridge: Harvard University Press.

Kingsbury, Jack Dean
　1979　　"The Figure of Peter in Matthew's Gospel as a Theological Problem." JBL 98:67-83.

Kitto, H. D. F.
　1950　　Greek Tragedy: A Literary Study. 2nd ed. London: Methuen.

Knierim, Rolf
　1973　　"Old Testament Form Criticism Reconsidered." Int 27:435-67.

Koch, Klaus
　1969　　The Growth of the Biblical Tradition: The Form-Critical Method. New York: Charles Scribner's.

Koester, Helmut
　1974　　"Physis." TDNT 9:251-77.

Korfmacher, William C.
　1934　　"Three Phases of Classical Type Characterization." The Classical Weekly 26:85-86.

Kümmel, Werner G.
    1972   *The New Testament: The History of the Investigation of Its Problems*. Nashville: Abingdon.

Lattimore, Richard A.
    1965   *Story Patterns in Greek Tragedy*. Ann Arbor: University of Michigan Press.

Macauley, Robie and George Lanning
    1964   *Technique in Fiction*. New York: Harper & Row.

McCarthy, Mary
    1961   "Characters in Fiction." *Partisan Review* 28:171-91.

McKane, William
    1979   *Studies in Patriarchal Narratives*. Edinburgh: Hansel.

Malbon, Elizabeth Struthers
    1986   "Disciples/Crowds/Whoever: Markan Characters and Readers." *NovT* 28:104-30.
    1989   "The Jewish Leaders in the Gospel of Mark: A Literary Study of Marcan Characterization." *JBL* 108:259-81.

Marxsen, Willi
    1968   *Introduction to the New Testament*. Philadelphia: Fortress.

Miller, Stuart
    1967   *The Picaresque Novel*. Cleveland: Case Western Reserve University Press.

Misener, Geneva
    1924   "Iconistic Portraits." *CP* 19:97-124.

Mudrick, Marvin
    1960-61   "Character and Event in Fiction." *The Yale Review* 50:202-18.

Muilenburg, James
    1969   "Form Criticism and Beyond." *JBL* 88:1-18.

Neusner, Jacob
    1984   *Judaism in the Beginning of Christianity*. Philadelphia: Fortress.

Osley, A. S.
    1946   "Greek Biography Before Plutarch." *Greece and Rome* 15:1-20.

Pelling, Christopher, ed.
    1990   *Characterization and Individuality in Greek Literature*. Oxford: Clarendon.

Raphael, D. D.
    1960   *The Paradox of Tragedy*. Bloomington: Indiana University Press.

Redford, D. B.
    1970   *Study of the Biblical Story of Joseph*. Leiden: Brill.

Rimmon-Kenan, Shlomith
    1983   *Narrative Fiction: Contemporary Poetics*. New York: Methuen.

Robbins, Vernon K.
  1984   *Jesus the Teacher: A Socio-Rhetorical Interpretation of Mark.* Philadelphia: Fortress.

Russell, D. A.
  1976   "On Reading Plutarch's *Lives.*" *Greece and Rome* 13:139-54.

Scholes, Robert
  1968   *Elements of Fiction.* New York: Oxford University Press.

Scholes, Robert and Robert Kellogg
  1968   *The Nature of Narrative.* New York: Oxford University Press.

Shuler, Philip L.
  1982   *A Genre for the Gospels: The Biographical Character of Matthew.* Philadelphia: Fortress.

Silverman, Kaja
  1983   *The Subject of Semiotics.* New York: Oxford University Press.

Stanton, G. N.
  1974   *Jesus of Nazareth in New Testament Preaching.* SNTSMS 27. New York: Cambridge University Press.

Sternberg, Meir
  1985   *The Poetics of Biblical Narrative: Ideological Literature and the Drama of Reading.* Bloomington: Indiana University Press.

Talbert, Charles H.
  1977   *What Is A Gospel? The Genre of the Canonical Gospels.* Philadelphia: Fortress.

Todorov, Tzvetan
  1980   "Reading as Construction." Pp. 67-82 in *The Reader in the Text: Essays on Audience Interpretation.* Ed. Susan R. Suleiman and Inge Crosman. Princeton: Princeton University Press.

Vermes, Geza
  1984   *Jesus and the World of Judaism.* Philadelphia: Fortress.

Weinsheimer, Joel
  1979   "Theory of Character: Emma." *Poetics Today* 1:185-211.

CHARACTER IN THE BOUNDARY: BAKHTIN'S INTERDIVIDUALITY IN BIBLICAL NARRATIVES

David McCracken
University of Washington

ABSTRACT

Character conceived in individual terms is inadequate for biblical character, which involves an essential relationship to others, an *inter*dividuality of the sort described by Bakhtin. The place between, where one encounters another, is the threshold or boundary. There questions of ultimate importance, posed by another, are responded to; there character is formed, reformed, and revealed in dialogic interaction at a moment of crisis. This view of character assumes that what we call the "self" is a spiritual category, a relation to the Other, never monadic, static, or fully realized by human characters. Biblical interdividual characters exist in relative, surprising freedom, in "transgredience" rather than with ingredients, in a present zone of contact with the reader, in an active relation to the author, and in discourse with another. In the gospels, the crisis on the boundary takes a particular form, as the character encounters in Jesus the possibility of offense. Thus, the discourse of the gospels is scandalous and eccentric, that is, potentially offensive and not centered in the normal, respectable world. In the gospels, character exists most crucially in the boundary between one and Jesus.

We have a variety of critical means for discussing literary character, among them the classical, Aristotelian concept of character as a fixed essence, subordinate to the action; the semiotic revision of this by Seymour Chatman, which elevates character as a "paradigm of traits" equal in importance to action; the complete displacement of character from story (as in the structuralists Vladimir Propp and Roland Barthes); and the more recent deconstructionist notion of the absent character, or fragmentary "instances of subjectivity," that the mobile reader informs (Docherty: xv). These theories have their various powers and uses, but they have not been formulated in response to the peculiar challenges of biblical character, which is of course different from Homeric or Sophoclean character and from characters in modern or postmodern novels.

I intend here to sketch an entirely different view of character, based on the work of Mikhail Bakhtin and others, which I believe is more adequate to the particular task of understanding biblical character. My use of nineteenth- and twentieth-century thinkers, Kierkegaard and Bakhtin, might seem odd in light of my interest in confronting the peculiar challenges of biblical character, but I want to argue that the ideas of these two thinkers have distinct biblical bases that make them appropriate to biblical character and that, apart from the biblical origins of their ideas, they prove to be remarkably applicable to biblical texts. My sketch will necessarily lead me first to some comments about the relevance of thresholds to biblical narratives, then to the relevance of the *skandalon*, or offense, to these thresholds, and then to a view of the self that undergirds this notion of character. This will prepare the way for me to discuss some qualities of dialogic character, and to describe the special kind of discourse that is found in gospels, though not only there. Finally I will argue that the gospels require this radically different sense of character—so different, indeed, that one might justifiably wonder whether our word "character" applies at all, though I want to insist on using it because the interdividual character makes little sense if it does not replace our usual senses of individual character in biblical contexts.[1]

Character on the Threshold

Interdividuality may be grasped by calling to mind moments of dramatic interaction in biblical narratives. For example, when Gideon, hiding from the Midianites, is flailing wheat, an angel of the Lord appears to him and says, "The LORD is with you, you mighty warrior" (Judg 6:12, NRSV, here and throughout). When this angel of the Lord appears, it is clear that a significant action impends, but its significance as action depends on Gideon's reaction. The angel's characterization of Gideon as a "mighty warrior" would seem to fix his character authoritatively. But it does not. Gideon as "mighty warrior" might be a divine desire, but the description will prove to be at best only partially or temporarily true, modified by hesitation, fear, and personal vengeance. During this encounter Gideon is emphatically not a mighty warrior; he is, he professes, the least in his family, and his clan is the weakest in Manasseh (6:15).

---

[1] The term "interdividual" I take from Girard, who speaks of *la psychologie interdividuelle* (1987: the title of Book III); Oughourlian (ix-x, 11-12, 15-21); and Webb (5, 216-17, 296-99). "Character" plus "interdividual" is something of an oxymoron, especially if one is using character in the original, Theophrastian sense, in which character is something stamped or impressed on substance (see Barfield: 168). A useful discussion of terminology that distinguishes among hero, protagonist, character, figure, self, individual, person, and presence may be found in Rorty. She, however, offers no single word that applies to the interdividual character. Oughourlian suggests "holon" (Greek "whole") for the entity made up of I and Other, but I will use the oxymoronic "interdividual character" since, although awkward, it captures something of the strangeness, difficulty, and newness (to many of us) of the concept. Bakhtin uses the traditional terms "hero" and "character."

Gideon presumably had heard the voice of the prophet, who explained why the Israelites are being oppressed, but Gideon certainly did not heed the words; in fact, he uses the prophet's reference to Egypt to the opposite end—to blame YHWH. "The LORD has cast us off," Gideon complains, "and given us into the hand of Midian" (6:13). At this, YHWH repeats the angel's earlier epithet and repeats Gideon's complaint in a way that might establish a Gideon-YHWH relation that will rescue the Israelites: "Go in *this might of yours* and deliver Israel from *the hand of Midian: I* hereby commission *you*" (6:14; my emphasis).

The I-Thou relation works through responsive words that have histories from previous speakers. In the Bible, character is created and communicated through such words. In this exchange with Gideon, we have no description from an omniscient narrator, and the descriptive words of one character about another are less important for their objective truth than for the response they elicit from the other. These responses are comprised of words—Gideon's, who gets his from "our ancestors" and perhaps from the prophet that was heard but not heeded, as YHWH's voice has not been heeded (6:10). Gideon is Gideon in relation to ancestors, prophet, clan, family, and Midianites. In this speech, he is Gideon in relation to YHWH, who posits a new character role, mighty warrior, which is not immediately enacted but which elicits a response that manifests Gideon's interdividual character. This character will change, even becoming, temporarily, a mighty warrior, but it will never be fixed, because it dwells in the between of assertion, response, and anticipated next response, conducted in words that have histories from earlier voices.

If we think of character as fluctuating roles, formed in response to another and expressed in anticipatory words that contain the voices of previous speakers, we might say that God's characterization, "You mighty warrior," is no description but a challenge to what Wayne Booth calls "hypocrisy upward," a "productive hypocrisy—aspiring and emulating" (252-54). Gideon is no mighty warrior at the moment but rather what we in the 1990s (thinking of the individual rather than the interdividual) might describe as someone with a strong sense of victimization and low self-esteem. He will come to try out the role of mighty warrior, with sometimes comic and sometimes grotesque effects. (I find him comic when his fear leads him to eavesdrop on his enemies and overhear a dream about a giant barley cake crushing a tent, which he finds far more persuasive than the voice of God, and grotesque when his personal vendetta leads to spiraling violence at Succoth and Penuel and with his son Jether.)

Similar moments, though all with different voices, are common in biblical narratives. When Saul, after a victory, has not utterly destroyed the Amalekites as God ordered but has spared what is valuable and destroyed only what is worthless, Samuel comes to him and says, "Why then did you not obey the voice of the LORD?" (1 Sam 15:19). Or when Nathan tells a story of a rich man and a poor man to David, who has just murdered Uriah, David condemns the unjust rich man to death, and Nathan responds, "You are the man!" (2 Sam 12:7). Or when a lawyer, wanting to justify himself, asks Jesus, "And who is my neighbor?" Jesus replies with a story, "A man was going down from Jerusalem to Jericho . . ." (Luke 10:29-30). Or when Martha, stuck with the hard work of hospitality, complains to Jesus about her unhelpful sister, Jesus refuses to intervene, saying, cryptically, "there is need of only one thing" (Luke 10:41).

In these moments we have characters existing in the boundary between themselves and another. We know some things about these characters, but the heart of the drama in each case lies not in the traits that define an essential character, not in some typical essence that is revealed in the next moment, but rather in what happens *between* what we usually call characters. Although these are special moments, they are also typical. As Shimon Bar-Efrat says, "We meet the biblical characters primarily in special and unusual circumstances, in times of crisis and stress, when they have to undergo severe tests" (78).

These characters are on a threshold, indeed we might say on *the* threshold, for in these cases they are encountering in some form the word of God. They are at a potential turning point, and their responses are unpredictable and unknowable until the moment when they respond to the words addressed to them. That moment is eternal time, when they face a question of ultimate importance.

These threshold encounters are crucial to biblical narratives, but of course narratives must live in ordinary, human time; the stories must continue. Gideon proceeds, hesitatingly, to his (temporary) heroism. Saul weasels and lies, trying to blame the disobedience on the people. David, perhaps surprisingly, given the despicable murder he has committed, accepts his self-judgment, saying, "I have sinned against the LORD" (2 Sam 12:13). But something quite different happens in my examples from the gospels: we are confronted here with the ambiguous and the unknown.

When, in Luke, the lawyer responds to Jesus, his response is not open to clear interpretation in which we can ascertain the lawyer's traits, as we might do (though only temporarily and inadequately) in the cases of Gideon, Saul, and David. Jesus asks, "Which of these three, do you think, was a neighbor to the man who fell into the hands of the robbers?"; the lawyer responds, "The one who showed him mercy" (Luke 10:36-37). This is the right answer, but what trait, what essential character, does it exemplify? What, in fact, does the lawyer mean? Is he still full of the desire to justify himself and full of "right" answers that miss the truth? Does he say "the one who showed him mercy" because he, like his tribe, cannot bear to utter the word "Samaritan" in any approving way, and cannot acknowledge that a hated Samaritan could obey the law better than priest or Levite? Or, on the contrary, has this lawyer—suddenly on the boundary where issues of ultimate importance are encountered—seen and understood "neighbor" in a new, and true, way that renders useless the conventional distinctions of priest, Levite, and Samaritan?

We will never know the answer to this, for the story moves on to a different place without explaining or interpreting the meaning of the words. In the new scene, the house of Mary and Martha, Martha's response to Jesus' words is not even capable of interpretation; it does not exist. After Jesus' response but before Martha's, the story shifts scene and characters once again. But where it has left Martha is really the essential place of character: the between, the threshold, the boundary, where the responsive word awaits its response. Martha is no reified, psychological entity, no fixed essence, but rather what Mikhail Bakhtin calls "a person on the threshold of . . . decision, at a moment of crisis, at an unfinalizable —and unpredeterminable—turning point for [the] soul" (1984:61). Martha, unlike Gideon, Saul, and David, is frozen in a state of eternal suspense, as she exists dialogically on the threshold, but without our knowing how she exists.[2]

It is surprising how many unresolved stories like Martha's there are in the gospels, where characters are narratively abandoned, so to speak, in the moment of crisis, and readers are left with the crisis dramatically defined but not resolved. But closure, or lack of it, is not the primary issue; Martha is typical of biblical characters in being brought by the narrative to a threshold, where a crucial decision is called for, and where her character can be said to *live*. This life is not individual, not within herself, but rather interdividual, between her and the other to whom she responds. "Life," Bakhtin says, "by its very nature is dialogic. To live means to participate in dialogue: to ask questions, to heed, to respond, to agree, and so forth" (1984:293). This statement, which Bakhtin means to be true in a general sense as well as true to Dostoevsky's novels, is also true with regard to the life of biblical characters: it is relational and occurs in the between.

---

[2] I discuss these two Lukan narratives and the relations between them at greater length—though not with regard to issues of character—in chapter 8 of *The Scandal of the Gospels*.

The Threshold and the Skandalon

To properly appreciate the importance of the threshold to the biblical notion of life, we need to reanimate an idea that dwells in the Greek word *skandalon*, our "scandal" or "offense" or "stumbling-block," a word used in the Septuagint to describe the actions of YHWH, and even YHWH, God's-self, who lays stumbling-blocks and is one to the Israelites (Jer 6:21; Isa 8:14-15). But the idea takes on its full force in the New Testament, where Jesus is the *skandalon*, the offense, to those who approach—and *all* are called to approach him.[3] When characters do approach Jesus, they encounter the possibility of offense embodied in the hero of the gospels—a man who is the Son of Man, or the Son of God, or the way, the truth, and the life, *and*, at the same time a mere man. He is, moreover, a mere man not in the sense of a normal and respectable man, but rather a marginal one, who chooses to consort with those on the margins of respectable society. Both of these contrary attributes contain a potential offense to anyone who approaches him. Repeatedly, Jesus posits the possibility of offense because those who approach him *may* respond with faith *only* by encountering the offense. As Jesus says, "Blessed is anyone who is not offended at me" (Matt 11:6; Luke 7:23).

The *skandalon* is a crucial narrative element, not only because of its importance in action—as Jesus repeatedly posits the possibility of offense—but also because of its importance in creating interdividual characters—namely, those brought to the threshold by Jesus, who is both (as Kierkegaard says) the sign of offense *and* the object of faith (1991:23). Those brought to the threshold include the disciples, the inhabitants of his hometown, Pharisees, Gerasenes, Samaritans, Romans, and so on (and blessed are they who are not offended at him). But it is not just characters in the text who are brought to the threshold; the gospels themselves act as occasions for offense to their readers.

The Kierkegaardian Paradigm of Self

My extension of this narrative element to readers makes it evident that in my view the interdividual character is no mere textual function (as it might be for a structuralist) but also an analogue of a person (as it might *only* be for an Aristotelian), including a person like the reader, whom twentieth-century Americans and Europeans are inclined to think of as an

---

[3] There is another *skandalon* in the gospels, when, for example, followers of Jesus are stumbling-blocks to each other, or to "little ones" (e.g. Matt 18:6-7; Rom 14:13). This *skandalon* plays an important role in the works of René Girard (1987:416-31; 1986:132-36). I am concerned here, however, only with a related, but different *skandalon*—the offense of Jesus.

individual self. Kierkegaard offers a view of the self that provides a useful paradigm for biblical character partly because crucial concepts in the paradigm are derived from the Bible. Certainly, what we think of as the existentialist self is a far cry from a first-century person or biblical character. But the Kierkegaardian self is also a far cry from most modern versions of the self, because Kierkegaard's person as a physical and mental phenomenon has no self. It is only when qualified by spirit that the possibility of becoming a self exists. Self is a possibility of spirit that involves a dying away from the world, from the natural, the esthetic, and the ethical categories. Self, for Kierkegaard, belongs to the category of spirit, immortality, the eternal, and it is therefore true to say, as Gregor Malantschuk does, that "only God is a self in the genuine sense" (Kierkegaard, 1975: 4:634). For the human, selfhood is a possibility, at best a becoming, and it comes into existence only when the individual stands before God, which requires a difficult venturing out (Kierkegaard, 1990:98-103; 1992:429). "Kierkegaard," Louis Dupré has said, "is the first modern philosopher to place man's relation to God in the very heart of the self" (525).

Becoming a self, then, is far from inevitable; indeed there is a contrary movement available, a turning away from God. Disobedience against the eternal is despair; it rejects God's forgiveness in an act that Kierkegaard calls offense. Now offense is the antithesis of becoming a self, in faith, standing before God (Kierkegaard, 1980:32, 122, 128-39). Offense and faith are Kierkegaard's contraries essential to the spiritual category; they require an encounter on the threshold with the sign of offense and the object of faith.

Something like this concept of self undergirds the gospel presentation of character, which has its dramatic presence in the moment of encounter, where the crucial issue of offense or faith is revealed. Offense or faith is revealed in the between, where character exists in the presence of the other and in the response to the other.

Character as Interdividual

Bakhtin's conception of character is clearest in his discussions of the novel, though he argues convincingly that the dialogic qualities of the novel derive in part from Hellenistic, and specifically Christian, narratives (1984:112-13, 119-21, 135-36). "The human being in the novel is first, foremost and always a speaking human being," Bakhtin says, and the "fundamental condition" of the novel is "the *speaking person and his discourse*," which is always a response, full of other voices, and itself anticipating another response (1981:332). Five distinguishing qualities of the

Bakhtinian interdividual character will suggest its applicability to biblical characters.

1. Character is relatively free and independent rather than closed, limited, and strictly defined from an objective authorial position. It is not finally a part of a system of structures, for there is something always unfinalizable in character; it is not reified, quantifiable, defined, or predetermined. This is perhaps a less elegant way of formulating what Robert Alter has in mind when he speaks of the "abiding mystery in character as the biblical writers conceive it," and of their "sense of character as a center of surprise," an "unpredictable and changing nature of character" that makes it unsusceptible to fixed Homeric epithets (126).

2. Character exists in dialogic relation with other characters, not simply as an I (or he or she), but as an I-thou, an I-other. Thus character is composed not simply of ingredients but is marked by what Bakhtin calls "transgredience," a term that designates elements of consciousness that are external to it but absolutely necessary for its being, or more precisely, its co-being (Todorov: 95).

3. Character exists in a real present, in a dramatic contemporaneity with the reader, and not in a distant past, and this constitutes a dialogic relationship with the reader. It is this contemporaneity that makes Martha's suspension in undramatized and unresolved narrative so powerful for us as readers, if we regard her as a dialogic character in a story rather than simply a figure in a cautionary tale, representing the bustle of the active, worldly life. She, like other characters, is placed in "a zone of contact" (Bakhtin, 1981:32) with the reader rather than distantly observed as an object.

4. Character is something that the author tends toward speaking *with* rather than speaking *about*. This (asserted more aggressively) is one of the main arguments of Bakhtin's book on Dostoevsky, and while I will not argue that the Bible is a Dostoevsky novel (or the reverse, that *The Brothers Karamazov* is the fifth gospel), I believe that Bakhtin's idea about the dialogic relation between author and character has important implications for the Bible. Biblical narrators are typically reticent about characters and their actions. They have no use for Homeric epithets, and they often withhold evaluation of character and action, even when some evaluation would be welcomed by the reader. On the other hand, dialogue—the activity of response—constitutes an unusually large part of biblical narrative, and it often stands on its own, without being dominated by an authorial voice. Both of these traits diminish the importance of speaking-about.

Furthermore, the omniscient biblical narrator stands in a close relationship to the omniscient God. The narrator of the Bible, far more than the narrator of a Homeric epic, is an analogue of God, with derivative authority, to be sure, but God-like in the ability to know all, across the boundaries of time or space, the public or the private (Sternberg: 89-90), *and* God-like in the restricted use of this ability. Author, narrator, and God, though distinguishable, share qualities, including the tendency toward speaking-with, which is most dramatically evident in God (or an angel of the Lord). "You mighty warrior" is emphatically a speaking-with rather than a speaking-about. Even God's descriptions of the Israelites' waywardness, spoken through the prophets, are provocations to response rather than mere assertions about the past. Like God, the author does not know in an objective and distant way the fixed essence of his characters, and the narrator does not tell the story primarily by asserting knowledge about them. Instead, the character is placed within an action and provoked, given the opportunity to respond, allowed to voice a view (Gideon: we are being victimized) over against another view (angel: you mighty warrior), both of which interact in the narrative with God's/the author's/the narrator's view, which is a response to the character's view. This view is only partially exposed (in this episode indirectly, in the prophet's voice), but it is implicitly present.

5. Most important, character exists in discourse. In the novelistic tradition of Fielding and Thackery, we often think of authorially represented character (Bakhtin would say "monologic" character) as being describable through the words of an omniscient narrator. But a dialogic character whose essential life is in the between (between I and other, and ultimately between I and God), whose life is manifest only in a contemporaneous moment of encounter, who constitutes a dialogical other with the author (and is not simply a mimetic creation of the author), and who is relatively free rather than puppet-like in his or her relational consciousness—such a character comes into being artistically in his or her discourse, in the language that he or she utters in response to the other and in anticipation of the other's response. Language in this context is not conceived as a formation (*Gebild*), as Buber says Western humanism conceives of it. Instead, language is conceived "as an event (*Geschehen*), an event in mutuality.... Its intent is not the person who is shut up within himself, but the open one; not the form, but the relation; not mastery of the secret, but immediacy in facing it; not the thinker and master of the word, but its listener and executor, its worshipper and proclaimer" (Buber: 215-16).

SCANDALOUS AND ECCENTRIC DISCOURSE

There is a special kind of dialogic discourse that Bakhtin calls the scandalous and eccentric, which is a characteristic of "carnivalized" discourse. This is especially pertinent to the gospels, which are narratives of dialogic encounters in which life is poised on the threshold that radically calls into question the normal world. The actual genre of threshold dialogues, as Bakhtin has shown, was widespread in Hellenistic and Roman literature, propagated chiefly through the Socratic dialogues and Menippean satires, the latter of which, Bakhtin maintains, had a great influence on ancient Christian literature (1984:135-56).

A Menippean element that appears in the gospels is the scandalous, an artistic category between the tragic and the comic, wherein the eccentric, the one out-of-center (viz., Jesus in the gospels) destroys the ordinary wholeness of the world by making a breach in what is normal, central, and official. This breach may potentially free the person approaching the eccentric, who posits the scandalous. But this can only occur on the threshold, between the normal, official, stable world and another "world," which in the gospels is the kingdom or reign of God. This is the good news, which is at the same time scandalous news.

The dialogic encounter requires a dialogic concept of self and character. It is this dialogic quality that accounts for the curious power of those characters suspended in the between—the lawyer (responding to Jesus' question about neighboring) or Martha (not yet responding to Jesus' refusal)—as well as the power of those characters whose stories are *not* interrupted in the moment of crisis—the Pharisees in various encounters, the Syrophoenician (or Canaanite) woman, or the priest, Levite, and good Samaritan. These latter stories continue from the threshold by resolving the scandal scene, by continuing in time from the encounter with the eccentric to the response, which may be either offense at the scandal *or* faith in an eccentric world (the kingdom of God).

There is, however, an important difference between the stories of the lawyer and Martha, on the one hand, and David, on the other. The lawyer and Martha encounter on the threshold another "world" that is a scandal to the world of laws and domestic customs, even traditional and revered customs like hospitality, but David on the threshold encounters the world of kingly duty and responsibility that *he* has scandalized by his unkingly behavior. Both involve dialogic encounters, but in the gospel stories the scandal or offense dwells in Jesus and in the world that he posits, the kingdom of God. Something like this can of course happen in the Hebrew narratives, but it is not the norm.[4] In the gospels, it is pervasive: blessed are they who are not offended in Jesus, but they must all encounter the possibility of offense.

---

[4] However, in Bloom's *The Book of J* it is the norm: YHWH is, in Bloom's interpretation, repeatedly scandalous.

Character, the World, and the Kingdom

A dialogic conception of character in a Menippean, scandalous setting is particularly appropriate to the gospels for several reasons. First, any conception of character as a fixed and stable entity is inadequate in a text where the kingdom of God is offered as a disruption of worldly fixity and stability and where the crucial issue about character is its relation to this disruptive kingdom. The good news is that the kingdom of God is at hand and also that the apparently fixed, stable, normal, respectable world is not the kingdom. The one who makes known the kingdom is not a conventional, respectable man or a military leader, as he ought to be in the normal world, but an eccentric. The important issue about character in the gospel is its relation to this protagonist, who is eventually crowned as a mock king and crucified as a criminal. These actions take place in a carnival setting—a celebration of the normal world turned upside down. But this is a carnival of violence, in contrast to the unspecified kingdom of God, a different kind of carnival. At the center of all of this is a character whose mystery or unknowableness and whose lack of closure are crucial to all the gospels, even if most flagrant in Mark.

Second, in conveying these "worlds"—the normal world, the carnival of violence, and the kingdom of God—the gospels focus not on who individual characters *are*, as essential beings, or on their roles as actants, but on their relational activity, as is evident in the recurring metaphors of walking and seeing. The question is not who they are, but how do they walk? Do they walk by faith, in the Spirit, in love, in the light? And how do they see? Do they look and perceive, or do they look and not perceive? People who walk in the light, and who see, may encounter stumbling blocks (*skandala*) without stumbling over them. We might well think that this could be done, literally, by any competent individual walker. But metaphorically, in the gospel sense, it is not achieved through competence or by individuals; it is done by the-Other-in-relation-to-the-one. Walking and seeing, the most common of activities, are the gospels' metaphors for life-giving, relational activity. Our literalness about the gospels' metaphoricity reflects a different consciousness of the person: a sense of walking as an individual's movements through space from A to B is radically different from a sense of walking as encounters with others between A and B.[5]

---

[5] Malina provides a useful alternative to what he calls the "mainstream U.S. . . . individualistic person" by contrasting it to the first-century Mediterranean "dyadic person, a person always in relation with and connected to at least one other social unit, usually a group" (127-28). See also Malina and Rohrbaugh on dyadic and individualist personality (229-31).

Third, although character-in-relationship is necessary, it is not sufficient. Gospel relationship requires an encountering of offense or faith on the threshold. Response is all.[6] Fixity of character, or gradually developing character, is not the stuff of the gospels. Mark's favorite word, *euthus* ("immediately") speaks to the instant change of responding characters on the threshold, encountering another.

Finally, the Jesus of the gospels is essentially discourse, pure voice, who is to be heard and understood by others—or, heard and *not* understood. Indeed, in Mark it is part of the scandal of Jesus that he tells parables *so that* people may hear and not understand (4:12). The scandalous and eccentric teller of parables is not an individual character but a speaking personality, consciousness, and view of an eccentric world (the kingdom of God), who exists in the gospels as the human manifestation of Kierkegaard's sense of a true self, and who exists dialogically, by means of voice or discourse.

The writings of Bakhtin offer an alternative to the study of biblical character as individual—or as paradigm, structural actantial role, or absent fragment of subjectivity, to use other critical discourses. The alternative is interdividual character, existing in a text relationally. Such a character is analogous to a person, like a reader who, in reading biblical narratives, is brought to the boundary and becomes part of the dialogic interaction. Such a reader becomes "*an-other* or other for the author," with "*surplus* that is determined by this otherness." For Bakhtin, narrative texts, the writing of narratives, and the reading of narratives all involve "active dramatic relations" and "voices" (1986:165). At the center of this, between authors and readers, are interdividual characters.

WORKS CONSULTED

Alter, Robert
    1981   *The Art of Biblical Narrative*. New York: Basic.

Aristotle
    1961   *Aristotle's Poetics*. Trans. Kenneth A. Telford. Chicago: Regnery.

---

[6] The importance of response, as "key," is emphasized by Malbon with regard to the exceptional Jewish leaders in Mark (275). She argues that "being a foe of Jesus is . . . a matter of how one responds to Jesus" and that "responding *appropriately* to Jesus . . . is not a simple matter either" (280).

Bakhtin, Mikhail
- 1981 *The Dialogic Imagination: Four Essays.* Ed. Michael Holquist. Trans. Caryl Emerson and Michael Holquist. Austin: University of Texas Press.
- 1984 *Problems of Dostoevsky's Poetics.* Ed. and trans. Caryl Emerson. Minneapolis: University of Minneapolis Press.
- 1986 *Speech Genres and Other Late Essays.* Trans. Vern W. McGee. Austin: University of Texas Press.

Bar-Efrat, Shimon
- 1989 *Narrative Art in the Bible.* Sheffield: Almond.

Barfield, Owen
- 1962 *History in English Words.* London: Faber.

Barthes, Roland
- 1982 *A Barthes Reader.* Ed. Susan Sontag. New York: Hill and Wang.

Bloom, Harold
- 1990 *The Book of J.* Trans. David Rosenberg. Interpreted by Harold Bloom. New York: Grove Weidenfeld.

Booth, Wayne
- 1988 *The Company We Keep: An Ethics of Fiction.* Berkeley: University of California Press.

Buber, Martin
- 1982 *On the Bible.* Ed. Nahum N. Glatzer. New York: Schocken.

Chatman, Seymour
- 1978 *Story and Discourse: Narrative Structure in Fiction and Film.* Ithaca: Cornell University Press.

Docherty, Thomas
- 1983 *Reading (Absent) Character: Towards a Theory of Characterization in Fiction.* Oxford: Clarendon.

Dupré, Louis
- 1963 "The Constitution of the Self in Kierkegaard's Philosophy." *International Philosophical Quarterly* 3:506-26.

Girard, René
- 1986 *The Scapegoat.* Trans. Yvonne Freccero. Baltimore: Johns Hopkins University Press.
- 1987 *Things Hidden since the Foundation of the World.* Trans. Stephen Bann and Michael Metteer. Stanford: Stanford University Press.

Kierkegaard, Søren
- 1975 *Søren Kierkegaard's Journals and Papers.* Vol. 4. Trans. Howard V. Hong and Edna H. Hong. Notes by Gregor Malantschuk. Bloomington: Indiana University Press.
- 1980 *The Sickness unto Death.* Trans. Howard V. Hong and Edna H. Hong. Princeton: Princeton University Press.

1990	*For Self-Examination/Judge for Yourself.* Trans. Howard V. Hong and Edna H. Hong. Princeton: Princeton Unversity Press.
1991	*Practice in Christianity.* Trans. Howard V. Hong and Edna H. Hong. Princeton: Princeton University Press.
1992	*Concluding Unscientific Postscript to Philosophical Fragments.* Trans. Howard V. Hong and Edna H. Hong. Princeton: Princeton University Press.

Malbon, Elizabeth Struthers
- 1989   "The Jewish Leaders in the Gospel of Mark: A Literary Study of Marcan Characterization." *JBL* 108:259-81.

Malina, Bruce J.
- 1989   "Dealing with Biblical (Mediterranean) Characters: A Guide for U.S. Consumers." *BTB* 19:127-41.

Malina, Bruce J. and Richard L. Rohrbaugh
- 1992   *Social-Science Commentary on the Synoptic Gospels.* Minneapolis: Fortress.

McCracken, David
- 1994   *The Scandal of the Gospels.* New York: Oxford University Press.

Oughourlian, Jean-Michel
- 1991   *The Puppet of Desire.* Stanford: Stanford University Press.

Propp, Vladimir
- 1968   *Morphology of the Folktale.* 2d ed. Trans. Laurence Scott. Austin: University of Texas Press.

Rorty, Amélie Oksenberg
- 1976   "A Literary Postscript: Characters, Persons, Selves, Individuals." Pp. 301-23 in *The Identity of Persons.* Ed. Amélie Oksenberg Rorty. Berkeley: University of California Press.

Sternberg, Meir.
- 1985   *The Poetics of Biblical Narrative: Ideological Literature and the Drama of Reading.* Bloomington: Indiana University Press.

Todorov, Tzvetan
- 1984   *Mikhail Bakhtin: The Dialogical Principle.* Trans. Wlad Godzich. Minneapolis: University of Minnesota Press.

Webb, Eugene
- 1988   *The Philosophers of Consciousness.* Seattle: University of Washington Press.

NARRATOR AS CHARACTER: MAPPING A READER-ORIENTED APPROACH TO NARRATION IN LUKE-ACTS

John A. Darr
Boston College

ABSTRACT

This essay plots a course for reader-response interpretation of the narrator in Luke's narrative. Fundamental to the argument is the notion that narrators are specialized kinds of characters; that is, they are "constructed" by audiences in much the same way that other characters are "built." As reading proceeds, a reader combines textual and extratextual data in particular ways to form a developing image of the narrator. Throughout this essay, James Dawsey's provocative study of the Lukan voice serves as a foil for demonstrating the need to attend carefully to factors like reader identity, narrative sequence, literary context, textual rhetoric, and extratextual repertoires. The article concludes with a brief preliminary proposal that suggests where an accurately mapped and carefully conducted reader-response approach to narration in Luke-Acts might lead.[1]

INTRODUCTION: NARRATOR QUA CHARACTER

The insight that narrators are but specialized characters is hardly novel. In his 1961 classic, *The Rhetoric of Fiction*, Wayne Booth observed that the main narrator of *Don Quixote* "has made of himself a dramatized character to whom we react as we react to other characters" (212).[2] Indeed, Booth noted, if the intrusive teller of a tale is to prove effective, "he *must* live as a character (219)."[3] But not just any old character: the narrator is always one of the most important characters—if not the most

---

[1] An earlier version of this article (then under the title "Discerning the Lukan Voice: The Narrator as Character in Luke-Acts") appeared in SBLSP 31 (1992:255-65). I wish to thank the members of the Literary Aspects of the Gospels and Acts Group of SBL (especially Robert Brawley) for their helpful comments on the essay. I am also indebted to members of the Boston Theological Institute's New Testament Group for their thoughtful suggestions.

[2] Booth cites earlier critics who made similar observations about narrators as characters with whom audiences are to identify (212-14).

[3] (My emphasis). Booth's basic ideas about narration remain valid even though he often failed to distinguish carefully enough among real author, implied author, and narrator (see Sheeley: 23 n. 2).

important character—of all, for he or she is designed to guide and control the readers' responses to everything in the story (215). Narrators are different from other characters in that they can interact with the audience outside of the story proper; and yet, the way readers come to know narrators is similar to the means by which they construe *dramatis personae*: through their speech (or "voice"), choices, actions, interactions with other characters, and so forth.

What these discrete ideas about narrators as characters seem to call for is a critical methodology that combines insights from reader criticism and character theory. As cogent and promising as such an approach may seem, however, it has not been mapped out by critics of the Bible or other literature. Hindering the entire project is the uncertainty that surrounds the issues of character in general and readers and reading in particular. Here we enter a theoretical minefield dangerous enough to frighten away all but the most intrepid or foolhardy of critics. The theoretical issues surrounding readers and reading are legendary; and, as one critic put it, "character is much more difficult to talk about than most other literary concepts" (Wilson: 730).[4]

The purpose of this essay is to sketch out a reader-oriented theory of characterization and make some preliminary observations about how such a model contributes to our understanding of Luke's narrator. My foil will be James M. Dawsey's unusually provocative book, *The Lukan Voice: Confusion and Irony in the Gospel of Luke*, which utilizes literary criticism to argue that original readers of the Third Gospel would have come to understand its narrator as unreliable and ironic. We turn first to Dawsey's argument.

LUKE'S NARRATOR AS IRONIC AND UNRELIABLE:
A PRÉCIS OF JAMES M. DAWSEY'S HYPOTHESIS

Dawsey mounts a controversial argument that has largely failed to receive support within the Lukan studies guild, although a full-scale refutation of it has yet to appear.[5] Attentive to discrete "voices" (speech, vocabulary, and points of view) in the story, Dawsey finds the narrator

---

[4] Kermode finds character to be a "source of opacity, of complex, various and never definitive interpretation" (75). These hermeneutical difficulties arise, of course, because character is the literary phenomenon that most blatantly confronts us with the human condition—the human self—and therefore with its attendant epistemological and ethical quandaries.

[5] Some who reject Dawsey's hypothesis: Tannehill (7); Wojcik (21, 43); Darr (181-82); and Sheeley (154). More positive is Moore (30-34), who, while pointing out overall theoretical weaknesses in Dawsey's study, applauds his "rigorous attention to contradictions and disjunctions" in Luke's gospel.

and Jesus at odds on such basic ideological issues as christology and eschatology. The fact that the narrator refers to Jesus as "Lord" identifies him as part of a "believing community" in the late first century, the very group for whom the narrative is written. According to Dawsey, however, this is hardly an ideal faith community. Rather, it is a group of self-contented and misguided Christians who misunderstand and misappropriate Jesus. The author—who somehow knows what the real Jesus was all about—designed the narrator to mirror these wayward believers, and then juxtaposed him with the "historical" Jesus in order to jolt the audience (who initially identify with the narrator) out of their complacency and unorthodoxy (125).

The crux of the problem, as Dawsey understands it, has to do with christology. The worshipful, but somewhat elitist, narrator is a triumphalist whose high christology leads him to focus on an exalted, miracle-working Lord and his glorious parousia. "In the eyes of the narrator, Jesus and God are almost indistinguishable, and both are worshiped" (144). But Jesus, speaking in the common (even vulgar) language of the lower classes, views himself as an eschatological prophet sent to gather the poor, downtrodden, and humble into the present but hidden Kingdom of God. He undermines attempts to worship him and claims that his exaltation will come only through suffering, humiliation, and death. The contrast is plain for Dawsey.

> There is a tremendous incongruity between Jesus' words that God has hidden the kingdom from the wise and understanding and revealed it to babes, and the words of the prologue written in high Attic style to a 'most excellent Theophilus,' so that he 'might know the truth concerning the things of which [he] has been informed' . . . On the one hand, the pattern of reversal stands at the center of Jesus' view. Society is being turned downside up, and only the very simple recognize that the awaited time of salvation has come. But on the other hand stands the dedication of the gospel, perhaps to a rich patron or even a provincial governor, . . . [and] written in a highly cultured style appropriate for an educated audience (147).

In short, the reader, who initially identifies with the voice relating the story, becomes increasingly distanced from the narrator as it becomes apparent that Jesus had a different agenda and ideology.

As implausible as all this may first seem, it is clearly within the bounds of literary possibility. One's initial response is to argue against Dawsey that Luke's narrator is omniscient and thus cannot be mistaken. But this line of reasoning is inaccurate (strictly speaking, there is no such thing as an omniscient voice in narrative) and ultimately moot, since even "highly privileged" narrators are sometimes ironic and unreliable.[6] Furthermore, we need not look far afield to find a striking example of an author using as negative paradigms characters with whom the audience initially identifies. Mark's ironic portrayal of the disciples' (especially Peter's) failure to grasp Jesus' true identity and the necessity of suffering and enduring persecution with him parallels Dawsey's notion of how the ironic narrator functions in Luke. Both are (ostensibly) rhetorical characterizations designed to entrap the audience (through initial identification) and then persuade them to modify their ideological/ethical stance (through subsequent distanciation via the speech and behavior of Jesus and other reliable characters).[7]

Despite his literary insight and an admirable willingness to look at the text from novel and unorthodox perspectives, however, Dawsey lacks a coherent literary methodology and, indeed, appears blissfully unaware of the voluminous work on narration in secular literary theory (aside from biblical scholars, Faulkner and Twain are the only moderns to whom he refers). Holding Dawsey's work up to a consistent reader-oriented model of characterization reveals strengths and weaknesses in his study, and signals directions for future work on narration in Luke-Acts.

READING READERS READING THE NARRATOR NARRATING

My approach to characterization is based on two interrelated observations about the production of literary character: readers build characters, and critics build readers.[8] We cannot go into all the implications and relationships of these dual constructive processes here; but we can sketch some pertinent aspects of this audience-oriented model. Although individual readers (and reading communities) exhibit idiosyncratic practices and agendas, certain reading dynamics are common to all. Reading is a temporal activity, largely cognitive in nature; it involves the processing of various kinds of information according to prescribed rules and inscribed (textual) stimuli (cf. Harker). As readers engage and begin to "move" into a narrative, they access both textual and extratextual data (including

---

[6] Harvey argued that "the distinction between reliable and unreliable narrators cuts clean across the categories of omniscient and indirect narration. We may often judge an omniscient narrator unreliable . . ." (76). On the slippery, imprecise terminology commonly used for narrators and narration, see Booth (158-61). For cogent arguments against the presence of a truly omniscient and fully reliable biblical narrator, see Gunn (57-60). Many critics now prefer to speak in terms of degrees of privilege for the narrator, rather than in terms of omniscience.

[7] The fullest and most recent treatment of the disciples as negative rhetorical figures in Mark is found in Tolbert.

[8] For a full description of this model, see Darr (16-59 and 179). The idea that readers build characters is also used by both Docherty and Burnett.

processing cues, or what we might call operating systems) and try to combine them in meaningful ways. Like other literary phenomena, characters are products of this creative process and cannot be rightly understood apart from it. The issue of what the reader *does*, then, is central to characterization theory; we shall address this notion in more detail below. First, however, we must confront another, equally fundamental question: Who is the reader to whom we refer? Since extratextual repertoires (what readers bring to a text) are conditioned by many factors (e.g. the reader's age, gender, economic status, historical era, social and cultural environment), readings of any particular text are bound to differ. Reader response critics must account not only for the text, but also for the reader reading and all of the "messy" factors implied thereby.[9] In short, the reader one postulates is at least partially determinative of how characters, including the narrator, are built. It is, therefore, incumbent upon critics to identify their readers.

Who Is "the Reader" of Luke-Acts?

An interpreter's search for "the reader" should always begin with a look in the mirror, for critics naturally tend to create readers in their own image. To a certain extent, "the reader" will always be *my* reader, a projection of my reading experience and a reflection of my own cultural conditioning. Appeal to a pristine, zero-degree, objective reader is wishful thinking; it cannot help us avoid the ultimate subjectivity of interpretation (cf. Fowler). In other words, the readers to whom critics refer are heuristic constructs whose design invariably imitates the individual critic. Contrary to what many (perhaps most) literary critics of the New Testament seem to think, however, these insights do not necessarily exclude the historical task or oblige us simply to overlook the fact that the texts before us were written nineteen hundred years ago for an intended audience with a very different language and culture from our own.[10] There is still great interpretive value in attempting to reconstruct a text-specific reader, that is, one who possesses the extratextual competencies assumed by the author (Culpepper: 7-8, 205-227; Tolbert: 52-55; Darr: 23-29). Although a full reconstruction is not possible, some of what the "authorial" audience was expected to know can be recovered. By comparing Luke and Acts with

---

[9] Moore shows how modern theory's developing awareness that the reader cannot be ignored in interpretation opened a Pandora's box of hermeneutical issues.

[10] Ironically, those advocating the ahistorical approach are loathe to abandon the most culturally-conditioned aspect of these ancient narratives, their language. On this glaring inconsistency see Darr (13-14). Similar observations have been made about those literary critics who attempt to treat the Hebrew Bible without an eye to its original language and historical context (Sternberg, 1985:10-11).

other literature of their time and culture, one can begin to draw some general inferences about the reading level and cultural repertoire of the intended audience.¹¹ This knowledge can, in turn, help us negotiate ambiguous terrain in the text.

The (my) reader of Luke is thus a heuristic hybrid, a fusion of ancient and modern cultural horizons. There are many blanks in the ancient horizon, but some things about it can be known with a degree of certainty. The reader is a member of the late first-century Mediterranean world and lives by the cultural scripts and social norms of that world. She or he knows basic historical, political, geographical, and ethnic facts about the Roman empire. Perhaps more to the point, the reader is at home in *popular* Greco-Roman literature. Luke-Acts was not written for a literary elite, but for those accustomed to low- to middle-brow fare like the romances. ¹² More specifically, the reader is familiar with the Septuagint, a fact that places him or her within the broad stream of the Jewish tradition (Christian or non-Christian Jew, God- fearer, or Gentile Christian). Beyond these general parameters, however, all is speculation.

Dawsey's take on the reader of Luke-Acts is instructive, for it involves several faulty moves ubiquitous in gospel scholarship, and goes a long way toward explaining why he sees the narrator as he does. At the heart of his model are historical *a prioris* about the real author, his audience, and his purpose. The author writes for his own faith "community," which is experiencing a theological or cultural crisis of some kind.¹³ His purpose is to help them deal with the problem at hand and get back on the right track. A further assumption is that one can define the so-called com-

---

¹¹ In my reference to "intended audience," the dreaded "i" word (intentionality) raises its ugly head. At the risk of moving too far afield, I would observe that the abandonment of all reference to intention would mean at one and the same time a jettisoning of the notions of textual discourse and rhetoric, and a retreat into a kind of constructivism (readers or reading communities construing all) that trivializes critical discourse. The famous "intentional fallacy," as originally coined, did not deny that literary texts exhibited perceptible patterns of intentionality, but only that a critic could (or should) attribute such intention to biographical trivia concerning the author. In other words, the argument against the "intentional fallacy" was a rebuttal of the excesses of romantic (author-oriented) criticism, and not an argument for the ultimate instability and ambiguity of language in general and texts in particular.

¹² Luke-Acts may be the most sophisticated of New Testament narratives, but, when viewed in its broader literary environment, it must still be grouped with popular literature: so Aune (7); Pervo (1-11); Tolbert (59-79); and Darr (27-28).

¹³ The notion that each evangelist wrote to his own somewhat idiosyncratic faith community has become such a part of the idiom of gospel studies that we fail to question it sufficiently. That Luke writes for a single, well-defined religious community in the Greco-Roman world would be very difficult to prove. Scholars seem not to have taken enough notice of Johnson's "cautious cautionary essay" on this subject. On the futility of defining a "community" on the basis of textual phenomena in Luke-Acts, see Darr (23-25).

munity and its problems by reference to characters, imagery, or rhetoric in the story. In this view, characters are allegories for persons in the real world, either believers themselves or those with whom they come in contact. And finally, if one digs deeply enough into these kinds of studies, one invariably detects beneath the veneer of historicity a modern theological purpose motivating the entire interpretive enterprise.[14]

The character that Dawsey identifies as representing what is "wrong" with the Lukan "community" is the narrator. He both tells the story and stands in as its wayward, intended reader. But this scenario, intriguing as it may be, proceeds from assumptions that simply cannot be proven with available historical evidence. It is difficult to avoid the conclusion that what drives Dawsey is an urge to make Luke speak to a modern church grown complacent in its worship and affluence, and unwilling to confront the discrete social ills that plague humanity. Dawsey's own admirable pastoral concerns come to the surface in statements like, "One of the main purposes in presenting the gospel, *then as now* [my emphasis], was to allow the community of believers to be confronted again with the Lord who appeared in history . . ." (125). The goal is to get the church off of its cushioned pews and out into the world, with a mission of "turning society upside down." One cannot fault such homiletic reading strategies, for they are what make the ancient written words relevant to the church's current situation. Whether or not they are historically sound, however, is a quite different question—one that demands a negative answer. Our conclusion that the intended reader is a lower- to middle-class type, for example, does not accord well with Dawsey's construction of the reader (and the narrator) as elitist. The reader to whom Dawsey refers sounds uncannily like a parishioner in a mainline American church, and not much like a Mediterranean person from many centuries ago.[15]

When we deconstruct Dawsey's presuppositions about the reader of Luke-Acts, his argument for its rhetoric—including his notion of an

---

[14] Brawley's work on the Pharisees in Luke-Acts provides an example of this kind of reasoning at work. Luke writes for and to his own Christian community in order to foster irenic relations between it and the non-Christian Jews with whom it is in contact. The Pharisees, whom Brawley sees as being somewhat positively depicted, represent the Jews whom the Christians are to respect. It is difficult not to see behind all this the honorable modern impetus toward better Jewish-Christian relations rather than any historically verifiable circumstances of Luke's intended readers. Such suspicions are reinforced by a closer look at the narrative: from a reader-response perspective, Luke's Pharisees consistently come off badly, even where Brawley understands them to be lauded. For pertinent discussions, see Brawley (92, 105) and Darr (90-91).

[15] Moore's comment on Dawsey's reader is telling: "He presents us with a narrative technique and a matching audience response almost two millenia out of time" (33).

unreliable and ironic narrator—also falls away. The lesson is plain for all who would study Luke's narrator: the audience we postulate conditions our perception of the narrator. A cynical or resistant reader, for example, will build an unreliable narrator. As Moore notes in his discussion of Dawsey, "it is instructive to see how easily such [disharmonious] data is accumulated when one goes to the gospel text with one's antennae adjusted to pick up contradictory voices instead of a noncontradictory authorial voice" (32). Still, it is difficult to imagine a fully resistant or highly cynical reader continuing to read beyond a few paragraphs. (The ultimate in resistance is putting the text down and leaving the room!) We need not think of an audience that is strictly in line with the ideology of the implied author, but some degree of openness, of willingness to suspend disbelief and enter the story world, would seem necessary to any realistic, non-aborted reading experience.

What Does the Reader Do?

As we noted above, reading is a temporal, cognitive activity that involves the processing of textual and extratextual data. In other words, it is a series of mental "moves" constrained by text and extratext. Stanley Fish described reading dynamics as "the making and revising of assumptions, the rendering and regretting of judgments, the coming to and abandoning of conclusions, the giving and withdrawing of approval, the specifying of causes, the asking of questions, the supplying of answers, the solving of riddles" (126-27). And all of these exercises are creative. Readers try to construct a consistent, meaningful work (including characters) as they move along the textual continuum. The interpreter's task is to trace and analyze this succession of creative activities on the part of readers.

In following the reader's building of characters, the critic must remain aware of these factors: (1) holism and context; (2) sequence and accumulation; (3) extratext; and (4) rhetoric. Each of these will be discussed below in relation to Luke's narrator.

Holism and Context. Much confusion and controversy surround the topic of holism within literary critical circles. Formalists have mistakenly held that the *text itself* is analogous to a solid object—whole, seamless, integrated. But the text is not holistic; it is full of gaps, indeterminacies, tensions, inconsistencies, and ambiguities. Holism should be used to refer not to the text, but to the literary *work* that a reader constructs on the basis of a schematic text. To speak of Luke-Acts as holistic is actually to speak of a reader's building of consistency among discrete textual data. Oscillating between retrospection and anticipation, readers attempt to "fit everything together in a consistent pattern" (Iser, 1972:288).[16] As opinions develop and expectations shift, the audience continually tries to build a consistent, coherent narrative world. Weaving together textual and extratextual information, readers are able to image patterns that often cover gaps, help resolve tensions, and clarify ambiguities. Even what the reader produces, of course, can never be whole and completely integrated. Nevertheless, the reader is able to build a coherent, adequately integrated work on the basis of Luke's text and the original extratext.

The point is that readers fully *expect* texts to provide them with sufficient data and guidance to construe a narrative world that hangs together and makes sense. And, of course, the complex world that the reader of Luke-Acts images is the proper context within which to understand its inhabitants, the characters. Most significant for analyzing characters is the extensive matrix of relationships that develops among the characters themselves (Harvey: 52-53). In other words, characters are delineated largely in terms of each other, much as we are defined by our relationships in real life.

Dawsey has certainly grasped the insight that characters are formed and evaluated in the crucible of relationships, for he has made the juxtaposition of Jesus and the narrator the crux of his argument. From John the Baptist to the Pharisees, most characters in the narrative are indeed formulated and assessed in terms of their interaction with Jesus. It is fitting then, that the reader also judge the narrator vis-à-vis Jesus. This is one of the many strengths of Dawsey's work and should not be ignored.

What Dawsey fails to comprehend, however, is that one cannot isolate and concentrate on a single kind of datum—voice, choice, actions, names, or whatever—in relation to just a few characters without skewing those characters (Tannehill: 7). The reader is not atomizing textual information, but, quite to the contrary, is trying to *combine* it in consistent, harmonious patterns. Such efforts may not succeed ultimately, but the reader response critic must at least ask how the audience attempts to carry them off. Ignoring this integrative, holistic reading dynamic while suppressing almost all textual information apart from voice virtually assures that characters in Luke will be perceived as idiosyncratic and (often) incompatible.

The narrowness of Dawsey's focus raises a host of contextual questions for the reader response critic. Given Dawsey's approach and results, where does Acts fit in? Why would an author write a second volume

---

[16] Iser's distinction (1972:288; 1978:118-29) between *text* (the bare-bones skeleton of verbal signs) and *work* (what a reader *actualizes*, or fleshes out in response to those signs) is clearly behind my argument here. The reader-response critic's focus should be the entire work (reader reading text), not the text alone.

using an unreliable narrator, and why would a reader want to peruse it?[17] Or would including material from Acts alter Dawsey's understanding of the narrator and his function? And what would happen to the notion of Jesus as simply prophet if one were to include his actions (especially the miracles) and not just his words in his characterization? Further, would adding other agents like God and the Holy Spirit to the mix make any difference? What all these significant questions imply is that characterization of the narrator is more complicated, and requires an analysis of far more material, than Dawsey realizes.

But even if one looks only at the limited kinds of data that Dawsey finds salient (speech and titles for Jesus), the idea that the narrator is elitist and unreliable appears faulty. By widening our lenses to include how other figures (not simply the narrator) use the title Lord, and by looking for the ways in which a reader would synthesize information, we find that the narrator is not at all idiosyncratic and misguided in his use of that title for the earthly Jesus, and, indeed, that he is fully sanctioned in doing so by other authoritative voices, including Jesus himself. Looking at *kyrios* in the concordance reveals the following. In Luke 1-2, the chapters that set the stage for the entire narrative, the title Lord is used interchangeably for God and Jesus. For example, Elizabeth refers to Mary as "the mother of my Lord" (1:43). When the angel heralds Jesus' birth, he says to the shepherds, ". . . for unto you is born this day in the city of David a savior, who is [*estin*, present tense] Christ the Lord" (2:11).

Later in the narrative Jesus refers to himself as Lord on at least two occasions before his passion. The reader who is already primed by chapters 1 and 2 to see both God and Jesus as Lord will perceive a double referent in Jesus' reply to Satan's temptation, "You shall not tempt the Lord your God" (4:12). In the grainfield episode Jesus concludes his refutation of the Pharisees with the forceful assertion that, "The Son of Man is Lord of the Sabbath" (6:5). And this is not at all out of line with Jesus' expressions of a very high christology elsewhere in the narrative. At 10:22, for example, Jesus states, "All things have been delivered to me by my father; and no one knows who the son is except the father, or who the father is except the son and anyone to whom the son chooses to reveal him." The "messianic moment" is already here in the ministry of the earthly Jesus; it does not await his passion and exaltation. To use

---

[17] There is some controversy about whether the narration in Acts is similar to that in the gospel. The question was initially raised by Walworth (7-11) and is currently being pursued by other Lukan scholars in an attempt to demonstrate a radical disjunction between Luke and Acts. But Sheeley's recent exhaustive study of narrative asides in both volumes led him to conclude that, "The voice which addresses Theophilus in the first volume is the same one which speaks to Theophilus to begin the second leg of the narrative voyage" (136).

Dawsey's unfortunate term, Luke's Jesus seems to be as "elitist" as his narrator.

A number of other positive characters, both major and minor, also call Jesus Lord (e.g. Peter [5:8]; the faithful centurion [7:6]), thus encouraging the reader to see this as an appropriate title. Not until 7:13 does *the narrator* refer to Jesus as Lord! But by this point in the story, the reader has been fully prepared to view this as an authorized title for the earthly Jesus; and so the narrator's use of it does not strike him or her as unusual or out of place. Luke's Jesus may well tend to speak of himself with other titles, but, given the narrative developments we have seen, the reader is easily able to harmonize that tendency with voices that call him Lord.

Sequence and Accumulation. Perhaps the most distinctive trait of reader-response criticism is its insistence on the significance of sequence (Resseguie: 317). Character is cumulative, and the means and timing of its accumulation must be taken into account by the interpreter. Given our redaction-critical heritage it is hardly surprising that we Lukan scholars still tend to gather discrete information from various parts of the text with little regard for its placement or the dynamics of linear accretion. As Moore rightly sees (34), Dawsey's approach has more to do with historical criticism's fragmentation and rearrangement of textual data than it does with more holistic and sequence-sensitive methods. Once again, the isolation and displacement of narrative evidence skews characterization.[18] One can create almost any character one wants by manipulating various data without regard to their textual order and settings. A reader-oriented analysis of Luke's narrator should begin at the prologue (an auspicious introduction indeed) and work through the story to its end with Paul in Rome. Earlier evidence strongly conditions a reader's reception of later evidence, so special attention must be accorded the prologue and the first two chapters of Luke.[19] My own preliminary research indicates that early on in the narrative several authority structures are established for the reader (see below).

The Extratext. What kind of narrator did the reader expect to encounter as the reading process began? That is, what knowledge of conventional Hellenistic and Jewish narrational modes might the authorial

---

[18] Only by disregarding or downplaying the sequential dynamic of the narrative, for example, can Lukan literary critics reaffirm the widespread notion that the Pharisees are somewhat positively depicted in Luke-Acts. On this tendency among interpreters, see Darr (85-126, esp. 87-91).

[19] On the reader-response argument that what comes first may well deserve to be weighted more heavily than what comes later in the narrative, see Sternberg (1978:93-96). It is quite clear that readers tend to place great stock in what they learn *first* in the narrative; and they will hold to it strongly in the face of other (later) evidence. Sternberg refers to this phenomenon of reading as "the primacy effect."

reader have brought to the text? Research of this vital subject has just begun.[20] What is already clear, however, is that ancient readers would not have expected to find a narrator at odds with the fundamental catalog of values in the narrative. That is, they might have looked for factual mistakes on the part of the story-teller (narration is a human endeavor, after all), but not for the wholly ironic and unreliable narrator that Dawsey images. As Scholes and Kellogg assert, "the idea of creating an unreliable fictional eye-witness is the sophisticated product of an empirical and ironic age" (264). And, of course, if the audience did not at all expect an ironic narrator, they most probably would not have seen one even if the textual evidence can be construed to support such a phenomenon. The reader would probably understand Luke's narrator as an *histor*, an inquirer "constructing a narrative on the basis of such evidence as he has been able to accumulate" and "seeking to convince the audience of his authority and competence to deal with the subject at hand" (Scholes and Kellogg: 265-66). As for the eloquent language of the prologue, it too is conventional for narrators and thus would not have caused the reader to categorize the narrator as an elitist. The Septuagintalisms of the narrative are just that, intertextual echoes of the Septuagint, and not indicators that the narrator is trying to inject a "specialized language of worship" back into the story of Jesus.[21] Taking on different dialects seems to have been an expected part of the competent narrator's repertoire. How the reader built Luke's narrator was, at least in part, due to a knowledge of all these—and other—extratextual factors.

Rhetoric. Narrators are always central to the rhetoric of the narratives they mediate. All of the information (shown and told) that the reader receives is filtered through the narrator's particular point of view. He or she even tells us what the other characters say and think. The effect of a truly unreliable and ironic narrator, therefore, is not just to present himself badly, but to destabilize the entire narrative. What can or should the reader believe if the teller of the story cannot be trusted? Is the Lukan narrator's depiction of Jesus reliable? What about his references to God and the Holy Spirit? It is doubtful that Dawsey realizes the true consequences of positing an unreliable narrator for Luke, for in doing so he has pulled one of the linchpins from the narrative and sent it spinning out of control.

---

[20] Sheeley (40-96, 179-182) compares Luke-Acts with thirteen Greco-Roman literary pieces (romances, biographies, and histories) in terms of how they use parenthetical commentary by the narrator.

[21] Dawsey's claims along this trajectory (28-32) are simply not cogent from the perspective of reader-response criticism.

Preliminary Suggestions Concerning Luke's Narrator as Character

This is not the venue for a thorough examination of Lukan narration. By definition, the narrator is involved in *all* of the narrative, though the degree and type of narrator involvement may (indeed, does) vary substantially from episode to episode. This ubiquity and complexity should give us pause: the subject would best be treated in several large monographs or perhaps a multi-volume commentary. In response to Dawsey's forays, however, it seems fitting to suggest some alternative approaches to (1) the intended reader's perception of the authority and reliability of the Lukan narrator, and (2) the (primary) rhetorical function of that narrator. Both proposals are based on a reading of Luke's prologue (1:1-4)—the initial point of contact between reader and narrator—and on reader-response analyses of characterization in Luke-Acts.

First, how does Luke's narrator, as *histor*, try to "convince the audience of his authority and competence?" Since there is no such thing as absolute, universal, and unquestionable narrational authority in the abstract, the narrator must appeal to structures of authority that are already recognized by his intended readers; and he must link himself to those authorities in a credible way. In other words, the Lukan narrator's authority is *derivative* and depends heavily on the reader's credulity, on his or her investment in a certain theological world view, and on a certain set of literary conventions. By identifying himself immediately as the narrator of "the things that have been *fulfilled* among us" (1:1), the teller of the story locates himself within a long succession of those who recount the wondrous deeds of God in salvation history. The reading role one is encouraged to take up is that of a *theophilos* (1:3), a "friend of God" who (one soon learns) is thoroughly versed in the scriptures that provide the immediate background for the present story.

Fulfillment assumes prediction and promise, and so the reader is immediately directed outside the framework of this narrative and "toward a far broader salvation-historical horizon (it implies that relevant things have happened *before* and *since* the events related in the story) . . . Luke's story is but a part of a much larger, ongoing story in which God plays the major role" (Darr: 51). This divine frame of reference—which ultimately generates the narrator's authority—is carefully construed and cultivated in Luke-Acts. God, the super-agent who remains unseen, controls the action from offstage. However, it is only through the narrator and certain oracles, which the narrator identifies as certified by the Holy Spirit, that the reader learns what God has willed and accomplished, as well as the significance of God's acts. There is a palpable sense of control and unanimity operative here. God has a very specific and incontrovertible plan for the world; and the narrator, who assumes the audacious role of the ancient biblical narrators, speaks for God. It is the narrator who tells us God's will, God's plan, whom God favors, to whom God assigns various tasks. The narrator's view and that of the divine are thus to be seen as a pair of mutually reinforcing, highly reliable, and highly privileged perspectives serving as fully authoritative guides for the reader (cf. Darr: 50-53).

Less impressive, perhaps, but nonetheless important to the narrator's appeal for authority is his reference to "those who from the beginning were eyewitnesses and ministers of the word" (Luke 1:2). The story he tells has been handed down by reliable, respectable witnesses from a previous generation. Luke's narrator clearly identifies himself as a second or third generation believer who yet has had contact with the first generation among whom the events of the story took place.

Is Luke's narrator reliable? One cannot ultimately prove a narrator's reliability; and the issue is ambiguous if one ignores the intended audience with its particular extratextual repertoire and expectations, and if one chooses to concentrate on the text's inevitable gaps, ambiguities, and apparent inconsistencies rather than on the way authorial readers put the text together using its own indicators as well as assumed extratextual knowledge. Given the tightly controlled artifice of authoritative voices developed in the text, the literary conventions and historical linkages to which the narrator appeals, and the readerly tendency toward consistency-building, however, it is hard to imagine the original audience assessing Luke's narrator as unreliable.

Apart from his role as authoritative guide to characters and events in the story, however, how might Luke's narrator function? Elsewhere I have argued at length that the fundamental rhetorical thrust of Luke-Acts is the attempt to form its readers into *ideal witnesses*. There are, of course, two aspects to being a reliable witness: one must correctly and insightfully perceive the events in question, and one must faithfully report what one has seen and heard to others. Much of the story is devoted to inculcating and honing the first quality in the reader. From beginning to end, the text urges one to *see*, *hear*, and *respond* properly (i.e. according to the text's value system) to "the things that have been fulfilled among us." Especially through characterization, the reader is encouraged to value certain ways of seeing and hearing (=reading) and to reject others. In short, an analogy is drawn between the reader reading and the characters seeing and hearing the salvific personages and events. Many figures thus serve as positive (e.g. Simeon) or negative (e.g. the Pharisees) paradigms of perception.

But it is not enough to perceive; one must also bear witness to what one has seen and heard. The ultimate purpose of all this rhetoric is to transform the mere reader of the story into a bold re-teller of the story, that is, into one who exhibits the values of *parresia* and *autarkeia* (Darr: 147-68). The ideal character and, by analogy, the ideal reader will observe the divine, fully recognize it, comprehend its true significance, and testify about it to others.

This rhetoric of recognition and response begins immediately in the narrative, for the prologue identifies the insiders of the story as those who were *from the beginning* witnesses of the word, and who delivered that word to others. The narrator represents a second, but no less important link in a (hopefully) ongoing chain of such witnesses; he too has "traced everything closely from *the very first*," and now will pass on an orderly, accurate account to his reader. The narrator thus serves as a paradigm: even as the audience begins to hear the story, they have before them the very model of what they are to become—one who attends closely to the data from the very beginning and then recounts it to others. And at a significant juncture the narrator even steps on stage as one of those who "evangelize" with Paul. When Paul receives a vision and decides to direct his efforts toward Macedonia (and so Europe rather than Asia), the narrator accompanies him; and their speech to the women of Philippi results in the conversion of Lydia (Acts 16:9-15). In short, the narrator functions mimetically vis-à-vis the reader; he is an ideal witness, one who rightly perceives and boldly reports what he has seen and heard.

Conclusions

The literary-critical study of Luke's narrator is yet in its infancy. Dawsey's book has done much to spark interest in this vital but often-neglected area of Lukan studies. But his conclusion that the narrator of the Third Gospel would be seen by the reader as ironic and unreliable is not confirmed when one applies basic elements of a coherent reader-response model to the salient evidence. Rather, what comes under suspicion are Dawsey's methodology and presuppositions about Luke's intended audience. Our interaction with certain aspects of Dawsey's argument has led, however, to intriguing new prospects for understanding Lukan narration. Far from proving ironic and unreliable, the narrator actually appears as an authoritative, trustworthy guide, and serves as a model witness to and for the reader.

WORKS CONSULTED

Aune, David E.
    1987   *The New Testament in Its Literary Environment*. Philadelphia: Westminster.

Booth, Wayne C.
    1983   *The Rhetoric of Fiction*. 2nd ed. Chicago: University of Chicago Press.

Brawley, Robert L.
    1987   *Luke-Acts and the Jews: Conflict, Apology, and Conciliation*. Atlanta: Scholars.

Burnett, Fred W.
    1985   "Characterization in Matthew: Reader Construction of the Disciple Peter." Unpub. paper presented to the Literary Aspects of the Gospels and Acts Group of the Society of Biblical Literature (see his article in this volume).

Culpepper, R. Alan
    1983   *Anatomy of the Fourth Gospel: A Study in Literary Design*. Philadelphia: Fortress.

Darr, John A.
    1992   *On Character Building: The Reader and the Rhetoric of Characterization in Luke-Acts*. Louisville: Westminster/John Knox.

Dawsey, James M.
    1986   *The Lukan Voice: Confusion and Irony in the Gospel of Luke*. Macon, GA: Mercer University Press.

Docherty, Thomas
    1983   *Reading (Absent) Character: Towards a Theory of Characterization in Fiction*. Oxford: Clarendon.

Fish, Stanley
    1972   "Literature in the Reader: Affective Stylistics." *New Literary History* 2:123-62.

Fowler, Robert M.
    1985   "Who is 'the Reader' of Mark's Gospel?" *Semeia* 31:5-23.

Gunn, David M.
    1990   "Reading Right: Reliable and Omniscient Narrator, Omniscient God, and Foolproof Composition in the Hebrew Bible." Pp. 53-64 in *Essays in Celebration of Forty Years of Biblical Studies in the University of Sheffield*. Ed. David J. A. Clines. JSOTSup 87. Sheffield: JSOT.

Harker, W. John
    1989   "Information Processing and the Reading of Literary Texts." *New Literary History* 20:465-81.

Harvey, W. J.
    1965   *Character and the Novel*. Ithaca: Cornell University Press.

Iser, Wolfgang
- 1972 "The Reading Process: A Phenomenological Approach." *New Literary History* 3:279-99.
- 1978 *The Act of Reading: A Theory of Aesthetic Response*. Baltimore and London: Johns Hopkins University Press.

Johnson, Luke T.
- 1979 "On Finding the Lukan Community: A Cautious Cautionary Essay." SBLSP 18:87-100.

Kermode, Frank
- 1979 *The Genesis of Secrecy: On the Interpretation of Narrative*. Cambridge: Harvard University Press.

Moore, Stephen D.
- 1989 *Literary Criticism and the Gospels: The Theoretical Challenge*. New Haven and London: Yale University Press.

Pervo, Richard I.
- 1987 *Profit With Delight: The Literary Genre of the Acts of the Apostles*. Philadelphia: Fortress.

Praeder, Susan M.
- 1987 "The Problem of First Person Narration in Acts." *NovT* 29:193-218.

Resseguie, James L.
- 1984 "Reader-Response Criticism and the Synoptic Gospels." *JAAR* 52:307-24.

Scholes, Robert and Robert Kellogg
- 1966 *The Nature of Narrative*. London and New York. Oxford University Press.

Sheeley, Steven M.
- 1992 *Narrative Asides in Luke-Acts*. JSNTSup 72. Sheffield: JSOT.

Sternberg, Meir
- 1978 *Expositional Modes and Temporal Ordering in Fiction*. Baltimore: Johns Hopkins University Press.
- 1985 *The Poetics of Biblical Narrative: Ideological Literature and the Drama of Reading*. Bloomington: Indiana University Press.

Tannehill, Robert C.
- 1986 *The Narrative Unity of Luke-Acts: A Literary Interpretation*. Vol. 1, *The Gospel According to Luke*. Philadelphia: Fortress.

Tolbert, Mary Ann
- 1989 *Sowing the Gospel: Mark's World in Literary-Historical Perspective*. Minneapolis: Fortress.

Walworth, Allen J.
- 1985 "The Narrator of Acts." Unpub. Ph.D. dissertation. Louisville: Southern Baptist Theological Seminary.

Wilson, Rawdon
    1978/79   "The Bright Chimera: Character as a Literary Term." *Critical Inquiry* 5:725-49.

Wojcik, Jan
    1989   *The Road to Emmaus: Reading Luke's Gospel*. West Lafayette, IN: Purdue University Press.

SIGNS OF THE FLESH: OBSERVATIONS ON CHARACTERIZATION IN THE BIBLE

Alice Bach
Stanford University

ABSTRACT

In biblical texts a crucial ambiguity for the feminist reader revolves around the narrator's providing one version of how female characters behave within the situations in which they have been placed, and another *imagined* version that might be provided by the female figure—if one could reconstruct her story. A continuing concern of mine has been to find a method for retrieving the female character who may have been flattened or suppressed by the weight of the story that is not hers. A necessary first step is to abandon the Proppian idea that the characters are of no interest in themselves, but rather are agents of the plot, secondary elements necessary to the enactment of the story. In a male-driven plot, female agents are going to be limited functionaries. One way to shake off the strictures of the structuralists and to identify counter voices is to propose that character can exist in our consciousness as an element independent of the story in which the character was originally discovered. Chatman has observed that the experience of reading often involves the retention of our image of a character, not only apart from events but also long after we have forgotten the events of the story (118-19). The reader creates a "paradigm of traits," a more fluid concept of characterization than the one formulated by Forster and still common among biblical literary critics, of referring to round and flat characters, who derive their dimension and shape from the narrator's version of the story. Following Chatman's concept of characterization as an integral process of reader and text, I examine the biblical figure of Bathsheba, not as a passive nonperson, but first as an object of male sexual fantasy, seen and not heard, and then as a good mother, heard and not seen.

What is character but the determination of incident? What is incident but the illustration of character?
        Henry James, The Art of Fiction

Every story needs a storyteller. Within the Bible, the importance of recognizing the biblical narrator as a figure telling a slanted story has been undervalued. Recently Robert Alter has described the biblical narrator as "impassive and authoritative" (1989:176). While he acknowledges that ancient narratives may switch momentarily from the narrator's point of view to a character's angle of vision, he is content to describe prenovelistic narrative as containing "a high degree of uniformity of perspective maintained by an authoritative overviewing narrator" (1989:176). Alter allows no room for an iconoclastic reader like Gayatri Spivak, who describes her task as "to read it and run with it and go somewhere else. To see where in that grid there are the spaces where, in fact, woman oozes away" (145).

I want to suggest a mode of reading in which one imagines the biblical narrator as a storyteller with whom the reader must contend, as s/he does with characters within the story. Instead of being seduced by the narrator's version, I am attracted to a strategy that allows the reader to step outside the reader's appointed place in order to defy the fixed gaze of the male narrator. I realize the difficulty in conferring upon the narrator, or indeed upon characters in the story, more "reality" or verisimilitude than the text itself would offer. I am not suggesting a "true" or historical identity for the narrator, but rather a fictive one based upon his agenda and upon his role as storyteller. If one challenges the notion of the omnipotent voice of the impassive narrator, the female characters will not be in so much danger of oozing away.

In my reading, the narrator shares with the characters a narrative life in the reader's consciousness. A tension is thus set up between the reader's desire to form narrative conclusions concerning characters and the narrator's attempts to control the reader's understanding of characters within the story. By fleshing out the narrator, we flush out his intentions. By refusing to award him the transparency he seeks as omniscient voice of truth, the reader will be aware of the narrator's motives, what he's up to in fashioning his story. Because the redactors have spliced the biblical narrator's voice with that of the author and of God himself, one task of a literary critic who is suspicious of the narrator's identity as the authoritative voice of truth is to separate the role of the narrator as self-interested agent from the narrator as the teller of the tale. To make the narrator visible, and thus his agenda more identifiable to the reader, one needs to regard his version of the story as a self-conscious telling of the tale, intended to convince us that he has provided the true account of what happened.

One way to figure out the narrator is to shift our readerly identity from that of ideal reader, an individual who would believe, understand, and appreciate every word and device of the text, to that of suspicious narratee. In using the term narratee, I invoke Gerald Prince's concept of narratee-character as the fictive one addressed by the narrator. The signals that he sends out within the text to the narratee are then read by the reader to smoke him out. Prince argues, I think persuasively, that interpreting the signals sent to this narratee-character, a construct created by the author, allows one to categorize the narration *according to the type of narratee to whom it is addressed* (15). Even if the narratee is not explicitly addressed, as he is not in the majority of biblical narratives, when the narrator lavishes his opinions upon him, the narratee "becomes as clearly defined as any character" (Prince: 18). Thus, constructing a narratee within the biblical text is a technique that may help the biblical critic figure out the narrator's game since the narratee "constitutes a relay between narrator and reader, he helps to establish the narrative framework, and he serves to characterize the narrator" (Prince: 23).

A second strategy of reading characters, connected to the first, is to retrieve or reconstruct characters from the structuralist wasteland in which they are mere actants of the plot. By looking at sights not within the narrator's gaze, for instance, a reader may be able to "see" characters who are not primary agents of the plot. Literary techniques suggested by Seymour Chatman and Baruch Hochman focus the delineation of character within the insight of the reader rather than within the fixed gaze of the narrator. Shifting the gaze from the narrator's eye to the reader's "I" is especially important for feminist readers since the elements of structural analysis applied to character often deflate female biblical characters, who are not usually the focal point of narration.

SIGHTING THE BIBLICAL NARRATOR

Only recently has biblical criticism moved past the positivistic New Critical arena in which one assumes that there is *one* correct interpretation of story and characters that can be adduced from a *proper* analysis of form. Among the most totalizing of the presuppositions that underlie such a formalist reading of the text is that language has a stabilizing force, that it means what it says and says what it means. The New Critic looks for a balanced order, and not surprisingly, finds one. In contrast Bakhtin finds limitless textual diversity, although arguably because he is looking for diversity rather than singularity. Language for Bakhtin at any given moment of its historical existence is heteroglot from top to bottom: "it represents the co-existence of socioideological contradictions between the past and present, between differing epochs of the past, between different socioideological groups in the present, between tendencies, schools, circles and so forth, all given a bodily form" (291). As Ilona Pardes's eloquent study suggests, the Bible is just such a text of many tongues.

In a view related to the formalist ignoring of the effect of a reader on the text, many interpreters have continued to ignore the effect of a female reader upon the text. As I shall argue in this paper, too often biblical critics have been ideal readers, allied with the patriarchal narrator, and have not recognized that he was telling it slant. This kind of reader makes the desired audience stance explicit; he is the audience presupposed by the narrative itself. A bumptious narratee, on the other hand, will challenge the privileged role of the narrator and recast him as the fictive henchman of the author.

In traditional biblical interpretation, critics have commonly figured the narrator as omniscient and entwined with the divine voice without questioning his reliabliity as a narrator. Indeed the biblical narrator has a privileged position within the text, possessing the ability to move outside time and space. Since there is no textual distinction between the implied author and the public narrator, readers have equated the two voices, while considering themselves part of a universal audience. As Bakhtin has indicated, authorial discourse is "directed toward its own straightforward referential meaning," and authorial narrators possess a stronger voice than that of characters who are contained within the events of the story (187). Clearly the biblical narrator, not being content merely to tell his tale, has made himself such a significant literary presence.

Meir Sternberg has described the biblical narrator's function with great economy:

> the narrator enjoys free movement in time (among narrative past, present and future) and in space (enabling him to follow secret conversations, shuttle between simultaneous happenings or between heaven and earth). These two establish an unlimited range of information to draw upon or, from the reader's side, a supernatural principle of coherence and intelligibility (Sternberg: 84).

When the authorial voice is equated with that of the deity, as it is in the biblical narratives, the plot thickens. I am assuming that the narrator is male, like the community (ideal reader) he represents. Recently Harold Bloom has hypothesized a female author for the J material in the Torah. Since I understand the narrator to be a figure in the text, one whose authority is never questioned within the text, and I recognize the control the patriarchal society exerted upon woman, I find it hard to imagine a female in antiquity who would be credited with omniscience. I am surprised that Bloom did not use the occasion of his female designation to confront the politics of reading, exploring the convention generally assumed "that the voice of authority is male, albeit a comprehensive male voice in which sexual distinctiveness is to some extent neutralized" (Culler: 205). It seems that Culler has identified a more provocative question concerning the ways in which readers construct the identity of the narrator.[1]

---

[1] Lanser, expanding upon her observation that narrators as people all have gender, argues that in authored texts the reader assumes that the "presence of a female name on the title page signals female narrative voice in the absence of markings to the

The omniscient biblical narrator has a task of the utmost significance: he is the prophet of prophets. His most privileged job is to relate the word of the Lord, thus proving that the narrator's authority is secondary only to that of the deity, to whom he is scribe. The ultimate evidence of his omniscience is that he is privy to God's "feelings." His audience believes his explanations, that waters flooded the earth because the Lord repented of making human beings and "it grieved God in his heart" (Gen 6:6), and that Saul lost his kingship because God repented making Saul king (1 Sam 15:11). There is no episode in which the narrator's voice represents or supports a point of view different from that of the Bible's central ideology. In fact the choice of omniscient narrator strengthens the biblical view of an omnipotent deity and "serves the purpose of staging and glorifying an omniscient God" (Sternberg: 87).[2] Gérard Genette has described this narratorial function as providing the foundation of verisimilitude. When the narrator engages in extra-representational acts—"judgments, generalizations about the world, directly addressed to the narratee" (Lanser, 1992:16)—he renders the textual events (as well as characters' behaviors) more plausible (Lanser, 1992:17).

Sternberg does not resist the narrator's version, but rather describes how the text functions to preserve the only "correct" account by silencing "alien and erroneous viewpoints (not excluding criticisms of God or appeals to idols)." These voices that are not compatible with the norms of the implied author occur on the surface of the text, or on the level of story, but the narrator discredits these errant discourses, silences them. Sternberg claims that to allow a dissonant voice even a momentary breath of life would make the narrator "a maker rather than a shaper of plot" (128). By viewing the narrator as teller of the tale rather than the creator of the tale, Sternberg fuses the identity of the fictive narrator with the "real" author and thus avoids the morass of untangling sighs and whispers of voices other than the narrator/author. He cannot allow the narrator to become one of several possible narratorial voices directed to the narratee, because that would sever the indivisible authoritative troika: deity, author, narrator. The voice of the narrator is the "voice of the one and indivisible truth" (128).

---

contrary" (Lanser, 1981:166). While Lanser has offered an observation that critics have overlooked in plotting the conventions of reading, she is dealing with authored texts. Further work needs to be done on the assumptions made about narratorial identity in anonymous and multiauthored texts.

[2] Sternberg points to an important difference between the compositional nature of Homeric or Near Eastern texts and biblical composition that reflects a crucial difference in their epistemology and theology. In the Bible, according to Sternberg, the regulating principle is "the interplay between the truth and the whole truth" (89).

This statement of Sternberg's furnishes an important clue about his strategy of reading. By privileging or foregrounding rhetorical or structuralist techniques—e.g. persuasion, sound patterns, syntactical structures, narrative or thematic structures, repetitions, and motifs —and thrusting into the background the question of reading, as Sternberg does, one ignores many questions of interpretation.[3] Sternberg sees no ambiguities related to the identity or loyalties of the narrator, and certainly no possibilities of multiple or indeterminate readings engendered by the reader's suspicions of the narrator's version, because Sternberg endorses the ideology of the biblical narratives, seeing the rhetorical conventions as expressions of ideology and, quite properly from his perspective, a unified biblical theology controlling the forms and structures within the text. Sternberg calls this the "ideology of narration" (84-128).[4]

It would seem, as Freud suggested in *Moses and Monotheism*, that the establishment of patriarchal power is linked to the preference for an invisible God. In the biblical text the everywhere present and nowhere visible narrator relates the story of the omnipotent God of the Patriarchs. Freud's argument that the replacement of a matriarchal social order with a patriarchal one is an advance of intellect over "lower psychical activity" raises a question of whether the promotion of the invisible over the visible is not a consequence of the establishment of paternal authority, a consequence of the fact that the paternal relation is invisible. A similar process can be observed in traditional interpretations of biblical texts, whenever the role of the author and narrator are conceived as paternal. When the allegiance of the reader rests with this paternal pair, to whose credit everything in the text accrues, the reader has been unsuitably engaged: in other words, a simple case of literary seduction.

Like Sternberg, Alter is eager to please the father narrator and allows only for an ideal reader, one who believes that the events portrayed are "true." His observation that the role of the narrator helps the biblical authors express God's will to the community reveals his interpretive alliance with the author, projecting a straight line from author to narrator to reader.[5] Put another way, Alter does not leave room for a fictive or

---

[3] For a thorough examination of the elements of essential conflict in viewpoint between reader-response critics and structural critics, see Suleiman: 3-45.

[4] To smooth out the wrinkles in quirky characters, who sometimes do not reflect the divine message, Sternberg eliminates incongruities by arguing that the recipient of the divine point of view is the narrator and not the other characters (85-87).

[5] Alter is certainly not alone in combining the narrative and authorial audiences. Even so august a charter of readers' maps as Iser does not acknowledge a duality in the reader until the final chapter of *The Implied Reader*. Prince's distinction between real readers, virtual readers, ideal readers, and narratees leads to a more subtle analysis of readerly roles. See Gibson: 265-269 for an early acknowledgment of the problem of the identities of the reader.

implied narratee except for the complicit one who accepts the convention that the omniscient voice serves the pivotal function of reporting "God's assessments and intentions, or even what He says to Himself" (157). One technique for adjusting the tension between narrator and narratee is to posit that the narratee occupies a position similar to that of a fictive character and thus is "immanent to the text" (Leitch: 254). Imagining various types of narratees gives us a glimpse at the cards the narrator is holding. The portrait of the fumbling pharaoh in the account of the plagues in Exodus tells us that the narrator expected an anti-pharaonic attitude in his narratees.

Although the narrator doesn't like to cast his shadow across the biblical narratives, one instance of his performing as a character is to be found in the book of Deuteronomy, when he assumes the persona of Moses preaching directly to the community of Israel. The narratee, therefore, also materializes as the audience listening to Moses on the plains of Moab. Usually, however, the narratee maintains a more elusive presence. Although authors usually try to create the illusion that the gap between the narrator and the reader is narrow, the narrative audience is firmly planted within the elements of the fiction. Thus an irritable or suspicious narratee could question the story told through the narrator's fixed gaze and surreptitiously glance around the fictive landscape to pick up clues about the story ignored by the narrator. In the biblical narrative, irritable voices, like Miriam questioning Moses' power as sole prophet of Israel, are quickly silenced. Their cause must be taken up by an equally suspicious or irritable reader.

One interpretive strategy that can undermine the authority of this fictive narrator, and give us a clue about assumptions the author has made about the reader, is to pose the question, "What sort of reader would I have to pretend to be—what would I have to know and believe—if I wanted to take this work as real?"(Rabinowitz: 96). The answer to that question for critics of the Bible has usually been a "faithful reader." But what of the critic who refuses that role? S/he sets up a tension between author and audience, delineating a gulf between the narrative audience and the authorial audience. To read with suspicion, I construct just such a restive audience, very far from the ideal one projected by biblical critics who imagine only an audience harmonious with the agenda of the implied author.

Of course such a description of a fictive audience presupposes an acceptance on the part of that audience of the text as fiction, making the double-level aesthetic of true/not true possible. For some interpreters of biblical texts, it is not within the scope of their inquiry to imagine a fictive biblical text, an implied reader or audience, and an unreliable narrator.

Alter and Sternberg, then, have acknowledged that the biblical author has designed his work rhetorically for a specific hypothetical audience, but neither critic addresses the question of a narrative audience or an implied narrator at variance with the author. In order to peel the ideology of the text away from the story, a necessary task for the feminist critic, the hypothesis of a volatile narrative audience is helpful.[6]

An ideal reader himself, Alter does not question the biblical convention of describing God's intentions with precision. Alter's view of the narrator does, nonetheless, offer a valuable observation in comparing the anonymity of the narrator to the more historically designed "characters" who interpret and mediate God's will to the reader, the biblical prophets. The lack of information about the personal history of the narrator "assumes for the scope of his narrative a godlike comprehensiveness of knowledge that can encompass even God Himself" (Alter, 1981:157). I would add to Alter's theory that the more invisible the narrator, the less likely he is to raise the hackles of dissident readers. The more blurred the portrait of the narrator, the easier it is for the reader to "forget" the narrator's alliances. Faithful readers share the narrator's theological code, male readers the gender code, and those whose political stripe matches that of the narrator the political code. Suspicions arise when the reader does not share the social, political, and gender codes of the narrator. The more codes one does not share with the narrator, the more incongruent the reading (Bal, 1988a:5). Thus, the narrator, like the characters in the text, will come to exist as a figure possessing various attitudes in the consciousness of the reader.

Theorists focusing upon modern literature have been concerned with questions of how the reader "sees" what the narrator describes. A literary convention that acknowledges the voice of the narrator as separate from the story being narrated is referred to as framing. Genette attempted to fine-tune the concept of point of view or narratorial voice by distinguishing "focalization," or the consciousness that absorbs a narrative (the reader), from "voice," the discourse that tells the narrative (the narrator).[7] As Bal points out in her counterargument to Genette, to identify narrative point of view one must make a distinction between the vision through which the elements are presented and the identity of the voice that is narrating that vision. To put it succinctly one must distinguish between "the one who sees and the one who speaks" (Bal, 1985:101). Bal awards

---

[6] This hypothesis would be a parallel to the hypothesis of a female reader reading male-authored texts suggested by Elaine Showalter in her pivotal article, "Feminist Criticism in the Wilderness." Showalter contends that the *hypothesis* of a female reader changes our understanding or vision of a text. In other words shifting the gaze of the reader/viewer creates another story.

[7] See Genette, especially chapters related to *mode* and *voix*.

different status to the one who sees and the one who narrates (Bal, 1985:110-114). When the reader's squint reveals something other than what the biblical narrator expresses, the reader can conclude only that the narrator is not omniscient. The story that he tells can thus be read as a version or modified retelling of an autonomous story, rather than the story. Literary readings of this two-tiered model point directly to a narratorial perspective that is limited, not omniscient. As Bal has demonstrated, the technique of focalization can re-view female biblical characters, while at the same time making the reader conscious of the narrator's role in shaping a version of the autonomous story (Bal, 1988 a & b). As I shall argue below, the narratorial focalization of Bathsheba has been central to traditional interpretations of the encounter between her and David.

Characters Seen

In biblical texts a crucial ambiguity for the feminist reader revolves around the narrator's providing one version of how female characters behave within the situations in which they have been placed, and another *imagined* version that might be provided by the female figure —if one could reconstruct her story. A continuing concern of mine has been to find a method for retrieving the female character who may have been flattened or suppressed by the weight of the story that is not hers. A necessary first step is to abandon the Proppian idea that the characters are of no interest in themselves, but rather are agents of the plot, secondary elements necessary to the enactment of the story. In a male-driven plot, the functions of female agents are going to be limited. In the process of constructing character out of the text, the reader reads her own experience into the text, giving expression to what Pardes calls "the counter female voices which attempt to put forth other truths" (4).

One way to shake off the strictures of the structuralists and to identify these counter voices is to propose that character can exist in our consciousness as an element independent of the story in which the character was originally discovered. In reading, as in life, a sequence of events can lend itself to various interpretations depending upon the perspective or context in which the observer places the material. The literary work is more than a detailing of events. In the sphere of the reader's mind, character does not have to be reduced to minimal functions. Hochman, in his persuasive study of the dynamic "existence" of characters, argues that "a work of literature is an entity made up of things not there, a conjuring of absent nonexistent parts" (33). Thus, we do not respond passively to characters as they have been presented within the story, but rather we respond actively to them or even appropriate them (Harvey: 54, 73, 111).

When we respond to the narrator in a negative way and reject his codes, we may reject his story. At the same time, one of the characters from that story may live on in the reader's mind. The details of Miriam's outrage at Moses that result in her being isolated from the community for seven days may blur, the reader may reject the alliance between God and prophet that results in punishment of Miriam, but the figure of Miriam, contentious in speech and vulnerable in illness, can live on in the reader's consciousness.

Chatman has observed that the experience of reading often involves the retention of our image of a character, not only apart from events but also long after we have forgotten the events of the story (118-119). The reader will then create a "paradigm of traits." From the collection of gestures, actions, thoughts, including what the narrator and other characters (both reliable and unreliable) report about the character, the reader transforms this paradigm of traits into a character. This process, described by Chatman as one of accretion of such elements as scene, setting, and character within the reader's mind, results in the character taking on an existence independent of the original story. This notion is helpful in moving away from the theory of characterization formulated by Forster and still common among biblical literary critics, which refers to round and flat characters, who derive their dimension and shape from the narrator's version of the story.

Using these strategies, I would like to try to retrieve Bathsheba from the end-of-the-road category of nonperson. Adele Berlin separates the figure of Bathsheba, as an object of adultery in 2 Samuel 11-12, from the active mother Bathsheba attempting to secure the throne for Solomon, her son, in 1 Kings 1-2. While Berlin uses the flattening structuralist term "actant" for the earlier portrait, she uses categories more akin to the paradigm of traits model suggested by Chatman for Bathsheba the Queen Mother, "with feelings and reactions developed beyond the needs of the plot" (Chatman: 30). I intend to collect the shards of Bathsheba's story from the narrator's ongoing tale of David, with the intention of giving Bathsheba a subjectivity apart from her role in the story of David.

The reader first sees Bathsheba when the narrator and David see her—from the monarch's rooftop, bathing. The scene invites the reader to assume the voyeuristic perspective of a spectator squinting at a keyhole. Let us assume for the moment that Bathsheba is unaware of our gaze. Within a few verses we are introduced to this female character through a list of intimate statements about her body. The reader is privileged to observe signs of the flesh through the narrator's gaze: 1. the woman is bathing (v. 2); 2. the woman is beautiful; 3. the woman is having sex with the king. She is identified for us in a traditional way: she is the daughter of Eliam and the wife of Uriah the Hittite. Then we are sent more sexual signals: 4. she has just been purified from her menstrual period and is presumably at the fertile time in her cycle; 5. she has conceived and is pregnant.

Her only direct speech describes her function in the story, "I am pregnant" (2 Sam 11:5; NRSV, here and throughout). The narration does not provide any details of her state of mind. Not even "I am pregnant with your child." We are not told if this turn of events in her life has thrown her into a panic. She is not given the pious extended speech patterns of Abigail, another of David's wives. Nor does she possess the acid tongue of Michal, who has chastised David a few chapters earlier for getting physical in the sight of Israel. By withholding from the reader Bathsheba's reactions to the sexual demands of the king or to her own act of adultery, the narrator has eliminated a direct route of sympathy between the reader and the female character.

Akin to the much-repeated question posed by Sternberg: "What did Uriah know and when did he know it?" at least one female reader has been drawn to reverse the question: What did Bathsheba know and when did she know it? Undoubtedly she was the first to know that she was pregnant by the king. But after she informs David of this messy development, she disappears inside her house. Not until the narrator has reported the incidents surrounding Uriah's death does he bring her out again to be glimpsed by the reader. The spectator will be disappointed if he expects another erotic fantasy. The scene has darkened. The woman is mourning for her husband. Paralleling the first scene, the monarch sends for her, brings the woman to his house, only this time it is a one-way trip. The narrator chooses two phrases that remind us of her function: she becomes his wife, and she bears him a son (2 Sam 11:27). This time there is no ogling of her naked beauty; no more is she the delicious fantasy figure, appearing wordlessly in bed while her husband is out of town. We can not look at her anymore, for she is the king's wife. In her proper role as royal mother, we will meet her again.

The question for me, if not for Sternberg, is how did Bathsheba feel about being brought to live permanently with the man who had seized her without a word? Figuring Bathsheba as an openly constructed character, borrowing Chatman's term, allows the reader the freedom to move beyond the printed page, to view characters as independently memorable (118). Following Chapman's suggestion that the audience reconstructs characters from evidence "either implicit or announced in an original construction," I want to imagine Bathsheba as an open-ended character by treating her "as an autonomous being, not merely as a plot function" (119). Wondering about her story prompts questions. Perhaps in lamenting for her husband, she is lamenting her own helplessness. She had no power to resist the king's sexual demands. Has she connected her carrying of David's child with Uriah's death? Is what the narrator calls mourning for her husband, perhaps lamenting for her own female destiny?

We are never told how Bathsheba feels about David. The story supplies no direct details about Bathsheba's reactions to her suddenly altered status as wife to the King of Israel and Judah. By comparing her story with that of the other narratively important wives of David, Michal and Abigail, we can excavate embedded signals that add to the laconically narrated portrait of Bathsheba.

While David sees Bathsheba first,[8] Michal is the one who gazes at David. The power of the male gaze shows us what is lacking in Michal's gaze. Men's desire naturally carries power with it. David's gaze carries the force of action and of possession, both lacking in the female gaze. The first item of information the narrator tells us about Michal is that she loved David (1 Sam 18:20). Her strong love causes her to rescue her outlaw husband from the deadly intentions of her father the king. But her gaze is not powerful enough to possess him sexually. The only time the reader catches David in bed with Michal, it is a stone image, an idol (1 Sam 19:16), not David in the flesh. The real David has escaped Michal and her bed. Michal does not possess the object of her gaze; David does. Before they have exchanged a word, David has pulled Bathsheba into his bed. Their exchange is sexual, not verbal.

In contrast there are *no* signs of flesh in the connection between David and Michal when she helps him elude Saul. No terms of endearment are exchanged; Michal could have been a loyal ally or soldier in her only direct speech to David, "If you do not save your life tonight, tomorrow you will be killed" (1 Sam 19:11). Even in this critical moment in which she chooses her husband over her father, there is no sign of intimacy

---

[8] In a private conversation, Professor Jack Sasson suggested to me that Bathsheba may have engineered the initial meeting with David, since she was bathing in the evening, a time marked by a distinct chill in the Jerusalem air. I tried to construct a reading in which a sly Bathsheba had noticed the monarch pacing his rooftop in the early evening and decided to make herself the object of his gaze. Neither surprised nor rendered helpless by David's rapacious actions, in this reading Bathsheba is actually the puppeteer pulling David's strings. Such a reading would support the idea that the pregnancy was a plot twist intended by Bathsheba, who schemed to become the mother of the future king. My continued resistance to such a reading has further underscored to me the strength of Chatman's argument, that the reader formulates hypotheses about characters based upon the reader's own gaze (116-26). Thus, Sasson's speculations and my own reflect the suggestion that there is a literary process in which character is openly constructed, a process that combines the investment of emotion and interest on the part of the reader with the poetics of character.

between Michal and David. Even though she has owned the gaze of the beloved, she could not dominate him.

Michal reappears in David's story after David has become king. The narrator reports that the king has taken "more concubines and wives; more sons and daughters were born to David" (2 Sam 5:13-16). The narrator gives a sharp signal of David's sexuality through his report of the names of eleven children who were born to the king in Jerusalem. None of them are children of Michal; her bed and her womb have remained empty. She is absent from the story until she catches sight of her husband "leaping and dancing before the Ark" (2 Sam 6:16). She is at the window, separated from the sexual heat of her husband. She can merely observe her husband leaping and dancing, verb forms that evoke David's sexuality. The reader observes Michal framed, enclosed, at the window observing David in a moment of physical abandon. Once again she is distanced from the flesh. From the window she cannot touch him or participate in the joyous frenzy. She is above it all. As her speech reminds us, David is a king without clothes, "*uncovering* himself today before the eyes of his servants' maids, as any vulgar fellow might shamelessly *uncover* himself" (2 Sam 6:20). Michal is a trenchant observer, but no longer one with a gaze of desire. Her no longer beloved David has been uncovering himself before concubines and wives for quite some time, as the report of the eleven named and other unnamed offspring confirms. She has observed the signs of his flesh, but she has not been a player.

In his rejoinder to the wife in the window, David makes clear that God has chosen him above the house of Saul, something Michal knows all too well. And he assures her that he will be even more contemptible in future days, which foreshadows his rapacious activity with Bathsheba a few chapters later. But just as David can risk leaping before the sacred ark of God, so he can leap with another man's wife and survive God's displeasure. Indeed he will even survive my readerly displeasure.

The narrator remarks tersely at the close of the narration called by Kyle McCarter "The Bathsheba Affair": "The thing that David had done displeased the Lord" (2 Sam 11:27b). Once again by reporting divine displeasure, the narrator reminds the reader of his privileged position, adding a frame of verisimilitude to his story. A narrator who knows the mind of God certainly must have got his story straight. The tantalizing ambiguity of the thing that David did, the sin he committed, remains to tease the reader. Is it his murder of Uriah? His taking of another man's dearest possession? Is there a chance that the sin (for both narrator and God) is that of seizing Bathsheba, first temporarily, then permanently? The answer to this question gives a clue about the loyalties of the reader. Sternberg refers several times to "Bathsheba's infidelity," ironically permitting her a moment of subjectivity that is also a characterization of blame. Sternberg reads the bedding of Bathsheba in another place as "the love affair between David and Bathsheba" (202). Whether this phrase is a courtly euphemism or blind sentimentality, the suggestion of rape as the sin David has committed would unquestionably make this reader uncomfortable. It even makes me uncomfortable. Suggesting such a violent filling of the gaps has been instructive. It has shown me that the analysis of a male fantasy of sexual primacy does not result in a reinvented text of female potency. No wonder Bathsheba grieves.

Bathsheba Heard

During her first scene in the so-called court history, Bathsheba is not a player. By the time her son Solomon has become an adult contender for the throne, however, she is ready. No longer the nubile bather, seen but not heard, she returns, empowered by what? Years of life at court? A slightly curdled mother's milk? Like Rebekah she angles for the prize for her son, unlike Rebekah she does not have to scheme alone. Nathan, the prophet who guided David, helps Bathsheba achieve the monarchy for Solomon.

The narrator picks up his tale with some information that evokes the earlier story of David and Bathsheba. David is cold and needs someone to warm his (c)old body. This time the narrator does not invite the reader to peep at the young woman. Abishag the Shunammite is brought to the king. He himself does not choose her or send for her. Like Bathsheba she is described as very beautiful. Abishag, however, is not the object of David's gaze or ours. She will attend David's body as nurse, not as lover. Abishag performs a traditional, and safe, feminine role, while the young Bathsheba, the object of male desire, had been a potential threat. In the narrator's tale of Abishag being brought to David, there is no hint of the eager sexual energy ignited when David saw Bathsheba. David's erotic energy typified by his seizure of Bathsheba in the early years of his reign has vanished. The king now requires a woman in his bed, explicitly not as a sexual companion. Might the omnipotent narrator be sneering at the king's lost potency?

Shooting Bathsheba

In conclusion I'd like to rerun the tale of David and Bathsheba one final time, casting the narrator as filmmaker. The most direct signal that the narrator is engaged in the eroticization of woman can be seen by the way he controls and limits what we see. The narrator performs the function of a camera, slowing panning over the female body. The first frame reveals the length of her entire naked body at her bath, and then a tight shot directs our gaze to a more intimate record, as the narrator discusses the woman's fertility cycle. She is primed to become pregnant. The narrator's report that David lies with her seems redundant. The taking of the woman is his erotic fantasy.

The woman's identity is not important. Learning that she is the wife of Uriah does not alter David's desire. The narrator shows his hand in these first few frames by emphasizing male ownership of the woman's body's fertility and its interiority; at the same time he shows her vulnerability since her body is not inviolable. The scene has been constructed for a male spectator. The woman has been completely objectified. The male figure commands the scene; he articulates the look and creates the action.

Signs of male domination remind us that the film story has been constructed by men for male spectators. While female spectators may be part of the audience, as Kaplan argues in *Women in Film*, they must either identify with the woman as object or they must appropriate the male gaze. When Bathsheba announces that she has conceived, David does not respond to her, but sends for Joab, his trusted intermediary, and Uriah, the man he has wronged. In a narration that reveals nothing of the woman's response to the king, her silence reinforces the power relationship between the king and a woman brought to his bed. A male viewer might well share the narrator's voyeuristic pleasure in this scene, picturing the woman as enigma, as other, viewed as outside of male language, in which deals are cut.

To cut the deal for Solomon to become David's successor, Bathsheba needs words. No longer the eroticized object of male sexual desire, she now plays the game like the loquacious Abigail, who convinced David to change his plans with honeyed words. Bathsheba in her plea to the king sounds much like Abigail, docile, compliant. The sexual Bathsheba has been replaced by a safer Queen. Speaking in the familiar cadences of a deferential wife, she is no longer dangerous. Like Michal who saved David from Saul, Abigail who saved him from bloodguilt, Bathsheba now plays an acceptable social role. She saves David from appointing the wrong son king.

But let us consider this final scene as a cinematic midrash employing elements of the earlier films/readings. Remember Bathsheba, the nubile young woman, rosy in her bath? Now she is seen as clothed, driving, ambitious, just like the men surrounding her. The camera eye records Nathan writing Bathsheba's dialogue with the king, signaling that her ambition is not to be feared. As she delivers Nathan's speech, the audience is assured that Bathsheba is supported by the divine prophet.

Bathsheba goes to David, who is seen being tended by Abishag, an asexual object. "What do you desire?" asks the king, an ironic twist evoking and recalling his sexual desire that is now dead. Bathsheba is all business, reminding the king that he had promised to make Solomon his heir. Like Abigail before her, Bathsheba uses a verbal strategy of flattery and humility to get David to change his mind at a crucial moment in Israel's history. Like Abigail, Bathsheba is the subject of this scene, reminding the failing king that it is within his power to alter the events of state and halt the power grab of Adonijah. "But you, my lord the king— the eyes of all Israel are on you to tell them who shall sit on the throne of my lord the king after him" (1 Kgs 1:20).

Another ironic signal in this scene of reversals. If all eyes had been upon Bathsheba bathing in the earlier scene, now all eyes are upon David faltering on the throne.

To give the necessary authority to the woman's request, Nathan backs up Bathsheba's story, another reversal from an earlier scene: the angry Nathan who had prophesied the death of the nameless infant son, the sexual connection between David and Bathsheba (2 Sam 12: 1-15), now speaks out in favor of Solomon, the second son of the pair. David then recalls a vow made in an earlier scene:

> As the Lord lives, who has saved my life from every adversity, as I swore to you by the Lord, the God of Israel, 'Your son Solomon shall succeed me as king, and he shall sit on my throne in my place,' so will I do this day.
>
> (1 Kgs 1:29-30)

But had he made such a vow to Bathsheba? Nathan's mention of the vow to Bathsheba (v. 13) is ambiguous. Is this a strategy to convince the muddled monarch that such a vow had been made? There is no textual mention of such a vow. One would also assume that if Bathsheba had been given assurance of her son's ascendancy to the throne, she would not have needed Nathan to encourage her to remind the king of his promise. While the origin of the promise from David to Bathsheba concerning Solomon is draped in obscurity, what is clear is that Bathsheba has been vindicated in the best tradition of patriarchal culture. She has become the triumphant mother, whose son triumphs over the sons of David's other wives. Finally Bathsheba is seen as the mother working to achieve for her son what God intends for him to have. Thus, she has been transformed from sexual object to Queen Mother. Finally, Bathsheba has been cast in the familiar role of good mother, working to protect and extend the tradition. In this final scene she is heard and not seen.

Conclusion

Although authors usually try to create the illusion that the gap between the narrator and the reader is narrow, the narrative audience is firmly planted within the elements of this fiction. We have followed the narrator's gaze, blinked when he blinked, turned a blind eye when he wanted acts concealed. I hope I have suggested possibilities for eye-opening readings in which an irritable or suspicious narratee can question the story told through the narrator's fixed gaze and can surreptitiously glance around the fictive landscape to pick up clues about the story that didn't tempt the narrator. In the instance of Bathsheba we can refuse to stand watch with the narrator and David on the rooftop. As feminist readers we can read it, avert our gaze, and go somewhere else. When faced with an authoritative overviewing narrator, we can cast a cold eye.

Works Consulted

Alter, Robert
    1981   *The Art of Biblical Narrative*. New York: Basic.
    1989   *The Pleasures of Reading*. New York: Simon & Schuster.

Bach, Alice
    1990   "The Pleasures of Her Text." Pp. 25-44 in *The Pleasures of Her Text*. Ed. Alice Bach. Philadelphia: Trinity Press International.

Bakhtin, Mikhail
    1984   *Problems of Doestoevsky's Poetics*. Ed. and trans. Caryl Emerson. Minneapolis: University of Minnesota Press.

Bal, Mieke
    1985   *Narratology: Introduction to the Theory of Narrative*. Toronto: University of Toronto Press.
    1988a   *Murder and Difference: Gender, Genre, and Scholarship on Sisera's Death*. Trans. Matthew Gumpert. Bloomington: Indiana University Press.
    1988b   *Death and Dissymetry: The Politics of Coherence in the Book of Judges*. Chicago: University of Chicago Press.
    1991   *Reading "Rembrandt": Beyond the Word-Image Opposition*. Cambridge: Cambridge University Press.

Berlin, Adele
    1983   *Poetics and Interpretation of Biblical Narrative*. Sheffield: Almond.

Bloom, Harold
    1990   *The Book of J*. Trans. from Hebrew by David Rosenberg. Interpreted by Harold Bloom. New York: Grove & Weidenfeld.

Chatman, Seymour
　1978　　Story and Discourse. Ithaca: Cornell University Press.

Cixous, Hélène
　1974　　"The Character of Character." New Literary History 5: 384-400.

Cohn, Dorrit
　1978　　Transparent Minds. Princeton: Princeton University Press.

Culler, Jonathan
　1988　　Framing the Sign: Criticism and Its Institutions. Norman: University of Oklahoma Press.

Forster, E. M.
　1927　　Aspects of the Novel. New York: Harcourt, Brace.

Freud, Sigmund
　1939　　Moses and Monotheism. Trans. James Strachey. London: Hogarth.

Genette, Gérard
　1972　　Figures III. Paris: Editions du Seuil.

Gibson, Walker
　1950　　"Authors, Speakers, Readers, and Mock Readers." College English 11 (Feb): 265-69.

Harvey, W. John
　1965　　Character and the Novel. Ithaca: Cornell University Press.

Hochman, Baruch
　1985　　Character in Literature. Ithaca: Cornell University Press.

Iser, Wolfgang
　1974　　The Implied Reader. Baltimore: Johns Hopkins University Press.

Kaplan, E. Ann
　1983　　Women and Film. New York: Routledge, Chapman, and Hall.

Lanser, Susan Sniader
　1981　　The Narrative Act: Points of View in Prose Fiction. Ithaca: Cornell University Press.
　1992　　Fiction of Authority: Women Writers and Narrative Voice. Ithaca: Cornell University Press.

Leitch, Vincent
　1988　　American Literary Criticism from the Thirties to the Eighties. New York: Columbia University Press.

McCarter, Kyle
　1980　　I Samuel. A new translation with introduction, notes and commentary. AB. Garden City: Doubleday.

Pardes, Ilana
　1992　　Countertraditions in the Bible: A Feminist Approach. Cambridge: Harvard University Press.

Prince, Gerald
   1980   "Introduction to the Study of the Narratee." Pp. 7-25 in *Reader-Response Criticism*. Ed. Jane Tompkins. Baltimore: Johns Hopkins University Press.

Rabinowitz, Peter
   1987   *Before Reading: Narrative Conventions and the Politics of Interpretation*. Ithaca: Cornell University Press.

Showalter, Elaine
   1985   "Feminist Criticism in the Wilderness." Pp. 243-270 in *The New Criticism: Essays on Women, Literature, and Theory*. New York: Pantheon.

Spivak, Gayatri Chakravorty, with Elaine Rooney
   1989   "In a Word, *Interview*." *differences* 2:124-56.

Sternberg, Meir
   1985   *The Poetics of Biblical Narrative*. Bloomington: Indiana University Press.

Suleiman, Susan R., ed.
   1980   *The Reader in the Text: Essays on Audience and Interpretation*. Princeton: Princeton University Press.

CYBORGS, CIPHERS, AND SEXUALITY: RE-THEORIZING LITERARY AND BIBLICAL CHARACTER

Laura E. Donaldson
Antioch College

ABSTRACT

Unlike other aspects of narrative, the concept of character has received relatively little attention and still remains theorized along the problematic poles of mimeticism and formalism. This essay attempts to retheorize character through the image of the cyborg and to reconceptualize the interpretation of character as the production of positions within a conflicted narrative field. The story of Joseph and Potiphar's wife (Genesis 39) offers provocative insights into how this process might work, since a cyborg theory of character allows us to read Potiphar's wife as a woman who uses her sexuality to prevent a male homosocial redistribution of the household rather than to sexually harass Joseph.

CHARACTERIZING CHARACTER

Some commentators have described the past several decades as the "Era of Theory"—a time of intense creativity that also witnessed a dramatic explosion in the realm of narrative poetics. In contrast to the burgeoning of hypotheses concerning point of view or focalization, however, the concept of character still remains the most neglected and problematically theorized aspect of narrative. This regrettable state of affairs results from a continuing articulation of the issue along the dichotomous poles of mimetic imagism, where characters mirror the socio-psychological complexity of real humans, or formalist reductionism, where they exist merely as ciphers, or literary spaces, in which textual forces meet (Culler: 230). For the former, characters are similar to real people who inhabit the narrative; for the latter, in the words of Roland Barthes, characters are "verbal scraps (physical appearance, thoughts, statements, feelings) held loosely together by a proper name" (as cited, Martin: 118-19).

Although construed as theoretical opposites, these approaches are nevertheless linked by their inadequate explanations of the textualized persons and personified texts that constitute character (Weinsheimer: 208). Indeed, each colludes with the other by treating character as a monolithic category and by obliterating "the fact that the character stands in a similar relation of interdependence with other characters, other textual elements, or higher levels of abstraction" (Bal: 108). Consequently, neither the mimetic nor the formalist position can account for what Shlomith Rimmon-Kenan calls "the specificity of fictional characters":

> Whereas in mimetic theories (i.e. theories which consider literature as, in some sense, an imitation of reality) characters are equated with people, in semiotic theories they dissolve into textuality. What remains? If both approaches end up canceling the specificity of fictional characters, though from different standpoints, should the study of character be abandoned, or should both approaches be rejected and a different perspective sought? Can such a perspective reconcile the two opposed positions *without* 'destroying' character between them? (33).

Some critics have tried to solve this riddle of characterological specificity by conflating character and structure after the manner of Henry James's famous declaration: "What is character but the determination of incident? What is incident but the illustration of character?" For example, Stephen Moore's otherwise sophisticated *Literary Criticism and the Gospels: The Theoretical Challenge* spends only one paragraph reiterating the orthodox Jamesian view that "plot and character are inseparably bound up in the reading experience" without ever saying exactly how "each works to produce the other" (15). Ultimately, however, Moore abandons even this position by resorting to E. M. Forster's widely disseminated mimetic distinction between round and flat, multidimensional and unidimensional, to analyze narrative character.

Forster defines "round" characters as those textual figures whose complex organization and dynamic development "give us new pleasure each time" we read about them (114); in contrast, flat characters exist statically because, unlike their round counterparts, they are constructed around a single idea or quality. This distinction is not neutral, however, since according to Forster flat characters are more "primitive" than round ones and do not represent as great a literary achievement (111). Unfortunately, this particular view seems to be the posture of many biblical scholars who venture into literary analysis.

While a detailed critique of Forster's schema lies well beyond the scope of this essay, it seems important to interject a cautionary note concerning its uncritical application to any written text, and most especially to those, such as the Hebrew or Greek Bible, classical epic poetry, and the Native American novel, that possess a significant residual orality. In his comparison of oral verbal performance with written narrative, Walter J. Ong reveals the ethnocentrism of Forster's distinction: "We know now that the type 'heavy' (or 'flat') character derives originally from primary oral narrative, which can provide characters of no other kind " (151).

According to Ong, the specific qualities of oral memory work most effectively with "flat" figures, such as heroic persons whose deeds are "monumental, memorable and commonly public," because they help to organize experience in a permanently memorable form (70).

The round character has its roots in the invention of chirographic technologies and, more specifically, of the written prose text (Ong: 152). Since "round" characters emerge from the highly privatized and deeply interiorized experience that writing mysteriously empowers (Ong: 153), Forster's schema cannot possibly do justice to the additive, aggregative, and participatory qualities of an orally based verbal performance. His theory of character—whose material context is an industrialized and highly literate West—not only leaves unanswered many questions about the relation of text and reality, but also risks the imposition of inappropriate evaluative criteria upon the narrative structures of other cultures and other times.

Seymour Chatman and Rimmon-Kenan attempt to transcend the limits of both mimeticism and formalism by joining rather than conflating the contributions that each view makes to the analysis of narrative. In his now "classic" *Story And Discourse: Narrative Structure in Fiction and Film* (1978), Chatman formulates an "open" theory of character that tenuously perches on the border between mimeticism and formalism. According to Chatman, perceiving character as an open-ended paradigm of traits, or "vertical assemblage intersecting the syntagmatic chain of events that comprise the plot" (127) enables the critic to resist not only the closed determinism of mimeticism but also the kenotic tendency of formalism to empty character of all sensuous detail. Although Chatman provides many useful insights and is still indispensable to any discussion of character, his trait-based theory still—after all is said and done —perpetuates the traditional Aristotelian view of character as inert and descriptive.

Rimmon-Kenan articulates mimeticism and formalism as different aspects of narrative; thus characters are conceived as "'at once persons and parts of a design' . . . In the text characters are nodes in the verbal design; in the story they are—by definition—non (or pre) verbal abstractions, constructs. Although these constructs are by no means human beings in the literal sense of the word, they are partly modelled on the reader's conception of people and in this they are person-like" (33). Because character and action are interdependent, Rimmon-Kenan suggests that the subordination of mimeticism to formalism or vice versa has more to do with different types of narrative than with absolute hierarchies (35).

A significant difficulty of this approach stems from its dependence on the framework of narrative androgyny to address the specificity of character: just as the androgyne combines a male and female essence to create a whole person, Rimmon-Kenan's "char-actor" inseparably joins the formalist processes of the text to its more mimetic dimensions. However, just as psychological androgyny integrates masculinity and femininity yet leaves their stereotypical definitions untouched, a narrative androgyny never questions the underlying assumptions of either mimeticism or formalism. Fusing together the equally mistaken positions of homology (naive worldliness) or arbitrariness (naive unworldliness) to create a whole text only spawns a distorted and deformed vision of the entire reading process.[1]

From this brief survey of recent attempts to theorize character, it seems abundantly clear that these efforts need "to be supplemented by more radical theories that redefine the very idea of character" (Martin: 120). Without wishing to sound too presumptuous, this is exactly what I propose to do through the image of the cyborg. Indeed, I would argue, neither the human nor the androgyne, but the cyborg—that uncanny and unstable hybrid of animate organism and inanimate machine—emerges as the paradigmatic figure for any theory of character. I have chosen the biblical narrative of Joseph and the character of Potiphar's wife (Genesis 39) as a test case of this assertion because no other narrative so brilliantly illustrates the critical issues involved in that particular production of meaning known as "character analysis."

In *Lethal Love*, Mieke Bal notes that the encounter between Joseph and Potiphar's wife moves the entire question of sexuality from margin to center (98). This literary and ideological movement is especially important for the purposes of my essay since it problematizes any attempt to perceive character either in a formalist vacuum or as a transparent reflection of reality. As we shall see, the question of sexuality provides the impetus for reconfiguring character in the image of the cyborg since "only a dialectic for which the outside is always already inside can open the problem to a solution. Then there is no disjunction between the realms at all, but rather complex modes of translation and transformation between them which must be carefully specified. Then the making of the text *as text* begins to be thinkable . . . ." (Terdiman: 18). And, I would add, the making of characters *as* characters begins to be thinkable only in those cyborgian terms that more adequately account for the complex modes of textual translation and semantic transformation that exist between characters, readers, and writers.

---

[1] For an extended discussion of this issue in both literary and film narratives, see Chapter Three, "The Con of the Text: Textualism, Contextualism, and Anticolonialist Feminist Theories," in Donaldson.

On Ciphers and Sexuality

> Mimetic criticism claims to be appropriate to the novel, semiotic to appropriate it. One plays slave to the text, the other master.
> (Joel Weinsheimer, "Theory of Character: Emma")

> Th[e] cyborg does not have an Aristotelian structure; and there is no master-slave dialectic resolving the struggles of resource and product, passion and action. S/he is not utopian nor imaginary; s/he is virtual. Generated, along with other cyborgs, by the collapse into each other of the technical, organic, mythic, textual, and political, s/he is constituted by articulations of critical differences within and without each figure.
> (Donna Haraway, "The Promises of Monsters")

The Bionic Woman, the Six-Million Dollar Man, the Terminator, Robo-Cop, and, yes, even Star-Trek's Jean-Luc Picard in service of the Borg—all these media icons indicate that cyborg ontology has saturated almost every layer of Western culture. One could also mention such other blurrings between human and machine as electronic pacemakers, in vitro fertilization, and computer-generated therapeutic counseling. As Donna Haraway declares in her manifesto for cyborgs, "by the late twentieth century, our time, a mythic time, we are all chimeras, theorized and fabricated hybrids of machine and organism; in short, we are cyborgs" (150). For Haraway, the cyborg is a creature who "has no truck with bisexuality, pre-oedipal symbiosis, unalienated labor, or other seductions to organic wholeness through a final appropriation of the parts into a higher unity" (150).

If character is a trope for human identity (Leitch: 148)—neither the same (mimetic) nor different (formalist), but signifying otherwise—then the cyborg figures the text as an unstable field and requires us to construct a radically different character for character itself. In his reflections on language and symbolic power, sociologist and critical theorist Pierre Bourdieu elaborates upon the uncanny, or uncomfortably strange, quality of such a re-visioning:

> Thinking in terms of a field requires a conversion of one's entire usual vision of the social world, a vision which is interested only in those things which are visible ... the notion of field presupposes that one break away from the realist representation which leads one to reduce the effect of the milieu to the effect of the direct action that takes place in any interaction. It is the structure of the constitutive relations of the space of the field which determines the forms that can be assumed by the visible relations of interaction and the very content of the experience that agents may have of them (1990:192).

A field is thus a structured space of positions whose "constitutive relations"—both hidden and seen—determine the content and form of the field's direct action. A cyborgian field requires us to negotiate these positions by articulating the critical and unstable differences that traverse the "within" and "without" of the meaning-making process.

Further, not only the positions but also the interrelations between positions in any given field are determined by the distribution of its resources, or "capital." This capital can be economic (money, property, or stocks), cultural (acquired knowledge and skills), or symbolic (accumulated prestige or honor) (Thompson: 14). Indeed, one of the most important properties of a field is its conversion of one form of capital into another—a Ph.D. for a lucrative academic position, for example (Thompson: 14). This dynamic of conversion implies that a field is always the site of a struggle either to maintain or to alter the distribution of its specific capital and, according to Bourdieu, participants possess differing chances of winning or losing depending on their location in the structured space of positions (Thompson: 14).

FIGURE 1

Joseph————————————————Potiphar's Wife
(object)   *(subject)*

A field representing traditional interpretations of Genesis 39 might look like the straight line in Figure 1, where the signifier "Joseph" functions as the harassed desired object and "Potiphar's wife," the harassing desiring subject. The specific "capital" of this field would presumably be physical attraction fueled by the uncontrolled libido of the woman: she struggles to change the sexual status quo while Joseph struggles to maintain it.

> Now Joseph was handsome and goodlooking. And after a time his master's wife cast her eyes on Joseph and said, "Lie with me." But he refused and said to his master's wife, "Look, with me here, my master has no concern about anything in the house, and he has put everything that he has in my hand. He is not greater in this house than I am, nor has he kept back anything from me except yourself, because you are his wife. How then could I do this great wickedness and sin against God?" And although she spoke to Joseph day after day, he would not consent to lie beside her or to be with her (Genesis 39:6b-10, NRSV).

In his commentary on Genesis 39, Walter Brueggemann adopts a prototypical stance towards Potiphar's wife when he differentiates the adulterous duplicity of the woman from the "single-minded determination of the man" (314). Brueggemann's analysis repeats the often-noted insight that the extremely curt "Lie with me" of Potiphar's wife allegedly suggests an intense and lustful passion, while Joseph's dignified and substantive refusal connotes sincerity and pious restraint (e.g. Jeansonne: 110).

Robert Alter sharpens this position by implying a libidinal voraciousness as the character's primary motivation: "The brevity of the sexual proposition on the part of Potiphar's wife is a brilliant stylization—for as Thomas Mann was to observe at great length, she *must* have said more than that!—of the naked lust that impels her, and perhaps also of the pre-emptory tone she feels she can assume toward her Hebrew slave" (73). Although Meir Sternberg equates the "poisonous repetition" of the woman's proposition with "sexual assault" (424), while Harold Bloom praises it as "great comic writing" (230), they nevertheless agree upon Mrs. Potiphar's "lustful" motives.

But perhaps the most revealing interpretation of this character emerges from a popular guide for adult Bible study groups—Sara Buswell's *The Challenge Of Old Testament Women: 2* (1987). In Buswell's analysis, Potiphar's wife becomes a "mistress of manipulation" whose attempted seduction of Joseph represents an outlet for her spiritual ennui and sexual disappointment:

> Attracted to the young, handsome, and successful overseer who had brought much prosperity to her household, Potiphar's wife was determined to enjoy a portion of the abundance for herself. With her husband devoting his attention only to the food he ate (Gen 39:6), this affluent aristocrat was apparently lonely or bored enough to "cast her eyes upon Joseph" (Gen 39:7, KJV) as a most likely source of entertainment. She was not flirting but flaunting her power when she demanded, "Come to bed with me" (120).

While the scholarly commentaries lack Buswell's rather lurid inventiveness, they similarly perceive Potiphar's wife in terms of an anarchic and threatening sexuality that is opposed to the reasonable godliness of Joseph.

However, the text's presentation of the actions in question "denaturalize" this interpretation of Potiphar's wife. Narratives—especially biblical narratives—often use a character's actions to reveal important traits and to create nuanced characterizations (Berlin: 38). Singular, or non-routine, actions manifest a dynamic aspect by often provoking a textual crisis, while repetitive actions expose a character's unchanging or static identity (Rimmon-Kenan: 61). In Genesis 39, the verbal actions in question are repetitive, i.e. Mrs. Potiphar directs them to Joseph "day after day," and they ultimately provoke both a psychological and textual crisis.

These alleged advances comprise the first half of Genesis 39:7: "And after a time his master's wife cast her eyes on Joseph." The common translation of the Hebrew preposition אחר and its object הדברים into the English adverbial phrase "after a time" or "after a while" assumes that the richly ambiguous literal meaning, "after these things," needs more denotative clarity. More importantly, however, this particular translation of the phrase allows biblical critics to posit a cause and effect relationship between Joseph's physical beauty and the actions of Potiphar's wife—a causal relationship that disintegrates upon closer inspection.

The midrashic tradition of the Joseph story can teach interpreters a great deal about the text of 39:6b-7, for its conundrums act as a narrative irritant that has produced many pearls of hermeneutic wisdom over the centuries. According to James Kugel, whose book *In Potiphar's House* charts the early interpretive life of Genesis 39, the Midrash Tanhuma foregrounds the linguistic ambiguities of "these things" by offering two ingeniously incompatible explanations:

> The first takes the Hebrew words *debarim* in our biblical text . . . not as "things" at all, but as "words" (an equally common meaning of the Hebrew term). What "words"? Why, words of Mrs. Potiphar—idle chatter, perhaps, or suggestive phrases, or little terms of endearment —anything to get him to desire her . . . the words themselves are not in the Bible, but their existence is hinted at in this phrase; and so, Tanhuma says, she "enticed him with *words*," and it was, therefore, "after these words" had been spoken that the rest of the story ensued. The other explanation put forward in Tanhuma is quite separate from this one and in fact incompatible with it, since it goes back to the other meaning of *debarim*, "things." What things? Things again unreported in the biblical text, but whose existence is being hinted at in the phrase "after these things," things designed to get Joseph to desire her. And so, in the absence of specifics in the Bible, our midrashist supplies them: Mrs. Potiphar kept changing her clothes, three times a day in fact, one spectacular dress after the next—"and to what purpose? Only that he desire her" (Kugel: 41-42).

Unlike many contemporary translators and interpreters, then, the Midrash Tanhuma refuses to discount the anomalous order of Genesis 39:6-7 as a semantic mistake (Kugel: 42),[2] and its creative solutions to these ambiguities illustrate a principal tenet of cyborg characterization: every identity is both a motivated production from without and a relational production from within.

The interpretation that Potiphar's wife's repetitive actions reveal her identity as a sexual harasser is in fact related to masculinist ideologies of

---

[2] The midrashic tradition raises a similar question about the ambiguous sequence of Joseph leaving his garments in the hand of Potiphar's wife (Gen 39:10-13). In Genesis Rabbah, Rabbi bar Nahman conjectures that Joseph went into the house when no one else was there and "actually tried, but found that he was not a man, i.e., could not have an erection." Rabbi Samuel rather euphemistically notes that "his 'bow' grew taut but then became flaccid." Clearly, both comments recognize the possibility that Joseph himself was implicated in this action. As editor Jacob Neusner pithily states: "Either Joseph wanted to but could not, or wanted to but did not, or wanted to but was saved by his father, with God's help" (235).

subjectivity and makes her a kissing cousin, so to speak, to the Enlightenment's most (in)famous woman: Sophy, the "promised helpmeet" to Jean-Jacques Rousseau's new bourgeois man, Émile. For Rousseau, God has endowed Sophy, or woman, with boundless erotic passions and has also given her the modesty to restrain them (Rousseau: 322). Émile, on the other hand, possesses an internal law that allows him to be "alike free and self-controlled; though swayed by these passions man is endowed with reason by which to control them" (322).

Because woman's passion is unreconstructed by reason, it must submit to the most severe strictures of decorum—a repression that threatens to spill over these boundaries and engulf its unsuspecting male victims. Indeed, Rousseau exclaims, "how can anyone fail to see that when the share of each [in reason] is so unequal, if the one were not controlled by modesty as the other is controlled by nature, the result would be the destruction of both, and the human race would perish through the very means ordained for its continuance" (Rousseau: 322). As a free agent of desire, then, Rousseau's woman can unleash catastrophic devastation upon the world (Kaplan: 156); as the free perpetrator of sexual assault invented by [a predominately male] biblical hermeneutics, Potiphar's wife exudes an irrational sexuality that springs from the very core of her being and wreaks havoc with the life of Joseph the man.

The straight line that traditional interpretation uses to depict the relationship between Potiphar's wife and Joseph both perpetuates the "lie of spontaneous desire" (Girard: 16) and flattens the text's hermeneutic possibilities. It also imbues Potiphar's Wife with the illusion of a culturally unmarked and unfettered autonomy. In a devastating double-bind, biblical criticism has positioned Potiphar's wife, like her cousin Sophy, within the patriarchal discourse of sexual difference, yet simultaneously abstracted from her any marks of gender, race, or class.

Without a more adequate understanding of character, even feminist criticism remains limited to criticizing the text's "simplistic and stereotypical [portrayal] of the foreign woman as temptress" (Jeansonne: 113). For example, in order to expose the paradigms that (male) biblical writers used to describe women and female behavior, Athalya Brenner's *The Israelite Woman: Social Role and Literary Type* uses a "literary model" approach that divides the paradigm of the "Foreign Woman" into its positive and negative embodiments (133). Potiphar's wife exemplifies the Foreign Woman's negativity because her status as the dangerous seductress "has fatal consequences" for her male victim (121). While this demystifying of ancient views comprises a necessary step in feminist criticism, its failure to dislodge the interpretation of Mrs. Potiphar as sexually threatening risks reinforcing the very stereotypes it seeks to deconstruct.

Toward a Cyborg Theory of Character

> So Joseph found favor in his [Potiphar's] sight and attended him; he made him overseer of his house and put him in charge of all that he had (Gen 39:4).

In contrast to either the endorsement or critique of Potiphar's wife as a dangerous seductress, a cyborg theory of character enables a different configuration of the field in Genesis 39. The struggle over narrative capital in fact concerns domestic status rather than irrepressible lust, for the story of Joseph marks a male homosocial redistribution of the בית, or household. Within this field, the character of Potiphar's wife rebels against her masculinist origins and uses her sexuality as a weapon to prevent the household's passing from man to man (from Potiphar to Joseph) rather than from man to woman (from Potiphar to Potiphar's wife).

According to Eve Kosofsky Sedgwick, "homosocial" describes bonds between persons of the same sex. It is also a neologism formed by analogy with and difference from the term "homosexual," which hypothesizes "a potentially unbroken continuum between homosocial and homosexual" (Sedgwick: 1).[3] Sedgwick uses "desire" structurally, i.e. as a signifier for the affective or social force that shapes an important relationship. Genesis 39 narrates a scene of desire in which the affective-social glue bonding Potiphar's wife to Joseph is the lure of domestic status within the household rather than sexual fulfillment.

An image that more adequately conjures the complex field embedding Joseph and Mrs. Potiphar might look like the triangle of Figure 2 rather than the straight line of Figure 1.

FIGURE 2

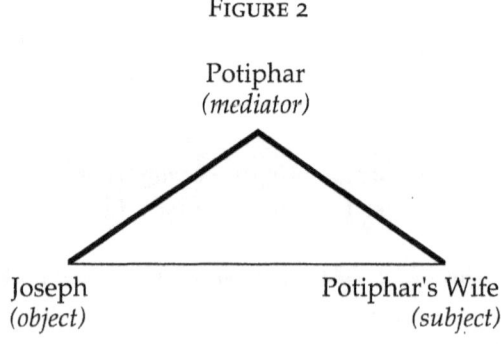

Potiphar
(*mediator*)

Joseph Potiphar's Wife
(*object*) (*subject*)

---

[3] In contrast to female sexuality, which occurs within the continuum between women's social and erotic bonds (negatively exhibited by the suspicion that all close relationships between women are lesbian relationships), male sexuality occurs within a disjunction between these two spheres. Sedgwick's term attempts to bring the social and erotic dimensions of men's sexuality back into provocative connection.

René Girard illuminates this image when he notes that the straight line of desire in the adventures of Don Quixote conceals the ubiquitous presence of a mediator: "The spatial metaphor which expresses this triple relationship is obviously the triangle. The object changes with each adventure but the triangle remains. The barber's basin or Master Peter's puppets replace the windmills; but Amadis is always present" (2). Although Girard uses *Don Quixote* to illustrate his point, we could just as easily insert the actors of Genesis 39 for those in Cervantes' novel. In Genesis 39, coveted objects such as Joseph might change, but Potiphar is always present. Whether one recognizes it or not, Potiphar acts as a mediator whose narrative point radiates both toward the desiring subject—his wife—and the desired object—Joseph. By abandoning the focus on the desiring subject and choosing the mediator himself as the origin of critical analysis (Girard: 12), we can produce a different set of positions within the narrative field of Genesis 39.

These previously transparent positions become opaque through the semiotics of Mrs. Potiphar's proper name—or, to be more accurate, her lack of one. It seems almost banal to remark that the ancient (and unfortunately still prevalent) custom of identifying a woman by her husband's name points to women's dependent ontological and legal status within diverse social structures. Nevertheless, this insight exists as a profoundly important constitutive relation between the characters of the story. According to Kenneth Hughes, the "proper" of a proper name is generically linked to "property" through the Latin term "proprius," which means "one's own" (136): "The proper noun (proprius) thus names "one's own" body as "one's own" property (proprius). One becomes property in order to potentially have property" (Hughes: 136). Because the vicariousness of Mrs. Potiphar's name signifies that she lacks the capacity to own her own body, we could conjecture that she becomes Potiphar's possession in order to claim the second meaning of "proprius": the potential for having property. And it is precisely this potential in the form of controlling the household of her husband that Joseph threatens. If biblical narratives often signify a character's identity through an appropriate, and often allegorical, Proper Name, then the lack of such a signifier makes Potiphar's Wife a powerfully visible statement about the entangling webs of ideology and character.

Lest my own production of meaning from the story seem too contemporary (although it is this static view of textuality that a cyborg theory of character resists), one should note that the rabbinic tradition often equated the word בית, or household, with "housewife"—a connotation that is semantically very close to the name "Potiphar's wife." Like the etymology of "proprius," then, this ancient Hebrew usage provocatively implies that the struggle over the household is actually a struggle over Mrs. Potiphar's own social identity. It suggests that she has metamorphosed from a figure reduced to the straight line of sexual harassment to one whose position becomes triangulated by the oblique angles of the narrative's male homosocial continuum.

However, rather than a "deadly symmetry" that excludes the historical accidents of gender, race, class, or sexuality, the cyborgian triangle of Genesis 39 instead becomes a "sensitive register for delineating relationships of power and meaning, and for making graphically intelligible the play of desire and identification by which individuals negotiate with their societies for empowerment" (Sedgwick: 27). And it is precisely in terms of a negotiation for empowerment that we can understand the actions of Potiphar's wife toward Joseph. By asserting herself sexually, she can potentially gain some leverage with the man who has so abruptly invaded her daily world. When that strategy fails, Potiphar's Wife hurriedly devises another ruse: a self-serving explanation of the incident that convinces her husband and effects the very removal of Joseph she so desperately desires.

I use the adjective "self-serving" advisedly since, although I am far from condoning her behavior, I wonder whether the moral outrage directed toward Potiphar's Wife stems from her literal self-centeredness and her blatant reclamation of what a patriarchal system has tried to wrest from her.[4] On a more repressed level, this outrage could also represent a deep sexual anxiety within the predominately male tradition of biblical criticism. If, as Girard claims, the impulse toward the object (Joseph) is ultimately an impulse toward the mediator (Potiphar)—in order to occupy his position and steal his very being (53)—then the character of Mrs. Potiphar is very threatening indeed.

At the very least, she has succeeded in questioning the prevailing critical approaches to character in Genesis 39. The idea of mediation, for example, encourages a kind of literary analysis that transcends the descriptive stance of both genre and thematic criticism (Girard: 23). In terms of characterization, an emphasis on mediation exposes the mimetic limits of both a generic typology of character (Potiphar's wife as "the for-

---

[4] Nelly Furman makes an interesting parallel to my argument through her semiotic analysis of the way garments take on meaning in Genesis 37-39. These garments not only function as tokens of identification but, according to Furman, also suggest a special bond between men. The "coat of many colors," for example, signifies the special love between Joseph and Jacob. When Joseph abandons his coat in the hand of his master's wife, "his stated reason is his respect for his master. In both cases, a piece of attire represents an emotional link, a trust *between men* [emphasis mine]" (143). I would add that we could also read the abandoned coat as a sign of Potiphar's wife's attempted intervention in this male homosocial genealogy.

eign woman") and an approach based upon moral themes (Joseph's mistress as immoral and sexually voracious). The notion of character as a determinate position produced within a conflicted narrative field also belies its formalist reduction to a loose collection of verbal scraps.

As the example of Genesis 39 has so aptly illustrated, neither mimeticism nor formalism can account for the complex translations and transformations and the interweaving of contexts and texts involved in character analysis. The cyborgian figure of Potiphar's wife thus suggests "a way out of the maze of dualisms in which we have explained our bodies and our tools to ourselves" (Haraway, 1991:181)—including the false dualism between representation and structure. She is simultaneously harassed and harasser, weak and strong, marginalized and centered, generated from within and produced from without: a "condensed image of both imagination and material reality" (Haraway, 1991:150).

If, in the words of Donna Haraway, cyborg imagery introduces the vision "not of a common language, but of a powerful infidel heteroglossia" (1991:181), then a cyborg theory of character must speak in many tongues. Its different voices are not benignly interdependent, however, since at every point they challenge and transgress each other, requiring a constant re-negotiation of the hermeneutic edifices we so confidently erect. The cyborg confronts us with our profound loss of innocence—or what I would call our ideological complicities—and necessitates that we consciously and often painfully recognize them in our theories of writing and reading.

Perhaps more importantly, a cyborg theory of character offers "a slightly perverse shift of perspective" (Haraway, 1991:154), which better enables traditionally suppressed readers (women, peoples of color, gays and lesbians, the working class) to "contest for meanings, as well as for other forms of power and pleasure" (Haraway, 1991:154) within the culturally charged realm of narrative. In my own counterstory of Genesis 39, for example, the straight line of sexual desire dissolves into a much more contradictory and subversive socio-narrative structure. Within a cyborg theory of character, Potiphar's wife resists both mimeticism and formalism—not to mention masculinism—evoking new critical grammars for their recoupling and, indeed, their regeneration.

WORKS CONSULTED

Alter, Robert
    1981   *The Art of Biblical Narrative*. New York: Basic.

Auerbach, Erich
    1957   *Mimesis: The Representation of Reality in Western Literature*. Trans. Willard R. Trask. Princeton: Princeton University Press.

Bal, Mieke
    1987   *Lethal Love: Feminist Literary Readings of Biblical Love Stories*. Bloomington & Indianapolis: Indiana University Press.

Berlin, Adele
    1983   *Poetics and Interpretation of Biblical Narrative*. Sheffield: Almond.

Bloom, Harold
    1990   *The Book of J*. Trans. David Rosenberg. New York: Grove Weidenfeld.

Bourdieu, Pierre
    1990   *In Other Words: Essays Towards a Reflexive Sociology*. Trans. Matthew Adamson. Stanford: Stanford University Press.
    1991   *Language and Symbolic Power*. Ed. and intro. John B. Thompson. Trans. Gino Raymond and Matthew Adamson. Cambridge: Harvard University Press.

Brenner, Athalya
    1985   *The Israelite Woman: Social Role and Literary Type in Biblical Narrative*. Biblical Seminar 2. Sheffield: JSOT.

Brueggemann, Walter
    1982   *Genesis*. Atlanta: John Knox.

Buswell, Sara
    1987   *The Challenge of Old Testament Women: 2*. Grand Rapids, MI: Baker Book House.

Chatman, Seymour
    1978   *Story and Discourse: Narrative Structure in Fiction and Film*. Ithaca & London: Cornell University Press.

Culler, Jonathan
    1975   *Structuralist Poetics: Structuralism, Linguistics and the Study of Literature*. Ithaca: Cornell University Press.

Donaldson, Laura E.
    1992   *Decolonizing Feminisms: Race, Gender, and Empire-building*. Chapel Hill & London: University of North Carolina Press; London: Routledge.

Forster, E. M.
    1927   *Aspects of The Novel*. New York: Harcourt, Brace & Co.

Furman, Nelly
  1989   "His Story Versus Her Story: Male Genealogy and Female Strategy in the Jacob Cycle." *Semeia* 46:141-49.

Girard, René
  1965   *Deceit, Desire, and the Novel: Self and Other in Literary Structure.* Trans. Yvonne Freccero. Baltimore & London: Johns Hopkins University Press.

Greimas, A.-J.
  1983   *Structural Semantics: An Attempt at a Method.* Trans. Ronald Schleifer and Alan Veile Daniele McDowell. Lincoln & London: University of Nebraska Press.

Haraway, Donna
  1991   *Simians, Cyborgs, and Women: The Reinvention of Nature.* New York: Routledge.
  1992   "The Promises of Monsters: A Regenerative Politics for Inappropriate/d Others." Pp. 295-337 in *Cultural Studies.* Ed. Lawrence Grossberg, Cary Nelson, and Paula A. Treichler. New York & London: Routledge.

Hughes, Kenneth James
  1986   *Signs of Literature: Language, Ideology, and the Literary Text.* Vancouver: Talonbooks.

Jeansonne, Sharon Pace
  1990   *The Women of Genesis: From Sarah to Potiphar's Wife.* Minneapolis: Fortress.

Kaplan, Cora
  1986   *Sea Changes: Essays on Culture and Feminism.* London: Verso.

Kugel, James L.
  1990   *In Potiphar's House: The Interpretive Life of Biblical Texts.* San Francisco: Harper Collins.

Leitch, Thomas M.
  1986   *What Stories Are: Narrative Theory and Interpretation.* University Park & London: The Pennsylvania State University Press.

Martin, Wallace
  1986   *Recent Theories of Narrative.* Ithaca & London: Cornell University Press.

Moore, Stephen
  1989   *Literary Criticism and the Gospels: The Theoretical Challenge.* New Haven & London: Yale University Press.

Neusner, Jacob
  1985   *Genesis Rabbah: The Judaic Commentary to the Book of Genesis, Vol. III.* Trans. Jacob Neusner. BJS. Atlanta: Scholars.

Ong, Walter J.
  1982   *Orality and Literacy: The Technologizing of the Word.* New York & London: Routledge.

Price, Martin
    1983   *Forms of Life: Character and Moral Imagination in the Novel*. New Haven & London: Yale University Press.

Prince, Gerald
    1982   *Narratology: The Form and Functioning of Narrative*. Berlin, New York & Amsterdam: Mouton.

Rimmon-Kenan, Shlomith
    1983   *Narrative Fiction: Contemporary Poetics*. New York & London: Routledge.

Rousseau, Jean-Jacques
    1911   *Émile*. Trans. Barbara Foxley. New York and London: J. M. Dent; E. P. Dutton.

Sedgwick, Eve Kosofsky
    1985   *Between Men: English Literature and Male Homosocial Desire*. New York: Columbia University Press.

Sternberg, Meir
    1985   *The Poetics of Biblical Narrative: Ideological Literature and the Drama of Reading*. Bloomington: Indiana University Press.

Terdiman, Richard
    1985   *Discourse/Counter-Discourse: The Theory and Practice of Symbolic Resistance in Nineteenth-Century France*. Ithaca & London: Cornell University Press.

Thompson, John B.
    1991   "Editor's Introduction." Pp. 1-31 in *Language and Symbolic Power* by Pierre Bourdieu. Cambridge: Harvard University Press.

Weinsheimer, Joel
    1979   "Theory of Character: Emma." *Poetics Today* 1:185-211.

CHARACTERIZING CHARACTER IN BIBLICAL NARRATIVE

Robert M. Fowler
Baldwin-Wallace College

The publication of these five essays on characterization in biblical narrative is fortuitous, for they have many points of intersection, and yet they also offer some instructive differences in direction or emphasis. I shall briefly describe the predominant areas of common interest, and then offer a few critical comments on each essay.

One common theme in these essays is that the theory of characterization is underdeveloped and underutilized, both in literary studies generally and in biblical literary criticism in particular. Several of the authors declare a need for more sophistication in the theory of characterization, and together these five essays contribute to that goal. For example, Forster's distinction between flat and round characters is regularly criticized as too simplistic. On a slightly different tack, both Burnett and Donaldson describe and then relativize a polarity between theories that regard characters as realistic representations of humans and those that claim that characters are only proper names in a text to which a reader attaches traits inferred from reading the text. Although the polarities they describe are similar, Burnett and Donaldson relativize them differently. Burnett allows his polarity to persist, but insists that a character must be allowed to slip freely back and forth between the poles of the text and the reader's activity. Donaldson wants to dismantle her polarity altogether by means of a "cyborg theory of character."

Most of these authors want to break away from static or monolithic views of characters. Most want to crack characters open, to give them some wriggle room, to allow for fluidity and multiplicity in characterization. This desire is acted out in several ways. McCracken wants to find wriggle room for characters within the text of the Gospels, in their "dialogic" discourse, which offers the reader not individual, but "interdividual" characters.

However, most of our authors prefer to accentuate not the text but the role of the reader in constructing character out of textual details. Thus, another feature shared by these essays is their enactment of the pervasive shift in focus to readers and reading in literary theory today. Burnett sketches some of the paradoxical dynamics of the text and reader interaction relating to characters; Darr makes a good case for a reader-oriented approach to characterization generally; and Donaldson and Bach offer specific instances of resisting reading of female characters in biblical narrative from a feminist perspective. Feminist readings of biblical characters signal a new day in understanding the reader's relationship to biblical characters and to the patriarchal narrators who portray them. Apparently it is now imaginable to read biblical narrative as a real, gendered, twentieth-century reader and not necessarily as an ideal, genderless, first-century reader; it is now imaginable to question the previously unquestionable authority of the reliable, omniscient, patriarchal, biblical narrator; it is now imaginable to read a biblical text against its grain.

With these points of common interest in mind, I shall now make a few comments on each of the essays.

Fred Burnett's essay offers the most thorough discussion of the theory of characterization, and so it is a good place to begin. Burnett starts by discussing the "realist" versus the "purist" views of character; namely, the view that characters take on a lifelike existence outside the text versus the view that characters are always only proper names in texts. Like others of our essayists, Burnett turns to Seymour Chatman, who tries to steer a middle course between these two extremes.[1] The realist versus purist debate is intertwined with the ancient discussion of the relationship between plot and character, which is a trade-off, as Burnett observes, constantly being adjudicated by the reader. Thus the slipperiness of characters is really a function of the slipperiness of reading.

A topic that arises repeatedly in Burnett's essay is the degree of individuality that can be attributed to characters in biblical and other ancient narrative. Burnett is sensitive to the fact that individuality is far more of a modern than an ancient psychological construct. He acknowledges that most characters in ancient narratives are "agents" or "types," rather than "characters" per se. Burnett's discussion of the evidence for individuality in Greek and Roman portraiture is interesting, for such inquiries could well add to our grasp of the "horizon of expectation" of a first-century audience's engagement with a literary character. Nevertheless, that Burnett has to go such lengths to find evidence of individuality in antiquity seems to validate the claim that it is not in fact the norm, but instead a predominantly modern predisposition.

Burnett's attempt to deal with a first-century horizon of expectations is commendable, but there are other significant resources available that he and the other authors of these essays fail to exploit fully. One is Bruce Malina's use of anthropological field studies to describe the "dyadic personality" in the first-century Mediterranean world; the other is Walter

---

[1] Chatman's *Story and Discourse* has achieved virtual canonical status, at least among biblical literary critics. Four of our five essays cite Chatman.

Ong's discussion of the "additive, aggregative, and participatory" (Donaldson) qualities of all discourse in oral cultures. Malina and Ong are not unknown to our authors—McCracken footnotes Malina briefly, and Donaldson cites Ong appreciatively in two paragraphs and then moves on to other matters. If one is concerned about how ancient audiences construed the characters in ancient narrative, then one had best deal with the anthropological work of Malina and others, as well as the orality and literacy studies of scholars such as Ong. But the attitudes of other audiences between the first and twentieth centuries would also be just as significant to investigate. The history of the self, or the history of what we might call psychological theory, could be attended to much better in theories of characterization. Whether we are interested in the reading experience of first-, tenth-, or twentieth-century readers, we could and should do much more to scrutinize the presuppositions about the self that readers bring to their encounter with characters.

If Burnett gives us a good survey of theories of characterization, John Darr gives us a helpful introduction to a "reader-oriented theory of characterization." He is interested in how "readers build characters," and he especially wants to consider the narrator of Luke/Acts as a character construed by the reader. Darr takes as a foil the provocative work of James Dawsey, but since Dawsey's thesis has not gained much favor in the critical guild, Darr may be picking on an easy target. Nevertheless, the Dawsey/Darr debate involves a number of points of interest. The main problems with Dawsey's argument, Darr claims, are that Dawsey fails to acknowledge the extreme unlikelihood of an unreliable narrator in any ancient narrative, and he does not employ a sophisticated theory of either characterization or of reader-response. Darr generally has the better end of this debate with Dawsey, but his reader-response machinery has some curious noises it in that invite inspection. Perhaps modern readers seek consistency and coherence in reading, but readers reading in a postmodern mode generally do not, and I doubt that ancient readers did either. Or if the ancient reader did seek consistency and coherence in characters, I daresay those qualities were at least understood far differently than they are today.[2] This returns us to the topic of the history of psychological theory. Consistency and coherence of characters surely

---

[2] For example, Burnett notes that the character of Creon differs markedly in three of Sophocles' plays. Or think of the variations in the characterization of Odysseus from the *Iliad* to the *Odyssey* or just from one episode to another within either one of those epic poems. What do these examples, which could be multiplied endlessly, imply about an authorial commitment to consistency and coherence in antiquity? Let us remember that the elaborate source theories of nineteenth-century philological-historical criticism were born out of the widespread perception of a lack of consistency and coherence in ancient narratives such as Homer and the Bible.

mean very different things in ancient, modern, and postmodern narratives. Surprisingly, none of these essays addresses directly the postmodern demise of the coherent, unified self, although McCracken's evocation of the Bakhtinian "dialogic character" and Donaldson's introduction of the cyborg are basically ways of getting at this very issue.

So, I question whether a first-century reader would seek out consistency and coherence in characterization, at least the way a modern reader would. But furthermore, even if Darr has figured out the implied first-century reader of Luke down to the tiniest detail, must we join him in honoring that reader and identifying ourselves with him? Here the essay by Bach throws down a challenge to Darr (and to anyone who cares deeply about biblical narrative): granting Darr his point that biblical narrators (Luke's narrator, for example) are typically presented as reliable and authoritative, nevertheless, must we bow to their authority? Bach's view is that if a patriarchal narrator (and how often in the Bible is there any other kind?) "flattens" or "suppresses" a female character, then a responsible reader may choose to read that character against the grain of the narrator's reliable and authoritative discourse. That is, a resisting reader may dare to reject the authority of a biblical narrator. Darr, on other hand, urges Dawsey and us to join him in recognizing and acquiescing to the trustworthiness of the Lukan narrator. I wonder which of the two Bach would find more congenial, Darr, the better informed and more sophisticated reader-response critic, or Dawsey, the more suspicious and resisting reader of Lukan authority?

If Darr gives us the best theoretical account of the reader's construction of character in biblical narrative, if not necessarily the most provocative practical application, David McCracken gives us the most thorough explication of the insight that biblical characters are "never monadic, static, or fully realized." The chief inspiration for McCracken's essay, signaled in his essay title, is the work of Bakhtin, who has been given too little attention to date in biblical criticism. Also featured prominently in the title is the key image of "interdividuality"—biblical characters are not adequately understood as solitary individuals, but as *inter*dividuals who are always to be found in relationship with others. McCracken's Bakhtinian theory of character is the most sustained discussion among these essays of their common theme of the slipperiness of biblical characters. It is an illuminating, helpful essay. However, problems began to take shape as I read of the *skandalon* that appears regularly in Gospel narratives, but much less so in Hebrew Bible narratives, and of a "Kierkegaardian paradigm of self." The difference between Hebrew narrative and the Gospels is simply asserted, not argued, although it may be so in

McCracken's recent book.³ The section on Kierkegaard in this essay is so brief that it distracts more than it adds.

Of the five authors, McCracken gives the most attention to the slipperiness of characters but gives the least attention to another common concern, the reader and the reading experience. This is unfortunate, because his Bakhtinian theory would lend itself beautifully to a fruitful dialogue with reader-response criticism, and because McCracken himself does evoke the reader strongly, if only occasionally. The absence of the reader in certain places in his essay is surprising. How can one who is as attuned to the reader as McCracken often is offer the sentence, "Response is all," and nowhere near it even mention readers or reading?

With the essays by Laura Donaldson and Alice Bach we cross over a threshold to encounter a truly scandalous kind of resisting reading of biblical characters. In dealing with Donaldson's essay, I would like to begin with her reading of the character of Potiphar's wife in Genesis 39, which is eye-opening, and then back up to her theoretical construct of the cyborg, which I do not find particularly helpful.

Similar to Bach's strategy in reading the character of Uriah's wife, Donaldson wants to read a "counterstory" about Potiphar's wife.⁴ Donaldson demonstrates that in the history of reading Genesis 39 the character of "Mrs. Potiphar" has regularly been reduced to that of a sexual adventuress with an overdeveloped libido. In contrast, Donaldson reimagines the story, not in terms of sexuality only, but more broadly in terms of household politics. Thus, Genesis 39 "concerns domestic status rather than irrepressible lust," a powerful rereading of a narrative that has been read so easily for so long that it is hard to see it with fresh eyes.

This reading is rich and provocative, but in spite of the cyborg, not because of it. I read Donaldon's essay at the same time that I was reading "cyberpunk" science fiction and "New Edge" journals such as *Mondo 2000*, so I was eager to see the cyborg model work well for her, but I was disappointed. The cyborg, "that uncanny and unstable hybrid of animate organism and inanimate machine," is Donaldson's choice for a way to do what most of our five authors are trying to do somehow, that is, to break open static perceptions of character and to find "a way out of the maze of dualisms" (Haraway), in this case especially the dualism of the sexes. But once into her reading of Genesis 39, she does not really need the cyborg. A reader does not need a cyborg to see either the triangle of the two men

---

³ This is a problem that McCracken shares with Donaldson and Darr. All three have published books closely related to their essays in this volume; each of their essays reads at times like a précis of a much longer exposition.

⁴ That Bathsheba is repeatedly called "Uriah's wife" and that Potiphar's wife is never named is of course immensely significant. Donaldson and Burnett both helpfully address the importance of the proper names of characters.

and the woman or the "homosocial" power arrangements between Potiphar and Joseph. Indeed, Donaldson, like McCracken, could have said most of what she wants to about the characters in Genesis 39 by using the vocabulary of Bakhtin, whom she does mention once briefly.

In the first half of her essay, Donaldson writes that character is "a determinate position produced within a conflicted narrative field." Its general fuzziness and poststructuralist jargon aside, this statement seems to shift the root metaphor of the essay from cyborg to field, and for a person raised on a farm the connotations of "field" are distinctly non-cyborgian. Later the root metaphor seems to shift again, this time to the realm of geometry, when Donaldson starts talking about "the cyborgian triangle of Genesis 39." So, is the cyborg in Genesis 39 the triangle of Potiphar, his wife, and Joseph? But elsewhere we hear about "the cyborgian figure of Potiphar's wife," so is Potiphar's wife really the cyborg? Or is the cyborg the "conflicted narrative field" in which all of the characters interrelate? So many things—a field, a triangle, and a figure—are so casually labelled "cyborgian" that the adjective quickly loses what little meaning it ever had. Ironically, although Donaldson's cyborg gets reduced to a vague and confusing adjective, her reading of Genesis 39 is excellent, so it remains unclear whether the cyborg has really helped her to accomplish that valuable reading. The cyborg has promise, but I do not see it fulfilled in this essay.

Finally, I turn to Alice Bach's essay, in which there is a superb combination of theoretical reflection and practical application from a feminist perspective. Bach states her central concern clearly: "A continuing concern of mine has been to find a method for retrieving the female character who may have been flattened or suppressed by the weight of the story that is not hers." Like Darr, Bach understands that biblical narrators are typically presented as reliable, authoritative, and omniscient. Unlike Darr, she reserves the right to challenge the authority of the biblical narrator, by reading in a suspicious, resisting fashion. Bach agrees with Burnett that biblical characters should be allowed to slip free of and to exist apart from the narratives that give them life. In this kind of reading the text may offer the first word about a character, but it does not have the last word. So Bach imagines a characterization of Bathsheba that the biblical narrator fails to gives her. (This is very reminiscent of Donaldson's recovery of a submerged story for Potiphar's wife.) Once Bach exposes the voyeurism of the narrator and proposes a cogent alternative point of view seen through Bathsheba's eyes, thus granting Bathsheba the object of male sexual desire a subjectivity of her own, I find it impossible to insist that the reliable, authoritative, biblical narrator must still be heeded, at least in his characterization of Bathsheba. After all, as Bach shrewdly observes, the narrator is telling David's story, not Bathsheba's. If Bathsheba's story is to be told, someone other than the narrator must step in to tell it.

As if it were not enough to have imagined the missing story of Bathsheba, the sexual object of David's gaze, Bach goes on to read that Bathsheba over against the later Bathsheba, who plots to place her son on the throne to succeed David. Thus Bach imaginatively reads two ironically incongruent Bathsheba characters, the powerless sexual object and the powerful Queen Mother. Instead of trying to construct a consistency and coherence between the two dissimilar characterizations of Bathsheba (or are there simply *two* Bathshebas?), Bach embraces and ponders the exquisite dissonances between them. Who says readers must read for consistency and coherence?

In conclusion, what do we learn from all of these essays? For one thing, we learn that the theory of characterization in biblical narrative is not dead or dying, but is alive and well in these essays, and it may even live to see a cyborgian future. Another thing, in the postmodern age, static, individualistic views of characterization are regarded with deep suspicion. Whether our language is spiced with talk of dialogue or cyborgs, these authors have a strong intuition that literary characters, like their human counterparts, are never solitary entities but are always to be found in relationships with others. Furthermore, readers and reading remain at the center of critical concern; in greater or lesser degree, all of these essays advocate a central role for the reader in the construction of characters. And finally, feminist approaches to characterization give us valuable room in which to maneuver in dealing with biblical characters, by encouraging us to imagine the missing stories of flattened or suppressed female characters.

But I wonder, what other kinds of stories are flattened or suppressed in the Bible? The kind of occluded story that has intrigued me in studying and teaching the Gospels for many years is the untold story of the clash between the biblical narrators themselves (Fowler: 228-60). The typical biblical narrator not only flattens and suppresses certain of his own characters, he also tries to do the same to his rival narrators. (The image of sumo wrestlers doing battle comes to mind.) I have wondered, what is at stake in the often bitter competition between these supposedly reliable and authoritative narrators? Who or what falls into the cracks between them? How is that they use such similar narrative techniques to tell often incommensurate stories? Should not this tip us off to question their narrative techniques? If the reply to all of these questions is in some form, "Well, you know, flattening and suppressing is the only way patriarchal authority knows how to operate," then I join the feminists in trying to imagine yet another story hinted at but so far missing from the Bible, the story of the postpatriarchal era of the biblical tradition.

WORKS CONSULTED

Fowler, Robert M.
    1991   *Let the Reader Understand: Reader-Response Criticism and the Gospel of Mark.* Minneapolis: Fortress.

Malina, Bruce J.
    1981   *The New Testament World: Insights from Cultural Anthropology.* Atlanta: John Knox.

IN OUR IMAGE WE CREATE HIM, MALE AND FEMALE WE CREATE THEM: THE E/AFFECT OF BIBLICAL CHARACTERIZATION

Ilona N. Rashkow
State University of New York at Stony Brook

Narratives—and biblical stories are no exception—are concerned with temporal events and incidents as well as characters and their personalities. Perhaps because Aristotle stressed the centrality of action and incident, literary criticism has tended to emphasize the importance of plot over character. Within the last several years, however, theories of "characterization" have become a focus of critical inquiry. As Alice Bach reminds us (using the oft-quoted words of Henry James), "What is [narrative] incident but the illustration of character?" Indeed, in James's view, the very purpose of literary narrative is to provide and elucidate the *varieties* of human characters and their eccentricities.[1] Although certain narratives are more action-oriented (and therefore more plot-centered) while others focus on the dynamics of interpersonal relationships, arguments over whether story-line or character is more "primary" to narrative are, as Frank Kermode suggests, somewhat "absurd given that the two elements are intricately related and mutually enrich each other" (77). Thus, the importance of plot notwithstanding, the *e*ffect and *a*ffect of biblical characterization is the object of interest in these papers.

THE PARADOX OF LITERARY CHARACTERIZATION

When asked to describe a person or a literary character, we mention a distinctive set of dominant qualities—a set of what Diana Meyers calls "characterological strands" (70). These strands can be stylistic qualities (the romanticism of the Shulamite or the melancholy of Qoheleth), virtues (the tenacity of Ruth), vices (the arrogance of Pharaoh), or foibles (the irrationality of Saul); they can be ways of processing experience (the careful pronouncements of Solomon or the quick intuitive reactions of Potiphar); or ardently held principles (like those of the Nazarites); they can be commitments to a role (Moses as community leader), to a career (Joshua as

---

[1] For a more in-depth analysis of the import of character for James see his "Preface to The Portrait of a Lady," *The Art of the Novel.*

warrior), or to other people (Rachel and her children). In "well-developed" characters[2] the same characterological strands are not in evidence at all times (Saul does not *always* behave irrationally). Moreover, a characterological strand is not invariably associated with the same evanescent traits. For example, the excitability of Moses is evident in both his determination to lead his people and his anger over the golden calf.

As James's quotation highlights, well-developed characters are often viewed as representatives of life and as such can be understood only if we assume that they are "telling a truth." This assumption allows us to find "conscious" as well as "unconscious" motivations, albeit in literary characters. Thus, the actions and language of Abraham, for example, reveal a great deal about him, despite the fact that all we will ever "know" is contained in the 1,534 verses of Genesis.

However, biblical characters are both more and less than real persons. It is generally agreed[3] that one aspect of characterization is *mimetic* (to represent human action and motivation), and another aspect is primarily *textual* (to reveal information to a reader or to conceal it). This presents a problem. Unfortunately, the more "realistic" a biblical character in the sense of responding fully and believably to his or her world (the mimetic function of characterization), the more difficult it may be to assign a complex of motives to him or her. Because "realistic" characters resemble "real people" (whose integrity is otherwise not in question), the same problems inherent in dealing with insights into conscious and unconscious actions surface—we cannot always "know" why people act the way they do. Further, if purely "unconscious" motives *are* there (and it is not without some irony that we can refer to the "unconscious" of a literary character), they are hard to locate: are Simeon and Levi *unconsciously* referring to their father when they ask "Shall he treat our sister like a whore?" or is this Meir Sternberg's father-son relationship surfacing (475)?

Just as the mimetic aspect of characterization causes difficulties in analyzing literary characters, the textual aspect (that is, pertinent

---

[2] Of course, not all biblical characters are "well-developed," and this aspect of characterization in biblical poetics has received considerable attention recently (see, for example, Gunn and Fewell, Sternberg, and Berlin). In this volume, Fred Burnett (following Adele Berlin) finds "'degrees of characterization' . . . a continuum that moves . . . from 'agent' to 'type' to 'character'" in his discussion of characterization in the gospels, a position with which David McCracken seems to agree: "gradually developing character is not the stuff of the gospels."

[3] Contra Edmond Cross, for example, who rejects "the referential illusion that would make a character something other than a product of writing and, apart from interpretations of its status, would lead us into psychological perspectives and presuppose the hypostatization of a real person" (107). See also Robert Alter who takes Harold Bloom to task for anthropomorphizing the biblical deity (22).

information about a character that is narratively presented and/or withheld) is problematic as well. The "textuality" of characters has no precise parallel in life (although it can be argued that real persons often resemble literary characters in the masks we present to the world). As a result, examining a narrative character is not risk-free. For instance, contradictory behavior in a biblical character may result from the psychic complexities the biblical writer imagined; however, they may result from the fact that the Bible is a literary narrative with a highly developed system of conventions. In other words, "character traits" may be more a function of the requirements of the story-line than personality. Thus, it can be argued that there is no room for "unconscious" motives in literary narratives, and that even those literary characters who seem like psychiatric textbook cases have objective correlatives for their behavior based on the needs of the plot. Viewed this way, the narrative world of the text explains, even if it does not always justify, what the biblical characters do. A character's behavior may be irrational, and characters may participate in the creation of comic or tragic chaos, but their behavior is determined by the writer's manipulation rather than divine, natural, or social causes. From this perspective, Saul's madness is part of the story-line and nothing else.

Following along this path, however, could lead us to the dangerous world of "authorial intent" that Fred Burnett seems to approach when he asks "does it also follow that ancient historiographers had no interest in the character as an individual since little of the character's inward life is presented?" David Gunn accurately describes the problems that arise when trying to determine authorial intent or interest, in this case, applied to characterization:

> The problems that arise in talking of the author's intention ... are not dissimilar to those which confront the critic who demands a precise knowledge of the story's original social context as the key to its exegesis, given the paucity of extant socio-historical data from ancient Israel and the problems of dating and identifying the author(s) and editor(s) of particular texts (1980:136n.6).

The Role of "The" Reader

Fortunately, poststructural literary criticism seems to have provided a way of resolving this paradox inherent in characterization theory by calling attention to the interaction between reader and text, thus challenging assumptions about the *nature* of literary characterization. In varying degrees, all of these papers discuss the way "biblical ... characters exist ... in a present zone of contact with the reader" (McCracken), how individual readers "build characters" (Darr) and "reconstruct characters" (Bach), and the extent to which "a 'character' is a construct developed during the reading process . . . [and] is also an effect of the reading process" (Burnett).

Interest in the unconscious existence of literary characters has led to questions about just where "character" or the "self" is located, especially as the interrelations of literature and other fields such as philosophy, anthropology, and sociology have been explored. Indeed, according to David McCracken, it is "a view of the self [defined by McCracken as "an analogue of a person . . . including a person like the reader, whom twentieth-century Americans and Europeans are inclined to think of as an individual self"] that undergirds . . . [the] notion of character." As a result, a literary character's distinction from his or her role and his or her world is no longer as clear as it once was. That is, since literature contributes to our imaginings of personal experience, literary characters carry their "psychology" within themselves, in the very structure of relations they embody, and invite us to form with them as readers. Thus, in some way (however obscure), literary characters contain their origins and significance as "psychologically coherent" (Schwartz and Willbern: 205), despite their fictive nature. As readers, we seek to experience and understand a literary character's role and world, even though we may acknowledge the narrative as fictitious.

This change in approach focuses on the "way" a reader and a character work together. By looking beyond the literal story, we challenge assumptions about the nature of reader-character relationships and relate narrative structure and conflicts to a drama within some *theoretical* human mind, a mind ambiguously located between the fictional characters of the text and that of a reader.[4] A natural consequence of this new perspective is a question posed by Darr: "Who is *the* reader to whom we refer [emphasis added]?" As Darr correctly notes, "individual readers (and reading communities) exhibit idiosyncratic practices and agendas."

The concept of "the reader" has been subjected to a searching analysis and is a matter of considerable controversy among literary theorists. "Is he the 'Actual Reader' (Van Dijk, Jauss), the 'Superreader' (Riffaterre), the 'Informed Reader' (Fish), the 'Ideal Reader' (Culler), the 'Model Reader' (Eco), the 'Implied Reader' (Booth, Iser, Chatman, Perry), or the 'Encoded Reader' (Brooke-Rose)?" (Rimmon-Kenan: 118). Despite different methodologies, what can be said with some measure of assurance is that all of the papers in Part I of this volume focus on both biblical characters *and* "the reader," be it the biblical authors' attitudes towards the ancient readers (Burnett), the kinds of readers various texts seem to imply (Bach), the role actual readers play in the determination of literary meaning (Darr), the

---

[4] For an elaboration of this see Rashkow, 1993.

relation of reading strategies to textual interpretation (Donaldson), the status of the reader's "self" (McCracken), or something else.

Burnett's paper is unique within the group in that he neither defines "the reader" nor discusses variations in readings based on factors that influence *individual* readers. Indeed, Burnett even seeks to explain how ancient readers constructed characters, once again coming perilously close to "authorial intent." Who is this "ancient reader?" Can we speak of *"the* ancient reader" with any more confidence than we can discuss *"the* modern reader"? The rest of the papers acknowledge that there is no monolithic read*er* and hence, no monolithic read*ing*. Bach identifies several potential readers ("faithful," "male," "politically sympathetic") and then paradigmatically establishes "the" reader of her paper as herself, a position with which most reader-oriented critics would agree. In other words, "the character" does not inhere completely and exclusively in the text. The "effects" of reading Scripture, psychological and otherwise, are essential to its "meaning" and hence character analysis. This seems to be borne out by the fact that each time we read a biblical narrative we see something new in its characters, not because biblical interpretation is inexhaustible but because each time we read a text we are at least slightly different people having experienced more of life's vicissitudes.

The Character We Call "Narrator"

Many of these "effects" of reading Scripture are based, in great part, on a character rather neglected in biblical scholarship until now, a character whom three of the papers address: the narrator. While Bach, Darr, and McCracken agree that narrators, as well as the rest of the characters, are "constructed" by readers and exist as figures within the text, Bach's view of the relationship between reader and narrator is quite different from that of Darr and McCracken. Darr views the narrator of Luke-Acts as an "authoritative, trustworthy guide . . . a model witness to and for the reader." Similarly, McCracken writes that "the omniscient biblical narrator stands in a close relationship to the omniscient God. The narrator of the Bible . . . is an analogue of God." Bach is less trusting. For her, the biblical narrator is a storyteller with whom the reader must *contend*. In Bach's reading, there is an adversarial relationship between narrator and narratee unless the reader and story-teller share either theological, gender, or political codes.

As a feminist, I find Bach's position more convincing. Certainly, for a female reader there are numerous examples in the Hebrew Bible in which the narrator does not act like Darr's "trustworthy guide." The Genesis story of Lot and his two daughters is a blatant example. Lot recognizes that the proposal of the townsmen to sodomize his supernatural guests is evil, but then he inexplicably tries to substitute an equally violent act: the rape of his daughters. The narrator never condemns Lot for offering his daughters as rape victims to the unruly crowd at his door, but instead remains silent in the presence of threatened sexual violence against these women, thus offering tacit approval. Could it be possible that the narrator believes that Lot's behavior is excusable? Does the narrator implicitly declare that all socially approved actions and societal values apply only to males (as the brutal story of Judges 19 would further illustrate)? It would appear so if one generalized Darr's reading of the narrator of Luke-Acts as "a model witness to and for the reader." What is even more frightening is an application of McCracken's thesis that "the narrator of the Bible . . . is an analogue of God"! Even non-feminists would blanch at that prospect.

The Politics of Characterization

Bach's position reflects what might be called the "politics" of characterization. If we define "politics" as ideologies, biblical narratives can be said to take sides in ideological debates, conflicts that center around issues of power. Donaldson, for example, uses the image of the cyborg to reconceptualize characterization as the "production of positions within a *conflicted* narrative field" (emphasis added). As a result, the story of Joseph and Potiphar's wife is a negotiation for empowerment wherein "Potiphar's wife resists both mimeticism and formalism—not to mention masculinism." For Donaldson, Genesis 39 is a struggle between two opposing political perspectives.

McCracken's position is more overtly political. McCracken construes the gospels as texts determined and shaped by the blatant partisan convictions of the authors. For McCracken, "any conception of character as a fixed and stable entity is inadequate in a text where the kingdom of God is offered as a disruption of worldly fixity and stability and where the crucial issue about character is its relation to this disruptive kingdom." McCracken's ideological analysis of characterization in the gospels examines the narrative voice and doctrinal perspective inscribed in the text. From whose point of view is the narrative being told? Whose class, gender, and ethnic interests are being served in the preservation and communication of this story? His answer is clear: the political sympathies of the author are the basis of literary characterization in the gospels. According to McCracken, New Testament characterization is not based upon *individual* characters as "essential beings," but rather upon their relational activity to a disruptive world. Based upon the carnival work of Mikhail Bakhtin, McCracken's concept of characterization in the New

Testament is a celebration of the normal world "turned upside down." The biblical author builds upon the prejudices and predilections of his audience by using the carnival genre as a rhetorical device that serves to "debunk, supplant, reinforce, coopt, caricature . . . [and] dismantle" the status quo in order to establish the ideology of the kingdom of God (Weems: 27). Individual characters are insignificant, and the dominant voice becomes the only one worthy of attention. Significantly for comparative theories of character construction, McCracken perceives this as a crucial difference between Hebrew Bible characterization and that of the New Testament:

> Both [Hebrew Bible and New Testament concepts of character] involve dialogic encounters, but in the gospel stories the scandal or offense dwells in Jesus and in the world that he posits, the kingdom of God. Something like this can of course happen in the Hebrew narratives, but it is not the norm.

Bach, on the other hand, confronts the tension between text and *reader* and the necessity to "retrieve or reconstruct characters from the structuralist wasteland in which they are mere actants of the plot." Bach's construct of characterization is a liberation struggle that requires a reader to "rescue" the Hebrew Bible from its implication in the dominant male ideology, both at the level of the text and, more importantly, at the level of its interpretation. Bach, in effect, urges a revolt of the reader based on the specificity of each reader's situation. For example, "feminist readers can . . . avert our gaze, and . . . cast a cold eye . . . towards an authoritative [male?] narrator."

Conclusion

In these papers, the old, "sensible" distinction between analyzing character, author, and reader has given way, and heretofore uninteresting or "inappropriate" parts of the text have come to be seen as aspects of characterization. As a result, while previously it was assumed that new readings could produce only small variations in a relatively fixed canon of ideas, the concepts that affect/effect literary characterization diminish the number of fixed, or relatively fixed meanings, and vastly increase the possibilities of new biblical interpretations. Indeed, the number of novel explications becomes endless.

That everyone responds to the Bible in his or her own way is not noteworthy in itself. But since Aristotle we have suspected that underlying our various responses there are principles to be described. If Aristotle is correct, a reader "identifies" with a narrative character. And since the Bible is viewed by many as a "spiritual" text, it is reasonable for a reader to assume biblical characters illustrate some sort of "ethical" precepts. As readers, we want and expect biblical characters to reflect the kind of world with which we know how to deal. But to quote Hamlet, "Ay, there's the rub." We identify with biblical characters, of course; but Freud teaches us that there are forms of identification that do not stem from admiration and imitation. Thus, the powerful effect of biblical characters on readers may be explained also in other than imitative terms. Fish and his concept of "community of like-minded readers" notwithstanding, there is little agreement about the moral principles operating in much of the Bible; and it is not improbable that an ancient reader had as difficult a time as a modern one understanding the characterization of a deity "hardening Pharaoh's heart" and then sending the plagues. Both might ask, "Did Pharaoh *really* deserve that?" Inevitably, our reaction to biblical narratives and biblical characters is individual. In reading the Bible, we try to shape the text and its characters until it is the kind of setting in which we can gratify our wishes and defeat our fears. In other words, readers *e*ffect characters who, in turn, *a*ffect readers.

WORKS CONSULTED

Alter, Robert
    1992   *The World of Biblical Literature.* New York: Basic.

Barricelli, Jean-Pierre and Joseph Gibaldi, eds.
    1982   *Interrelations of Literature.* New York: Modern Language Association of America.

Berlin, Adele
    1983   *Poetics and Interpretation of Biblical Narrative.* Sheffield: Almond.

Cross, Edmond
    1988   *Theory and Practice of Sociocriticism.* Minneapolis: University of Minnesota Press.

Fish, Stanley
    1980   *Is There a Text in This Class? The Authority of Interpretive Communities.* Cambridge: Harvard University Press.

Gunn, David
    1980   *The Fate of King Saul: An Interpretation of a Biblical Story.* JSOTSup 14. Sheffield: JSOT.

Gunn, David and Danna Nolan Fewell
    1993   *Narrative in the Hebrew Bible.* Oxford: Oxford University Press.

James, Henry
    1934   *The Art of the Novel*. Ed. R. Blackmur. New York: Scribner's.

Kermode, Frank
    1979   *The Genesis of Secrecy*. Cambridge: Harvard University Press.

Meyers, Diana T.
    1989   *Self, Society, and Personal Choice*. New York: Columbia University Press.

Rashkow, Ilona N.
    1993   *The Phallacy of Genesis: A Feminist-Psychoanalytic Approach*. Louisville: Westminster/John Knox.

Rimmon-Kenan, Shlomith
    1983   *Narrative Fiction: Contemporary Poetics*. London: Methuen.

Schwartz, Murray M. and David Willbern
    1982   "Literature and Psychology." Pp. 205-24 in *Interrelations of Literature*. Ed. Jean-Pierre Barricelli and Joseph Gibaldi. New York: Modern Language Association of America.

Sternberg, Meir
    1985   *The Poetics of Biblical Narrative: Ideological Literature and the Drama of Reading*. Bloomington: Indiana University Press.

Weems, Renita J.
    1992   "The Hebrew Women are not Like the Egyptian Women: The Ideology of Race, Gender, and Sexual Reproduction in Exodus 1." *Semeia* 59:25-34.

II

THE UNNAMED AND THE UNNAMABLE

ANONYMITY AND CHARACTER IN THE BOOKS OF SAMUEL

Adele Reinhartz
McMaster University, Hamilton, Ontario

ABSTRACT

One of the often-overlooked elements of characterization in biblical narrative is the presence or absence of a proper name. While all of the major characters in the Books of Samuel, such as Samuel, Saul, and David, and most of the secondary characters, such as Michal and Jonathan, Joab and Absalom, are named within the narrative, many members of the "supporting cast," that is, the minor characters with whom the major and secondary figures interact, remain unnamed. It will be the purpose of this essay to consider the effect of the withholding of the proper name on a mimetic reading of the narrative. We will argue that the anonymity of particular minor characters contributes positively both to the characterization of major and secondary characters and to plot development. After some general observations on the role of anonymity in mimetic literature, we will survey the anonymous characters in the Books of Samuel. The survey will be supplemented by a more detailed study of three anonymous women whose roles are developed more fully than most of the other unnamed figures in these books, namely, the medium of Endor (1 Sam 28:3-25), the wise woman of Tekoa (2 Sam 14:1-24), and the wise woman of Abel (2 Sam 20:14-22).

Like a Cecil B. De Mille epic, the biblical Books of Samuel boast a cast of thousands and more subplots than an afternoon soap opera. Yet, despite the complexity and sheer magnitude of this narrative work (1 and 2 Samuel were originally one book; see McCarter, 1980:3-4), its principal characters are vividly drawn and the structure of the causally-linked events in which they act—that is, the plot (Forster: 82)—is relatively clear. By the time we reach the end of 2 Samuel, we have "witnessed" the establishment of the monarchy of Israel under the guidance of Samuel the prophet and its fortunes under the first two kings, Saul and David. In the course of doing so, we have rejoiced with Hannah over the long-awaited birth of Samuel (1 Samuel 1), smiled at the earnestness of the young Saul in search of his father's lost donkeys (1 Samuel 9; cf. Exum and Whedbee: 21), and grieved with David over the death of his son Absalom (2 Samuel 19).

Credit for the relative ease with which the reader can pick a path through this work, and identify as well as identify with its major actors, must be given to the highly mimetic nature of the narrative. Despite the obvious distance between the world implied by these books and our own, the characters and their emotions, their intrigues and relationships, are remarkably realistic (as is true of biblical narrative in general; see Bar-Efrat: 92, and Licht: 10).

The mimetic nature of characterization in 1 and 2 Samuel is assumed by most studies of this work, ranging from the diachronic historical and source-critical work of Kyle McCarter to the synchronic structuralist analysis by David Jobling (5-24) and the more general literary-critical studies of specific figures, events, and/or pericopes (e.g. Gunn, 1978, 1980).[1] These diverse approaches have uncovered many of the narrative features that contribute to the mimetic quality of the characters of 1 and 2 Samuel as well as of the plot in which they act.

Largely overlooked, however, is one particular narrative feature shared by almost all figures in these books. This feature is the "possession" of a proper name. Insofar as the characters in this work are life-like, we may assume that they, like the humans whom they resemble, "have" proper names. Important for our understanding of characterization, however, is the fact that in a significant number of cases these proper names are not disclosed in the narrative. While all of the major characters, such as Samuel, Saul, and David, and most of the secondary characters, such as Michal and Jonathan, Joab and Absalom, are named, many members of the "supporting cast" (Samuel: 94), that is, the minor characters with whom the major and secondary figures interact, remain anonymous.

It will be the purpose of this essay to consider the effect of the absence of the proper name on a mimetic reading of the narrative. Throughout our discussion we will consider the contribution of this narrative feature for the construction of character and for the development of plot in the Books of Samuel. In doing so, we will assume the interdependence of plot and character within the narrative, in accordance with Henry James's famous formulation (174): "What is character but the determination of incident? What is incident but the illustration of character?" The simplicity and apparently axiomatic nature of this formulation have not prevented heated debates among literary critics on the precise relationship between, and relative importance of, plot and character in narrative (Rimmon-Kenan: 34-35; Chatman: 108-120; Forster: 91). While we will not enter into this theoretical debate, our examination will illustrate the integral relationship of plot and character in biblical narrative.

---

[1] The presence of mimetic assumptions is signalled by references to characters' traits (e.g. Jobling: 10, 21; Schulz: 123) and intentions (e.g. Van Dijk-Hemmes: 139). As Rimmon-Kennan (32) notes, speculation about characters' motives and personalities is characteristic of mimetic or realistic interpretation.

After some general observations on the role of anonymity in mimetic literature, we will examine briefly the range of the anonymous characters in the Books of Samuel. This survey will be supplemented by a more detailed study of three anonymous women whose roles are developed more fully than most of the other unnamed figures in these books, namely, the medium of Endor (1 Sam 28:3-25), the wise woman of Tekoa (2 Sam 14:1-24), and the wise woman of Abel (2 Sam 20:14-22).

Anonymity and Mimesis

The topic of anonymity and characterization has been discussed as rarely with respect to non-biblical mimetic literature as it has been with respect to biblical narrative.[2] More attention has been paid, however, to its converse, namely, the role of the proper name in the construction of character. Literary theorists agree that the proper name in and of itself is a "sign" or signifier that is initially empty of meaning. As such it is a gap that must be filled by the reader from the other data in the narrative (Docherty: 47). Once introduced into the text, however, it functions as the single most important unifying factor, a "peg" on which all of the other data of characterization may be hung (Rimmon-Kennan: 39). In doing so, the proper name provides a convenient way of referring to that character, thereby differentiating one character from another (Weinsheimer: 195). The two main functions of the proper name in the construction of character are therefore the unification of character and the differentiation of that character from other figures within the narrative.

The presence of the proper name in itself encourages a mimetic reading of literature since its function in literature mirrors that of the proper name in everyday life. According to J. Searle (172),

> The uniqueness and immense pragmatic convenience of proper names in our language lie precisely in the fact that they enable us to refer publicly to objects without being forced to raise issues and come to agreement on what descriptive characteristics exactly constitute the identity of the object. They function not as descriptions, but as pegs on which to hang descriptions.

A mimetic reading of character assumes a certain commonality between fictional and "real" people, while at the same time recognizing that they are not identical. What literary characters and real people have in common, argues Baruch Hochman (7), "is the model, which we carry in our

---

[2] The role of the proper name in the construction of character is generally discussed in the context of the use of anonymous characters in postmodern literature, such as, for example, the novels of Nathalie Sarraute and Alain Robbe-Grillet. In these works, anonymous characters are used precisely in order to avoid a mimetic rendering of character. See Docherty; Jefferson.

heads, of what a person is. Both characters and people are apprehended in someone's consciousness, and they are apprehended in approximately the same terms, yet they are clearly not identical."

That we build our conceptions of fictional characters in ways similar to those in which we construct "real" people is emphasized by Seymour Chatman (125-26). In understanding the traits that fictional texts ascribe to fictional characters, the audience "is asked to read out characters in the same way as it does real people . . . ." He continues,

> It is enough to distinguish the narrative from the real-life case by adding "narrative" or "fictive" to remind us that we are not dealing with psychological realities but artistic constructs, yet that we understand these constructs through highly coded psychological information that we have picked up in ordinary living including our experiences with art.

If the proper name plays such an important role in character construction, what are the implications of the absence of a proper name for the reader's construction of and response to particular characters? The mimetic model pointed to by the use of a proper name would suggest that the function of anonymity in mimetic literature might parallel the phenomenon of anonymity in everyday life.

That such a parallel is valid is supported by the studies of anonymity in mundane experience undertaken by the phenomenologist Maurice Natanson. While Natanson does not explicitly examine anonymity in literature, he does suggest that such study would be fruitful (1986:xiii, 117), particularly because of the essentially realist or mimetic impulse that in his view underlies much of literary interpretation (1974a:239). "In literal terms," suggests Natanson (1986:23), "being anonymous is being nameless. Anonymity, in general parlance, means the state of being unknown, without identity, a kind of hiddenness." In the structure of the social world, most individuals are anonymous to most other individuals (1986:24). They are known to one another not in the fullness of their individuality—i.e. as persons—but only in the typified roles they play or the functions they perform—as agents (1986:25). Although it is only persons who take on typified roles, the affirmation of a role means relinquishing personhood for the time being, resulting in a bracketing of the person him or herself (1974b:163, 164, 170). To the extent that the agent achieves dominance in the role-taking, to that extent the person is set aside or obscured. The opposite of anonymity or pure agency is recognition, in which "the person is recovered in his full integrity" (1974b:164, 168).

On this model, there is a direct relationship between our ignorance of another's proper name and our tendency to perceive that person solely or primarily as an agent, performing a typified role. If the parallel between life and literature holds true, the reader's response to literary anonymity—that is, the encounter with unnamed characters in a literary text—would be to interpret those characters as agents in typified roles with respect to other characters in the narrative and/or in the development of the plot.[3]

UNNAMED CHARACTERS IN THE BOOKS OF SAMUEL

Anonymous characters, precisely because of their anonymity and relatively fleeting roles in the narrative, tend not to attract the attention of the reader of the Books of Samuel. Once alerted to and interested in their presence, however, we find them everywhere and in countless numbers. The soldiers, servants, messengers of the kings and their enemies, the elders of the people, the men of God, and the angels—almost all remain unnamed, whether they appear in crowds, smaller groups, or as individuals. In this survey we will not attempt to refer to all such anonymous characters or character groups. Rather, we will provide a system of classification that will illustrate the role of anonymity in the construction of character and plot development.

Two broad categories of anonymous characters or character groups may be distinguished on the basis of the degree and type of relationship to the principal characters in the Books of Samuel—Samuel, Saul, and David—or to such secondary characters as Joab and Absalom. The first group consists of characters who are described as dependents of specific named characters. The second group consists of autonomous characters whose definitions are independent of those of any named character. We will discuss each group briefly, paying attention to the contribution of anonymity to characterization and plot development.

1. *Dependent Characters*

This group may be further divided into sub-categories reflecting both the degree and nature of their relationships to named major and secondary characters as well as the numerical size of the group: the smaller the group, the more intimate the relationship with a named character and the more detailed the characterization of the unnamed character.

---

[3] In the latter sense, the anonymous agent as a crucial actor in the plot is similar to the agent identified by Berlin (23) as one of the three categories of character (full-fledged, type, and agent), as opposed to the usual two categories — "round" and "flat" (Forster: 65-75). According to Berlin (32), "the agent is a function of the plot or part of the setting."

a. Armies or Troops

The anonymous character-groups that arguably have the most members are the various armies whose activities form such a large part of the narrative action in 1 and 2 Samuel[4]: not only the army of the king of Israel but also those of his enemies, from within (e.g. Absalom's troops in 2 Samuel 15-18) or without (e.g. the Philistine army in 1 Samuel 13). Most often these character groups are identified minimally, as members of a particular national group, or as being loyal to a particular leader within Israel. The designation "the Israelite army" might be considered clearly unified and also differentiated from the armies of other nations, and therefore in itself might be considered to function as a proper name. The same cannot be said, however, of the troops involved in the conflict between David and Absalom. Indeed, the issues of both group and individual loyalty and disloyalty comprise a major theme in 2 Samuel 15-18 (e.g. 2 Sam 15:32-37). This theme in turn hinges on the very lack of referential clarity regarding the terms "all the people" (2 Sam 15:17; 16:14; כל העם), which seems to refer to those loyal to David, and "all the people, the men of Israel" (2 Sam 16:15; כל העם איש ישראל), which seems to refer to Absalom's followers. Hence this term, כל העם, does not function mimetically as a proper name, since it neither unifies a character group nor differentiates one from another. Rather, it both contributes to and mirrors the confusion and sense of civil anarchy generated by this portion of the narrative.

Aside from the clarity or lack thereof regarding their group identity, examples of this character group are portrayed minimally, as simply doing those things characteristic of armies: going in, going out, and fighting. One example of many is 1 Sam 11:11, in which we are told that "Saul divided the troops (העם) into three columns; at the morning watch

---

[4] While it might seem that the "people of Israel" itself would constitute an anonymous character group, we omit it from consideration for two reasons. First, if one function of the proper name is differentiation, it may be argued that "people of Israel" in fact performs this function for this group, which throughout the course of biblical narrative, and particularly after the Exodus, is clearly differentiated from other "peoples" and also possesses certain traits, including a unique, shared history, of which the other tribal or national groupings in these books do not partake. Even the "elders of Israel," which as a character is sometimes distinguished from and other times interchangeable with "the people" as a whole, may be considered the equivalent of a collective "proper name" of a unified and unique character group. Second, if one looks at biblical narrative as a whole, it is clear that at certain points there is an attempt to name as many individual members of the "people of Israel" and its elders as is possible within the narrative medium. See, for example, the list of elders in Numbers 1 and the census list in Numbers 26.

they entered the camp and struck down the Ammonites until the day grew hot."[5]

In some cases, the presence, absence, or activity of the army is important as a backdrop or stage setting for the personal lives and adventures of a principal character. A case in point is 2 Sam 11:1, in which we read that, "at the season when kings go out [to battle], David sent Joab with his officers and all Israel with him, and they devastated Ammon and besieged Rabbah" while David remained in Jerusalem. As Meir Sternberg (193-96) has pointed out, this brief notice throws into full, ironic relief the question of why David stayed home at the season when kings do battle, and warns us that he may be up to no good. Furthermore, the army and the battle-front continue to play an important role as the story develops, as the place where Uriah, Bathsheba's husband, is at the time of David's advances, the place from which David has him return in the vain hope of covering up the king's adultery, and, finally, as the place to which he sends Uriah to meet his death.

In the above passages, the army as a group character, while dependent for its identity upon the king, is characterized only minimally. In doing the military work of the king, would-be king, or general, the main character trait of this group is obedience.[6] In other passages, however, this group character is portrayed in more detail, revealing other aspects of its relationship to its leader. One example of such characterization is 2 Sam 18:1-4, in which King David explains his battle-strategy to his men (העם) and declares his intention to go out to battle with them against Absalom's forces. Instead of obeying unquestioningly, however, they collectively voice a critique of their king's decision, causing David to change his mind, saying, "Whatever seems best to you I will do" (v. 4). This critique is, of course, important in its characterization of David as a king who respects the advice of his cohorts. It also has a crucial role in the plot by explaining —and emphasizing—the absence of David from this battle. This absence permits Joab's killing of Absalom (2 Sam 18:14-15), thereby contributing to the narrative tension of the plot segment in which the death of Absalom is revealed to David (2 Sam 18:19-19:1).

The "army" is therefore a typified character group, composed of numerous anonymous individuals. Though dependent on the king or other military leader for their group identity, these men are not intimate with, or even necessarily personally or abidingly loyal to him. Their anonymity

---

[5] All biblical quotations are from the new Jewish Publication Society translation of the *Tanakh* (1985).

[6] At times narrative interest is conveyed precisely by the way in which this character trait is portrayed, as in the case of Joab, who obeys but at the same time sabotages the king's orders with respect to Uriah. See 2 Sam 11:15-17 and Sternberg (213).

in itself deflects attention away from soldiers as individuals to their group identity as well as its typical characteristics. Their typified portrayal serves both to expose character traits of the leaders themselves, for example, ambition, ruthlessness, or capability of accepting advice, and to advance the plot, usually by their acting as the instruments through which the leader's military goals are achieved, or, as in 2 Samuel 18, by orchestrating or justifying the strategic absence of the king from the battlefield.

b. Courtiers and Servants

This category consists of character groups who are part of the household or entourage of a major character but not family members. These groups are both smaller and in closer proximity to their master than are the armies or troops discussed above. As with the armies, however, the primary characteristic of this grouping of anonymous figures is obedience. For example, in 2 Sam 13:29, Absalom's servants (נערי אבשלום) obey his command to murder Amnon for the rape of his sister Tamar. More loquacious in their obedience are the officials (עבדים) loyal to David in his conflict with Absalom. In 2 Sam 15:13-16 these men express their readiness to obey David's order to flee Jerusalem in order to escape from Absalom:[7] "Whatever our lord the king decides, your servants are ready" (2 Sam 15:15). Both of these events—the murder of Amnon and the flight of David—propel this segment of the plot line (chaps. 13-20) and help to illuminate the complexity and intensity of David's feelings towards Absalom, which form a major point of narrative interest.[8]

The role of the king's entourage, like that of the army, is not always limited to unquestioning obedience. 1 Sam 16:16 portrays courtiers as the king's counsellors. In their concern for their king, who is tormented by an evil spirit, Saul's servants advise him to find a lyre-player, so that ". . . whenever the evil spirit of God comes over you, he will play it and you will feel better." Having obtained Saul's agreement, they find David, who becomes not only his lyre-player but also his armor-bearer (16:21), a role that, according to the narrator, demonstrates Saul's great affection for him. Thus begins the long and ambivalent relationship between Saul and David played out in 1 Samuel 17 to 2 Samuel 1.

These examples allow us to see the anonymous groups of servants or courtiers in their typified roles, characterized by obedience to their mas-

---

[7] One wonders, however, exactly what behavior was expected of, or fate anticipated for, the ten anonymous concubines left behind to "mind the palace" (2 Sam 15:16).

[8] The servants are not always silent, however. In 1 Sam 25:40, David's servants must speak in order to comply with his command to take Abigail to be his wife, though their speech is not reported.

ters and solicitude for their well-being. The masters, for their part, not only give them orders but also accept their advice. In keeping with their anonymity, no attention at all is paid to the identities of the individual members of these character-groups; no differentiation is made between the personal identities of one servant and another, or indeed, one group of servants and officials and another, except in the identity of their master. As in the case of the armies, this latter aspect seems to be incidental to their typified behavior: the military and personal attendants of David engage in the same typified behavior as those of Saul or Absalom.

In their typified roles, these groups shed light on the characters of their masters: Absalom is shown as vengeful and ruthless; Saul as tormented and despondent. They also facilitate important turning points in the plot, such as the initial encounter between Saul and David and the outlawing of Absalom.

c. Personal Servants

Closer still to their respective masters are the individual anonymous personal servants, valets, or armor-bearers of various named characters. In most cases, these are described in more detail and emerge more distinctly than the members of the character groups we have considered above. Several examples will illustrate the nature of their characterization in the narrative and allow us to describe their typified roles.

When the young Saul and his "boy" (1 Sam 9:1-10) are searching for his father's donkeys, the boy brushes aside Saul's suggestion that they turn back to avoid worrying Saul's father, Kish, and presses Saul to consult the local "man of God." After some discussion, it is the boy's plan that prevails, with results that change the course of Saul's life. The close relationship between Saul and his servant is indicated repeatedly in the Hebrew, in which נערו, featuring the personal possessive ending ("*his* boy") is used. The rather resourceful and patient advice of Saul's boy provides a sharp contrast with his more immature, impatient, and worried master; our assessment of Saul as king, both in God's favor and, later, out of it, must surely be affected by this initial contrast. Furthermore, the boy's actions contribute directly to plot development by creating the opportunity for the encounter between Saul and Samuel, who will anoint Saul king. Having facilitated this encounter, however, the boy must be removed from the scene (1 Sam 9:27), since Samuel's message about Saul's future kingship was for Saul's ears alone.

Whereas boys like Saul had personal servants, the kings and the members of their families had armor-bearers who were in a similar position of trust. 1 Sam 14:1-15 describes the devotion of Jonathan's armor-bearer, who accompanies Jonathan to the Philistine garrison (vv. 1,

6) and willingly participates in a very dangerous mission, declaring: "Do whatever you like. You go first, I am with you, whatever you decide" (v. 7).[9]

Similarly devoted is the unnamed armor-bearer of King Saul. 1 Sam 31:4-6 describes his refusal to kill Saul in defiance of the latter's order, and their subsequent double-suicide. This episode exposes and plays out the potential conflict between the main traits of the anonymous servant. This armor-bearer finds himself in the dilemma of having to choose between the obedience he owes to his master and his concern for his master's well-being, which renders him incapable of taking his master's life with his own hands.

The armor-bearer with whom Saul closes out his career, and indeed, his life, is the narrative counterpart to—and forms an *inclusio* with—the "boy" of the young Saul, whose guidance led to the encounter that brought Saul to power in the first place. In this way the Saul saga, opened by an episode featuring an anonymous servant, is closed out neatly and symmetrically in the same way. In both cases, the servant demonstrates his complete and personal devotion to his master, a devotion that requires the refusal to acquiesce to his master's suggestion (1 Samuel 9) or obey his express command (1 Samuel 31; cf. Fokkelman: 625).

Despite the greater detail of his characterization, the anonymous personal servant or armor-bearer plays a typified role, characterized by intimacy, personal devotion, and effacement of self. The focus of the personal servant's attention is on his master, a focus that is therefore also consistent with, and perhaps even sharpened by, his own narrative anonymity. His devotion requires him to obey, but also at times to act in what he perceives to be his master's best interests, even when those negate the express wishes of his master. In their devotion, armor-bearers contribute to the characterization of their masters and in some cases present a unique perspective on them. By the end of the Saul saga, for example, after the reader has been fully impressed with the depth of Saul's hatred of David and his relentless efforts to kill him, the utter love and devotion of Saul's armor-bearer, so similar to that of the servant of his youth, implies a different, much more positive evaluation of his character. These relationships, therefore, in a small way, mitigate or qualify the negative impression of Saul created by the plot of the Saul story (cf. Gunn, 1980).

---

[9] This verse is translated more literally — and evocatively — in the *Revised Standard Version*: "Do all that your mind inclines to; behold, I am with you, as is your mind so is mine." The devotion implied here is further underscored by descriptions of the brave acts of Jonathan and his armor-bearer in vv. 11-14.

d. Family Members

A fourth category of anonymous dependent characters is comprised of anonymous family members of major or secondary characters. These are few, probably because it is the general biblical convention to provide proper names even for those family members who do not appear as actors in the narrative (e.g. 1 Sam 14:49-51). By looking at the two principal examples in the Books of Samuel, we shall be able to consider how this group compares with the ones we have already examined, particularly with respect to the narrative role of their anonymity.

The first example is the pregnant daughter-in-law of Eli, the wife of Eli's evil son Phinehas (1 Sam 4:19-22). She is described as giving birth and dying upon hearing the news that the ark of God was captured and that Eli and Phinehas were dead. When spoken to by the women attending her, "she did not respond or pay heed" (v. 21). We are told, however, that she named her baby Ichabod, meaning "the glory has departed from Israel." By "glory" she meant not her scoundrel of a husband (cf. 1 Sam 2:12) or her righteous father-in-law, but the ark of God, as indicated by her pronouncement: "The glory is gone from Israel ... for the Ark of God has been captured" (v. 22). These words have a prophetic ring to them, focusing not on her personal loss but on the divine judgment on the people of Israel represented by the capture of the ark by the Philistines. Hence this unnamed character, unlike the group and individual characters considered earlier, does not contribute primarily to the portrayal of the named characters to whom she is related. Rather, by her words as well as by her death, she punctuates and draws attention to a turning point in the narrative, as well as to the symmetry between the fortunes of Israel and the fortunes of the family of Eli. Her anonymity is a symbol of this national misfortune, of her death, and, despite the life to which she gives birth, of the moral barrenness of the house of which she is a part.

Similarly tragic, and symbolic, is the unnamed first child of David and Bathsheba (2 Sam 12:16-19). Whereas Eli's daughter-in-law, as well as all of the anonymous soldiers, servants, and armor-bearers in the narrative, surely had proper names within the story world, the child born of the adulterous union between David and Bathsheba is not named at his birth, as are Ichabod (1 Sam 4:21), Solomon (2 Sam 12:24), and many other biblical babies. As a newborn, he clearly could not be given a speaking role in the narrative; even so, the only important features of his characterization are the facts of his illegitimate conception, his illness, and his death. It was his conception that led to the death of Uriah and the marriage between David and Uriah's widow. His birth and his illness provide the occasion for the description of David's grief and the puzzlement that its mode of expression engenders in his servants (cf. 2 Sam 12:21). Finally, his death atones for the sin of David, legitimizes morally the marriage of David and Bathsheba, and clears the narrative path for Solomon, the next-born son, to the throne as David's successor. In this way, the child, unnamed and only barely present in the story, contributes to the characterization of his father in his torment, guilt, and grief, adding depth and surprise to his character. As in the case of Eli's daughter-in-law, the anonymity of this child is consonant with his tragic role, the main feature of which is his death and effacement from the story and the Davidic line.

These anonymous family members are not portrayed stereotypically, in that they do not act out the roles that in biblical narrative are typical of daughters-in-law or first-born sons. Yet the roles they play may be described as typified in the sense described by Natanson. First, these characters are not available to us in their individuality; only the bare facts of their lives and deaths are important. Second, they are present at pivotal moments in the plot. Finally, they act as vehicles for the moral judgment of the narrator upon the characters (in the case of David's son) or the events within the narrative (in the case of Eli's daughter-in-law).

2. Autonomous Characters

These characters, unlike those in the previous category, are autonomous: their definition within the narrative is independent of any named character. Their importance to the narrative therefore consists not in their inherent relationships to the major and secondary characters but in their interactions with them. Three types of autonomous characters may be distinguished on the basis of the degree and type of interaction with such main characters. Each category contains both group and individual unnamed characters.

a. Incidental Characters

There are characters who appear or act only briefly, in one or two verses within a given pericope, and may have little or no interaction with a major or secondary named character. A representative example is the series of unnamed individuals involved in Absalom's search for Ahimaaz and Jonathan, David's allies, in 2 Sam 17:17-20:

> Jonathan and Ahimaaz were staying at En-rogel, and a *slave girl* would go and bring them word and they in turn would go and inform King David. For they themselves dared not be seen entering the city. But a *boy* saw them and informed Absalom. They left at once and came to the house of a *man* at Bahurim who had a well in his courtyard. They got down into it, and the *wife* took a cloth, spread it over the mouth of the well, and scattered groats on top of it, so that nothing would be noticed. When Absalom's servants came to the woman at the house and asked where Ahimaaz and Jonathan were, the

woman told them they had crossed a bit beyond the water. They searched, but found nothing; and they returned to Jerusalem [emphasis added].

In this pericope, the underlined figures have only "bit parts" in the overall plot, though their presence and the vividness of the scene as a whole do serve to create dramatic interest. They do not interact directly with David and Absalom, the principal characters named in the pericope. Their actions and words, however, do have some impact on those characters. For example, by hiding Ahimaaz and Jonathan, the woman thwarts the plans of Absalom and furthers the goals of King David.

The anonymity of the "bit players" serves to maintain the narrative focus on the conflict between David and Absalom. The anonymous characters are portrayed only insofar as they contribute to the vignette in which they act, that is, in their actions vis-à-vis Absalom's pursuit of David. In this sense they may be considered agents of the plot (Berlin, 1983:32). Furthermore, one might argue that the lack of extraneous detail and description, including the absence of their proper names, contributes positively to the narrative impact and role of this pericope. The sparseness of this narrative allows the reader to perceive and focus on its humor, which also involves the appreciation of the quick thinking and action of the woman of Bahurim.

The anonymous characters also function as a vehicle for the expression of narrative point of view. 2 Sam 17:1-16 presents in some detail the conflicting advice of Absalom's advisors regarding the best way to eliminate King David. Lest we readers believe that this plan, however it is carried out, meets with the approval of the narrator, we are informed in v. 14 that in fact the Lord nullified the advice of Ahithophel, which was the soundest from a strategic point of view, in order to bring ruin upon Absalom. From this narrative comment we learn that the narrator, being on the Lord's side, is also on David's. From this perspective, the event at Bahurim, in which the action is propelled by anonymous characters, clearly expresses the narrator's glee at the comeuppance of Absalom's aides.

b. Messengers

The Books of Samuel contain frequent references to anonymous individuals who function within a given pericope as messengers, agents whose role is to facilitate communication. In 1 Sam 4:12-18, for example, a man of Benjamin carries news of the defeat of his armies and the death of his sons to King Saul. In 1 Sam 31:9 the Philistines send messengers to carry good news of Saul's death to the houses of their idols and to the people. In 1 Sam 30:11-16 an Egyptian provides information and scouting services to David in exchange for safety. In 2 Sam 1:1-16 the death of Saul is conveyed to David by a messenger from the camp of Israel, who is then killed for his role in Saul's death. In 2 Sam 15:13 the messengers from the camp of Absalom convey to David that the "loyalty of the men of Israel has veered toward Absalom," whereas in 2 Samuel 18, which describes the climax and tragic resolution of the conflict between David and Absalom, the news of David's military victory and Absalom's death is conveyed to David by a Cushite messenger.

The anonymous messengers serve as agents essential to the playing out of the story-line by carrying messages from one party to another. For example, although the conflict between David and Absalom was effectively resolved with the death of Absalom, the resolution of the story requires David's knowledge of Absalom's death, conveyed by the Cushite messenger. The interest of the narrator is not primarily in the identity and fate of the messengers themselves, though these are sometimes conveyed (cf. 2 Sam 1:13; 18:21), but rather in the content of the communication.

The anonymous messengers contribute not only to plot development but also to the characterization of the king or other principal character who receives the communication. Hence, for example, David's violent response to the Amalekite messenger's information about the death of Saul in battle (2 Sam 1:15-16) is of interest not primarily because of concern for the messenger himself but because it contributes to the picture of David's complex and ambivalent feelings towards Saul and the kingship.

In order to fulfill their typified role, messengers must bridge the spatial distance between the two parties and convey to a "receiver" the words given to them by the "transmitter." The fact of their humanity or personhood, however, is not incidental to their role but, rather, is often exploited by the narrative in order to create interest and tension. Because these are human messengers, the possibility always exists that they will not convey the precise message that they were asked to deliver. As Meir Sternberg notes, for example, the messenger sent by Joab to inform David of the battle outcome—and Uriah's death—"spoils Joab's point in transmission" (217) by making subtle changes in the order and manner in which this information is conveyed.[10]

c. Functionaries

In the preceding section we considered autonomous individuals or groups who perform the function of messenger. While it is possible that some of these were professional messengers, others appear to be performing this task on an ad hoc basis. 2 Sam 18:21, for example, implies that the

---

[10] On the motif of the deceptive or lying messenger, see Meier: 168-71. The unreliability of the messenger may have been one motivation for the use of letters, as in 2 Sam 11:14-15. See Meier: 171-72.

Cushite is not a messenger by profession but was simply asked by Joab to perform this task on one occasion only. In contrast, there are a number of anonymous characters who are described according to roles that apparently are part of their identities in the story world. In some cases, their actions or words are of incidental and limited interest. For example, the progress of the Cushite messenger and Ahimaaz is watched and reported to David by the watchman, who also identifies the latter self-appointed messenger by his manner of running. This watchman acts in his official capacity, and his role in the narrative is to help the reader focus on the desperate impatience with which David is awaiting news from the battlefront (2 Sam 18:25-26).

In other cases, however, the role of the functionary is central to the plot. 1 Sam 2:27 refers to a man of God who comes to Eli to deliver the Lord's prophecy regarding the death of his sons. In 1 Sam 9:5 a man of God, whom the reader and Saul later identify as Samuel, provides information regarding the whereabouts of Saul's donkeys. In 2 Sam 24:16 the narrator refers to an angel of the Lord who is systematically ravaging the population, thereby carrying out the divine judgment for the wickedness of the nation and their king David. Also in this category are the Philistine priests and diviners, whom the Philistines ask for advice on what to do with the ark of the Lord (1 Sam 6:2).

In all of these cases the unnamed characters are presented as agents in formally typified roles that, in the case of men of God and angels, entail access to and/or mediation of divine knowledge and judgment. The narrative therefore conveys no interest in them as private individuals, as it does with respect to Samuel, Saul, or David. Rather, it focuses the attention of the reader on their autonomous roles or functions. The functionaries therefore remain separate from and non-subservient to the main characters in the narrative.

3. Conclusion

Our survey of anonymous dependent and autonomous characters points to an important difference between them. Whereas the characterization of dependent characters focuses on their inherent relationship to a more important narrative actor, the portrayal of autonomous characters focuses on their interaction with a principal actor. Both groups, however, are portrayed in their typified roles. This typification involves various aspects. First, the anonymous characters we have looked at are portrayed only minimally. Almost no information extraneous to their role in the plot or interaction with the principal characters is conveyed to the reader. Hence these characters remain anonymous not only in the sense that the narrator does not name them but also in the sense that they are pure agents, in whom the narrator appears completely uninterested as unique and discrete individuals. Second, in some cases, the content of the typified role comes from a social role known in biblical society, which may be inferred from these and other passages in biblical narrative. Hence armies do battle, messengers convey messages, servants serve and obey, watchmen watch, men of God prophesy. In most cases, however, the agent's role is played out not only with respect to the social world assumed by the narrative but also, or even primarily, in the poetic techniques of the narrative itself, particularly the plot. Although the richly-portrayed characters like Samuel, Saul, and David provide the greatest narrative interest and serve as the pivotal actors in the plot, our survey has shown that anonymous agents in their typified roles are essential for keeping the action moving along.

It is not only anonymous characters, of course, who act in typified ways, contribute to the characterization of other figures, and move the plot along. There are plenty of named family members, men of God and prophets, messengers and servants. Many of these play typified roles very similar to those played by the anonymous characters we have looked at and act as agents in plot development.

What is unique about the anonymous characters, however, is their very anonymity. This aspect of their characterization works in two ways. In the first place, it deflects attention away from them to the named characters with whom they interact. Second, insofar as readers do notice them, it is their typified roles rather than their names and other aspects of their personal identities that come to the fore. As pure agents, they focus the reader's attention on the main characters and the plot. In doing so they also function as vehicles for narrative point of view. Therefore anonymity works negatively in the construction of the anonymous characters themselves, deflecting attention from their characters as such. At the same time, however, it contributes positively to the construction of the more important named characters with whom they interact and to the development of plot.

Unnamed Women in 1 and 2 Samuel

Our survey thus far has indicated that anonymity in the Books of Samuel does seem to work mimetically. Unnamed characters function within the narrative as agents and may be understood as analogous to anonymous people in our experience of everyday life. The opposition of agency and personhood, anonymity and recognition, would appear to be as appropriate to biblical narrative as it is to a phenomenology of the mundane. Lest we be tempted to rest content with these neat distinctions and tidy conclusions, however, the Books of Samuel present us with three anonymous characters who would challenge this typification of anonymity. Because of the amount and nature of their participation in the narrative, the medium or "witch" of Endor (1 Sam 28:3-25), the wise woman of Tekoa (2 Sam 14:1-24), and the wise woman of Abel (2 Sam 20:14-22) emerge as rather clearly differentiated characters despite their anonymity. A brief analysis of their narrative roles will therefore supplement, qualify, and correct our understanding of the role of anonymity in this narrative text.

These anonymous women share similarities that not only justify considering them as a group but also would seem to fit them into the model of anonymity that we have constructed above. First and most obviously, these women are anonymous, identified only by a brief description (אשת בעלת אוב, אשה חכמה) and place name (Endor, Tekoa, Abel).

Second, in all three cases, their proper names are unknown not only to the reader but also to the principal named characters with whom they interact. This anonymity contributes to the impression of distance between the partners in these narrative relationships. The medium of Endor is chosen by Saul for his nocturnal visit precisely because of her distance from his capital city. Such discretion is essential in light of the fact that in visiting her he is violating the ban that he himself had imposed on mediums and wizards (1 Sam 28:3). Similarly, Joab hires a wise woman from Tekoa who is not likely to be recognized by the king to whom she tells her fabricated tale (2 Sam 14:2). Therefore the anonymity at least of these two characters is not merely a function of their typified role as agents but is thematically important for the narrative itself.

Third, all three have communication as their primary function. Like the messengers that we have already discussed, these women mediate the communication between two parties. The medium allows Saul to consult the dead Samuel (1 Sam 28:11-14), who would otherwise be inaccessible to him. The wise woman of Tekoa speaks to David the words that Joab has put in her mouth (2 Sam 14:3, 19) "in order to change the course of affairs" (2 Sam 14:20). The wise woman of Abel acts as the spokesperson for her city in order to avert the attack of Joab and his troops.

Fourth, the emphasis in these passages is on the professional function or role of these women. This is indicated in several ways. As in the case of the angel of the Lord or the men of God, the narrator's first reference to each of these characters clearly designates her not only as a woman but as a specific sort of woman: as a medium (אשת בעלת אוב) or as a wise woman (אשה חכמה). That such designation is not simply a character description is clear in the case of the medium; the term obviously describes her function and profession, as does her inclusion in that class of professionals whom Saul had just banned (1 Sam 28:3; Brenner: 73). Many scholars have taken the term "wise woman" to refer primarily to a particular quality in the woman's personality. Hoftijzer (429), for example, comments that the wise woman is one "who knows how to present her case and how to act in a given situation." For Fokkelman (141), her wisdom consists in the fact that she is "in complete control of the situation," demonstrating through her speeches "depth, great eloquence, and a wealth of facts, persons, colour, expression, and emotion." According to McCarter (1984:345), the designation "wise" is indicative of a skill in uttering lamentations.

A contrary interpretation is possible, however. S. D. Goitein (10) suggests that "the wisdom of the wise woman is more than a natural talent. It is the complete ensemble of traits and training by means of which a woman acquires leadership among women, and sometimes among the public in general." A similar point is made by Claudia Camp (14), who argues convincingly that the wise woman represented one significant political role available to women in the period of the monarchy.[11] As she notes (17), "The audience . . . must have had some prior image of these two nameless figures who stand so boldly before a king and general . . . ."[12] This conclusion can be supported by details of the narrative episodes themselves. The fact that Joab seeks out this particular woman from Tekoa implies that she had experience and a professional reputation in performing the kind of service of which he was in need. The initiative of the wise woman of Abel in contacting Joab and her delivery of the head of Joab's enemy in return for the safety of Abel connote her importance in that city as well as her right to negotiate on behalf of its denizens. Hence "wise woman," like "medium," would appear to denote a profession or prominent social role rather than a one-time activity or character trait.

In addition, these women function as agents not only in the social world implied in the text but also in the development of the narrative plot and in the characterization of the named characters with whom they interact. The medium of Endor, at the request of King Saul, calls forth the dead Samuel, who advises Saul of his imminent demise (1 Sam 28:19). The wise woman of Tekoa convinces King David to allow his banished son Absalom back into the kingdom (2 Sam 14:21). Her Abelite counterpart averts the conquest of Abel by handing over to Joab, David's general, the head of his enemy Sheba, son of Bichri (2 Sam 20:22). These events mark important turning points in the saga of monarchy and military adventure, which is the subject matter of 1 and 2 Samuel. Saul's encounter with the

---

[11] Camp, however, does not refer to Goitein.
[12] That the woman is a functionary has also been suggested by Gevaryahu (11), who sees her as a type of official mourner, and Brenner (37).

medium of Endor shows him to be a desperate man, who must break the laws that he himself promulgated in order to obtain the information that his usual sources—the Lord, the Urim, or the prophets (1 Sam 28:6) —have denied him. David's discussion with the wise woman of Tekoa demonstrates his ability to listen and to change his mind, even once he has penetrated her ruse (2 Sam 14:19). Joab's willingness to accept the bargain suggested by the wise woman of Abel implies a pragmatic nature that is not interested in conquest for its own sake.

Finally, the role played by these women points up particular moral and/or theological problems, as did some of the other anonymous characters, such as Eli's daughter-in-law, David and Bathsheba's first born son, and Saul's unnamed armor-bearer. Saul's recourse to the witch of Endor brings home to the reader his utter desperation, which caused him to violate his own legislation, and his utter rejection by God, indicated by the failure of more conventional means of oracular communication (1 Sam 28:6). The Tekoite woman's dramatization of David's plight provides insight into the complexity of David's feelings towards Absalom and the complex relationship between personal emotion and political behavior. The pragmatic attitude of the wise woman of Abel, and her shockingly cold-blooded solution to the security problems faced by her city, touch on the issue of the rights of the individual versus the rights of the community in matters of life and death.

These three women are therefore characterized as autonomous functionaries, play typified roles characteristic of their professions, and act as agents in the sequence of events that constitute the plot and define its main actors. Thus far, therefore, it would appear that they fit squarely into the category of autonomous functionaries that we have already discussed.

In significant ways, however, these three women do not fit the mold of anonymous characterization. The most obvious difference is the amount and quality of their communication with the principal characters. The medium interrogates Saul with respect to her own culpability before agreeing to call upon the dead Samuel. Similarly, the wise women of Tekoa and Abel are not too shy to speak at length and in detail in order to express their situation and their advice to the powerful men with whom they interact.

Even more striking is the contrast between their ostensibly self-deprecating language and the bold tone and presumption of mutuality that characterize the words of these women to their male partners in dialogue. In 1 Sam 28:21 the medium insists: "Your handmaid listened to you; I took my life in my hands and heeded the request you made of me. So now you listen to me; . . ." The wise woman of Tekoa challenges the king in a forthright tone reminiscent of the classical prophets: "Why . . . have you planned the like against God's people? In making this pronouncement, Your Majesty condemns himself in that Your Majesty does not bring back his own banished one" (2 Sam 14:13). The wise woman of Abel is the least obsequious of all. She calls out to Joab from the city as his troops are about to break down the city walls (2 Sam 20:15-16) and arranges for the decapitation of Sheba, son of Bichri, in order to avert the conquest of Abel, thereby achieving a goal important to herself and her community.

Finally, although the emphasis of the characterization of each of these anonymous figures is on what we might consider her official profession or role, there are elements of each passage that would appear, at least initially, to reinforce her personal identity as a woman. The medium of Endor assumes a nurturing role in her insistence that Saul eat before departing (1 Sam 28:22-25),[13] though this role may hide a more selfish agenda by averting the potential embarrassment or worse of having Saul die in her home (cf. Berlin, 1988). The wise woman of Tekoa pretends to be a widow asking the king to intercede on behalf of her son. This role clearly could not have been played by a man who would have had difficulty fabricating a story that would act in as powerful a way to change the king's mind regarding Absalom. The wise woman of Abel speaks of that city as a "mother city in Israel" (2 Sam 20:19). Although the exact meaning of this phrase is unclear (Camp: 27; McCarter, 1984:430), it depicts this woman as acting out the protective role of mother for the city in her intercession with Joab (for an example of woman as protector, see 2 Kgs 11:1-3). Hence these women are portrayed not only in their typified roles as functionaries or agents but also to some degree at least in their more personal identities as women.

While these behaviors may seem to be typically female, however, they are not exclusively or even predominantly associated with women in biblical narrative. The role of hospitable host who quickly kills a fatted calf for her royal guest is more reminiscent of Abraham than of any female character (Gen 18:7; Simon: 165).[14] Although only a woman could convincingly act out the role of widow as required of the Tekoite wise woman, the biblical teller of tales is typically male.[15] Similarly, it is not normally women who act as the protectors of cities in war-time, as does

---

[13] Cf. Judg 4:18-24, in which Yael "nurtures" Sisera before murdering him.

[14] Simon (164) implicitly recognizes that the medium of Endor has departed from her typified role when he comments that in urging Saul to eat, she is no longer speaking as a witch but as an ordinary woman. As we have noted, however, her behavior is in fact more typical of male hosts than of the ordinary woman as portrayed in biblical narrative.

[15] 2 Samuel 14 is often considered form-critically as a juridical parable, similar in structure to 2 Sam 12:1-4; 14:4-7; and 1 Kgs 20:39-41. For discussion, see Coats.

the Abelite wise woman (see the all-male cast of participants in the battles recounted in 2 Samuel 8-10).

The anonymity of these three characters, therefore, while drawing attention to their typified roles, does not efface them as unique, unusual, even atypical, individuals. Their relatively detailed characterization and the prominent roles in the narrative segments in which they appear focus our attention as readers not only on their official, formal roles or professions but also on their autonomy and independence from the king or his general and on their unstereotypical actions as women. In these ways they are individuated to a greater degree than most of the other anonymous characters in the Books of Samuel.

Conclusion

What we have developed in our discussion of the role of anonymity in a mimetic reading of the Books of Samuel is in effect a model of anonymity as a literary convention. As such, it is one element in that "elaborate set of tacit agreements between artist and audience about the ordering of the art work . . . [that constitutes] the enabling context in which the complex communication of art occurs" (Alter, 1981:47).

This convention is characterized by a cluster of features in addition to the absence of a proper name. We have noted that, by and large, anonymous characters play typified roles as agents in the social world implied by the narrative, in the characterization of the major and secondary named characters with whom they interact, and in the development of the plot. They generally receive little characterization or description beyond the bare minimum needed to accomplish their typified roles. But in their contribution to the portrayal of other characters as complex, full, "lifelike" figures, and to the plausible progression of events that constitute the plot, anonymous characters clearly have a major function in a mimetic reading of the narrative that is belied by their relatively brief appearances.

As Robert Alter has noted (1981:62; 1983:119), however, biblical narrative does not adhere mechanically and inevitably to the conventional structures that it itself establishes. Rather, it transforms, recasts, redeploys, and occasionally even flagrantly subverts these conventions, not only in order to create dramatic interest but also to convey historical and theological meaning (Alter, 1981:59). The three anonymous women whom we have studied add aesthetic pleasure and texture as well as theological and moral depth to the reading experience, as do many of the other anonymous characters in these books. What differentiates these women from other unnamed figures is the degree and nature of their characterization. In their portrayal, anonymity is not merely incidental and symbolic of a typified narrative role, but it is a positive thematic component of the story itself: they are anonymous not only to the reader but also to the named characters with whom they interact. Their portrayal not only contributes positively to the characterization of others but also allows us to envision these unnamed women themselves as persons with their own concerns and agendas and not merely as agents of king, general, or narrator. Hence, while they are anonymous in the literal sense of being unnamed, they are not without personal identity.

The study of anonymity in mimetic interpretation of biblical narrative allows us to focus on what is most naturally ignored and, indeed, has been overlooked by many scholars of these books.[16] In forcing us to attend to what is absent from the text, it also alerts us to what is present, namely, a literary convention that works together with others in the skilled creation of mimetic narrative.[17]

WORKS CONSULTED

Alter, Robert
    1981   *The Art of Biblical Narrative*. Philadelphia: Basic.
    1983   "How Convention Helps Us Read: The Case of the Bible's Annunciation Type-Scene." *Prooftexts* 3:115-30.

Bal, Mieke
    1987   *Lethal Love: Feminist Literary Readings of Biblical Love Stories*. Bloomington: Indiana University Press.

Bar-Efrat, Shimon
    1978   "Literary Modes and Methods in the Biblical Narrative in View of 2 Samuel 10-20 and 1 Kings 1- 2." *Immanuel* 8:20-22.
    1989   *Narrative Art in the Bible*. JSOTSup 70. Sheffield: Almond.

Berlin, Adele
    1983   *Poetics and Interpretation of Biblical Narrative*.

---

[16] The fact that McCarter's extensive and detailed commentary (1980:239-42; 440-44) omits any reference to the anonymous armor-bearers illustrates a tendency of scholars to ignore the role of anonymous characters. See also Fokkelman (53-57, 625), who draws attention to the relationship between the armor-bearers and their masters but does not consider their anonymity.

[17] I wish to thank Adele Berlin, Elizabeth Struthers Malbon, George Savran, and Barry Walfish for their helpful comments on earlier versions of this essay.

Sheffield: Almond.

1988 "Literary Criticism and Biblical Interpretation." Paper delivered at conference on "The Hebrew Bible: Sacred Text and Literature," Wayne State University, Detroit, Oct. 30-Nov. 2, 1988.

Brenner, Athalya

1985 *The Israelite Woman: Social Role and Literary Type in Biblical Narrative.* Biblical Seminar 2. Sheffield: JSOT.

Camp, Claudia

1981 "The Wise Women of 2 Samuel: A Role Model for Women in Early Israel?" *CBQ* 43:14-29.

Chatman, Seymour

1978 *Story and Discourse.* Ithaca: Cornell University Press.

Coats, George W.

1981 "Parable, Fable, and Anecdote: Storytelling in the Succession Narrative." *Int* 35:368-82.

Docherty, Thomas

1983 *Reading (Absent) Character: Towards a Theory of Characterization in Fiction.* Oxford: Clarendon.

Exum, J. Cheryl, and J. William Whedbee

1984 "Isaac, Samson, and Saul: On the Comic and Tragic Visions." *Semeia* 32:5-40.

Fokkelman, J. P.

1986 *Narrative Art and Poetry in the Books of Samuel*, vol. II. Assen/Maastricht, The Netherlands: Van Gorcum.

Forster, E. M.

1927 *Aspects of the Novel.* London: Edward Arnold.

Gevaryahu, Chaim

1969 "The Return of the Exile to God's Estate in the Parable of the Wise Woman of Tekoa." *Beth Mikra* 36:10-33.

Goitein, Solomon Dov

1988 "Women as Creators of Biblical Genres." *Prooftexts* 8:1-34.

Gunn, David M.

1978 *The Story of King David: Genre and Interpretation.* JSOTSup 6. Sheffield: JSOT.

1980 *The Fate of King Saul: An Interpretation of a Biblical Story.* JSOTSup 14. Sheffield: JSOT.

Hochman, Baruch

1985 *Character in Literature.* Ithaca and London: Cornell University Press.

Hoftijzer, J.

1970 "David and the Tekoite Woman." *VT* 20:419-44.

James, Henry
    1986   "The Art of Fiction." Pp. 165-83 in *Henry James on the Theory and the Practice of Fiction*. Ed. William R. Veeder and Susan M. Griffin. Chicago: Chicago University Press (originally published 1884).

Jefferson, Ann
    1980   *The Nouveau Roman and the Poetics of Fiction*. Cambridge: Cambridge University Press.

Jobling, David
    1978   *The Sense of Biblical Narrative: Three Structural Analyses in the Old Testament*. JSOTSup 7. Sheffield: JSOT.

Licht, Jacob
    1978   *Storytelling in the Bible*. Jerusalem: Magnes Press.

McCarter, Jr., Kyle
    1980   *I Samuel*. AB 8. New York: Doubleday.
    1984   *II Samuel*. AB 9. New York: Doubleday.

Meier, Samuel A.
    1988   *The Messenger in the Ancient Semitic World*. HSM 45. Atlanta: Scholars.

Natanson, Maurice
    1974a   *Phenomenology, Role and Reason*. Springfield: Charles C. Thomas.
    1974b   "Solipsism and Sociality." *New Literary History* 5:237-44.
    1986   *Anonymity: A Study in the Philosophy of Alfred Schutz*. Bloomington: Indiana University Press.

Rimmon-Kennan, Shlomit
    1983   *Narrative Fiction: Contemporary Poetics*. London and New York: Methuen.

Samuel, Maurice
    1955   *Certain People of the Book*. New York: Knopf.

Searle, John R.
    1958   "Proper Names." *Mind* 67:166-73.

Schulz, Alfons
    1991   "Narrative Art in the Books of Samuel." Pp. 119-70 in *Narrative and Novella in Samuel*. Ed. David M. Gunn. Sheffield: Almond (German original published 1923).

Simon, Uriel
    1988   "A Balanced Story: The Stern Prophet and the Kind Witch." *Prooftexts* 8:159-171.

Sternberg, Meir
    1985   *The Poetics of Biblical Narrative: Ideological Literature and the Drama of Reading*. Bloomington: Indiana University Press.

Van Dijk-Hemmes, Fokkelien
    1989   "Tamar and the Limits of Patriarchy: Between Rape and Seduction (2 Samuel 13 and Genesis 38)." Pp. 135-56 in *Anti-Covenant: Counter-Reading Women's Lives in the Hebrew Bible*. Ed. Mieke Bal. Sheffield: Almond.

Weinsheimer, Joel
    1979   "Theory of Character: Emma." *Poetics Today* 1:185-211.

THE NARRATIVE FUNCTION OF ANONYMITY IN FOURTH GOSPEL CHARACTERIZATION

David R. Beck
Duke University

ABSTRACT

Recent examinations of Fourth Gospel characterization have neglected one aspect of Johannine characterization that distinguishes it from characterization in other biblical narratives. Although every gospel has unnamed characters within the text, in the Fourth Gospel anonymous characters function differently than anonymous characters in the synoptic gospels. Literary theorist Thomas Docherty has argued that naming is a distinguishing act that maintains the identity distinction of the reader from the named character. Anonymity erases that distinction, invites the reader's subjective identification with the unnamed characters, and frees the reader to enter the narrative world of the text. In the Fourth Gospel the anonymous characters that are given significant textual treatment are also those whose encounters with Jesus produce a faith response. Included among these are Jesus' mother, the Samaritan woman, the royal official in chapter 4, the lame man in 5, the blind man in 9, and the woman caught in adultery in 7:53-8:11. After the man born blind in chapter 9, the only significant anonymous character to appear is the beloved disciple. His textual presentation as the paradigm of true discipleship is enhanced by his anonymity. The anonymous characters who precede the beloved disciple in the text draw the reader into subjective participation in the narrative and into identification with the beloved disciple, enabling participation in the paradigm of discipleship he represents.

INTRODUCTION

A prerequisite to a reading of the Fourth Gospel, or any narrative, is the explicit identification of the "social location" of the reader (Segovia: 25). The biblical scholar must recognize that the only reading one is capable of is the one shaped and molded by one's own experience and training. I am incapable of reading as a naive first-time reader, as a member of another gender or nationality, or as one who is not involved with the claims this narrative presents. My reading is necessarily shaped by my participation in the community of faith that has long held this narrative as a sacred text. I am also one of the privileged elite of the world, spending my entire life within the borders of one of its wealthiest nations. I have never known first-hand the experiences of war, poverty, or persecution. I also read as one trained within the interpretive community of biblical scholarship. This places me in a specific reading role as a reader/critic. Robert M. Fowler has defined this role as follows: "(1) to affirm the enduring power of the Bible in my culture and in my own life and yet (2) to remain open enough to dare to ask any question and to risk any critical judgment" (31). This does not replace or eliminate the need to be sensitive to how other readings of this narrative would be produced and even necessitated by persons whose social locations are vastly different from my own.

The Analysis of Character

One theory of characterization that has frequently been used in the analysis of biblical narrative can be traced back to E. M. Forster, who distinguished between essential characters and those that only contributed to the overall effect. He designated the essential characters as "round" with complex personalities. Lesser characters are "flat" and not fully developed (73, 81). It has been noted that when discussing these character types, a shift is made from the technical function of the "flat" character in the text to the psychological essence of the "round" character (Fokkema: 23). This traditional approach to characterization assesses characters in narratives according to the degree of psychological complexity they possess, making them more or less believable as representatives of human beings (Fokkema: 28). This approach to characterization is found in the poetics of biblical narrative of both Adele Berlin and Alan Culpepper.

An opposite view of characterization prevails in structuralist theory and has its roots in the work of A. J. Greimas. Character (a term usually replaced by "actants" or some other designation) is a narrative function that cannot be analyzed through comparison to human beings. These plot functionaries are abstractions that fill one of six potential functions in a narrative: sender, receiver, object, subject, helper, and opponent (176-80). Plot is given primacy, and the concept of character is replaced with relations of opposition and correlation (Fokkema: 31). This understanding of character is evident in Robert Funk's poetics.

These opposing views of character in narratives both fail to consider how characters function in the reading process to entice the reader into participation in the narrative. John Darr has recently designed an interpretive model for understanding characterization that recognizes the interdependence of plot and character without subordinating either to the other. He acknowledges that readers "build" character (16) and that through the process readers are themselves "being positioned and maneuvered—indeed shaped—by the rhetoric of the text" (59). His model is largely dependent on the reader-oriented theory of Wolfgang Iser. The reader's response to a narrative is facilitated by the "indeterminacies and gaps" within the text (Iser, 1974, 1978). The purpose of this study is to examine a particular indeterminacy characteristic of the Fourth Gospel: anonymity.

The study of characterization in the Fourth Gospel has focused primarily on character types and their roles as plot functionaries. Alan Culpepper has rightly noted that the Johannine characters "represent a continuum of responses to Jesus which exemplify misunderstandings the reader may share and responses one might make to the depiction of Jesus in the Gospel" (104). This study will explore how the text invites the reader to participate in the narrative by identifying with the characters' misunderstandings and responses via the anonymity of several significant Johannine characters.

The anonymous characters in the Fourth Gospel are atypical of most biblical narrative. Jeffrey Staley has stated that unlike in Hebrew narrative, anonymity in the Fourth Gospel is not an indication of textual insignificance (1991:71). In addition, anonymous characters in the Fourth Gospel appear to have more textual significance than anonymous characters in the synoptics. Anonymous characters do appear in the synoptic gospels, frequently in miracle stories. Unparalleled in the synoptics, however, are the anonymous Johannine characters who enter into lengthy dialogue with Jesus and are granted a large amount of textual space, such as the Samaritan woman in chapter 4 and the man born blind in chapter 9. Also unparalleled in the synoptics are the anonymous Johannine characters whom readers might expect to be named, Jesus' mother and the beloved disciple.

This study will define characters with narrative significance as those characters given significant textual space whose encounter with Jesus produces a faith response. This is in contrast to named characters such as Nicodemus, who appears in the text in the role of an interlocutor whose query prompts a lengthy discourse from Jesus and whose textual absence during that discourse goes unexplained. Among these significant Johannine characters who are nameless are Jesus' mother in 2:1-5 and 19:25-27, the Samaritan woman in 4:4-42, the royal official in 4:46-53, the lame man in 5:2-16, and the blind man in 9:1-41. Despite the pericope's textual problems, the woman caught in adultery in 7:53-8:11 also fits this pattern. After chapter 9 the narrative spotlight focuses on the anonymous beloved disciple. The well established scholarly practice of capitalizing his designation has subverted his anonymity by making a name of this label. Scholarly consensus has long recognized the beloved disciple as the Johannine paradigm of true discipleship; this study will examine how his anonymity invites the reader to identify with and participate in that paradigm.

Nomination, Anonymity, and Narrative

The name of a character in a narrative has a greater function than merely to collect all the data the text has previously provided into a neatly bound package. The naming of a character is an act of distinction that sets that particular character apart from the narrative environment, other characters, and the reader (Docherty: 43). The previous traits, actions, feelings, and conversations of that character are gathered into the proper name designation and contained there for the reader. According to the realist or essentialist understanding of nomination, the name is the unchanging identifying mark of a character that collects the various attributes and characteristics that the text reveals concerning the character. Docherty recognizes that this is accurate for some narrative forms that are plot-oriented and where the character's function is subordinated to the plot (49). In other narratives the proper name has an existential or historical use in which the name is a culmination that the character achieves through the narrative (56). One indicator of this can be the initial absence of the proper name.

Names can also serve a subversive function that thwarts and overturns reader expectations through the non-conventional use of names. This practice has been analyzed in the novels of Raymond Queneau. These novels use several names for one character, name characters of one gender with names usually reserved for the other gender, and use names for non-human figures without explicitly identifying them as such. Using names in this manner destabilizes character in the text and creates "the uncertainty of a character's ontological status" (Campbell-Sposito: 732). This uncertainty is reinforced by the disclaimer at the beginning of *Le Dimanche de la vie* that reverses the expected: "Les personnages de ce roman étant réels, toute ressemblance avec des individus imaginaires serait fortuite" (Queneau). If this unconventional play of names in Queneau can subvert the reader's expectations, what effect on the reader is realized by the absence of a character's name?

Attention was drawn to the subversive function of namelessness in the Fourth Gospel narrative by Staley in his earlier work on the victimization of the implied reader in the Fourth Gospel. He noted that one of the examples of this reader-victimization was the sudden and unexpected appearance in chapter 13 of the anonymous disciple, whose unidentified presence overturns the reader's superior understanding (1988:108-9).

A character's anonymity in a narrative could function in several ways. It could serve to signal the unimportance of this particular character, who remains unobtrusively in the background of the narrative stage or passes across the stage for a moment only to disappear from the narrative and not return. Another possibility is that the name is unnecessary for the reader's perception of the character. An example of this type of unnamed character in the Fourth Gospel occurs in 2:9 at the wedding in Cana. Two unnamed characters are present, the steward and the bridegroom. Neither have significant textual space or narrative function. Their designations (steward, bridegroom) explain their actions in terms of their roles, and their disappearance from the narrative prevents the reader from being dissatisfied by the sparseness of textual information concerning them. The lack of a name could serve to divert the reader's attention from the unnamed character to the named character in whose presence the unnamed character is seen. This explanation could be used to understand the absence of names in gospel texts where Jesus is present with other unnamed characters, such as the Samaritan woman in chapter 4 or the blind man in chapter 9. Neglected by these possibilities, however, is a consideration of how anonymity can serve to further a reader's identification with a character.

Docherty identifies three functions of names in the reading process. The first is as an indication of authority, the second is as a locus for the gathering of traits and qualities to facilitate characterization, and the last is to provide the reader with a point of view from which to observe the narrative world (74). These functions can only be present when names are used consistently in a narrative. When names are not used consistently, or are lacking entirely, the tendency is towards the decentralization of the self, not just for the characters in the narrative but for the reader as well (80). A result of this decentralization is the shift on the part of the reader from sympathy for a character that maintains the reader's separateness from the character, to empathy wherein the reader is "quite literally involved in and positioned within an other's subjectivity," namely that of the character (83).

When names are absent, the reader has an option for the freedom of subjectivity, whereby the reader "impersonates many positions, and informs his or her subjectivity by losing identity as a nameable self" (86). Anonymity erases the identity distinction of the name and instead creates a gap that the reader is invited to fill with her/his own identity, entering into the narrative and confronting the circumstances and situation of the character in the text. As a gospel that is the product of a community of believers and makes no secret of its propagandizing intent, the Johannine narrative sustains Docherty's view that "the reader's identity is not free

Identification with Characters and Identity Formation

The understanding of reading as an act of identity formation has been explored in the work of Norman Holland. He views reading as a process whereby the reader's identity re-creates itself. Holland sees three modalities at work in the reading process. First the reader interprets the experience in ways consistent with her/his characteristic response to the world so that her/his adaptations are matched. These adaptations are the typical ways the reader copes with the world. Next the reader extracts from the work fantasies that correlate to her/his movement towards gratification. In this modality the match is not nearly so exact as in the previous adaptation stage. The content of the fantasy the reader locates in the text is actually the expression of her/his own desires. The reader re-creates the text on the basis of her/his own identity theme. Holland's understanding of identity is borrowed from Heinz Lichtenstein, who defines identity as "the infinite sequence of bodily and behavioral transformations during the whole life of an individual" (Holland: 120). In the final modality the reader's identity is re-created from the literary work "to synthesize the experience and make it part of the mind's continuing effort to balance the pressures of the drive for gratification, the restraints of conscience and reality, and one's inner need to avoid emotional and cognitive dissonance" (126).

It has been suggested that Holland's view of identity formation through the reading process is one in which the text is re-formulated as a re-creation of the reader's pre-existing self identity that remains unaltered by the text. This is refuted by Marshall W. Alcorn and Mark Bracher, who note that Holland himself states that the reading process can significantly alter the variations of an individual's identity theme, arguing that these variations on a reader's identity theme actually constitute a re-formation of self (343). Following the analyst/patient model of psychoanalysis, they assert that projective identification is always also introjective, leading to an alteration and re-formation of self. This is accomplished through reader identification with literary characters or persona (350). The anonymity of those characters facilitates this process of identification and ultimately results in the alteration and re-formation of the reader's self.

The phenomenon of reader identification with characters in narratives has been investigated using both children and adult subjects. In a 1984 study Paul E. Jose and William F. Brewer tested second-, fourth-, and sixth-graders to determine whether reader identification with characters increases in proportion to the perceived similarity between the character and the reader. The sophistication of the character identification process increased with the age of the children. The second-graders related perceived similarity directly to story liking, while among fourth-graders the influence of perceived similarity on story liking is indirect as it is channeled through the process of character identification. By sixth grade another step is added between character identification and story liking, "empathic identification" whereby the reader steps into the character role (919).

In a later study Jose tested the hypothesis that adult subjects would identify more with story characters with a gender role orientation similar to theirs, regardless of actual gender correlation. For this study, stories were written with male and female characters who behaved in either a stereotypically masculine or feminine manner, though not necessarily corresponding to the character's gender. Subjects were given two commonly used gender role questionnaires to determine their gender role orientation. The stories were not suspenseful but were character sketches emphasizing motives and feelings. The study demonstrated, as expected, that a reader more readily identifies with a character displaying a gender role orientation similar to the reader's own. However, an unexpected finding of the study was that actual gender similarity between reader and character had little correlation with character identification (710). The implication of this for the Johannine narrative is the potential for reader identification with any anonymous character with whom the reader's experience correlates, and the potential for identification with the discipleship paradigm presented by the beloved disciple regardless of gender correlation.

Anonymous Johannine Characters

The Johannine narrative begins with a concern for identity, and it designates the unnamable presence of God as Logos. The reader is informed that the privilege of being God's child awaits those who believe in the Logos' name, a name as yet unrevealed. The crisis of recognizing Jesus' identity and responding appropriately remains current throughout the narrative. The first named character in the Fourth Gospel is John (designated the Baptist in the synoptics but not in the Fourth Gospel), whose identity is revealed by the process of negation. His reoccurrence in chapter two continues the negation of his identity. In response to the straightforward question of who he is, he responds with descriptions of function, not a name.

This correlation of identity concerns and anonymity in the Fourth Gospel has been explored by William Watty, who correctly notes that "names can exclude as well as identify." He suggests that the overriding emphasis on the life-giving name of Jesus makes all other naming acts irrelevant and obscures them into anonymity (12). Margaret Pamment has recognized the function of anonymous characters in enabling reader identification with the narrative "particulars of individual historical events," recognizing their role as representative figures (363). She fails, however, to assess the function of the anonymity of these characters in creating an identity gap that the reader is enticed to fill.

The first significant anonymous character appears in this text at the Cana wedding. The lack of a name for Jesus' mother is all the more surprising if it can be assumed that members of the Johannine community would have known her name from the Jesus tradition of the earliest Christian communities. This immediately signals the reader that identity is not easily established in this narrative but a question open for consideration. Her anonymity in this text is disconcerting for the reader, opening up questions of her identity, replacing certainty with indeterminacy, and creating the potential for reader identification with her character. Her response of faith is remarkable, following as it does upon Jesus' filial rebuke. This rebuke draws the reader's attention to the importance of a correct identification of Jesus superceding that of parent/child relations and confronts the reader with a challenge to her/his own understanding and response to Jesus' identity. Interpreters have variously identified her character as a representative figure of Judaism who finds her home in the Gentile Christianity represented by the figure of the beloved disciple (Pamment: 365) and as the church who is entrusted to the leadership of the Johannine community and/or the church as the mother of all beloved disciples, all intended readers (Kurz: 104-5). It is doubtful that a reader would identify this anonymous mother of Jesus either as Judaism finding her home in Gentile Christianity or as the church as the mother of all beloved disciples without the direction of an interpreter.

The next character to encounter Jesus is Nicodemus. His naming discourages the reader from completely identifying with his character, which is appropriate to his limited textual function. His character lacks a recorded faith response. Instead his query produces a lengthy monologue from Jesus and then he vanishes from the text. He stands in the narrative as one whose potential for discipleship remains unfulfilled. This is in marked contrast to the next textual encounter with an individual, the Samaritan woman. The lack of a recorded response for Nicodemus makes him a foil for the woman, whose anonymity invites the reader to identify with her response to the revelation of Jesus' identity (Pazdan: 148).

The unnamed Samaritan woman, in contrast to Nicodemus, is not the initiator of a monologue but a participant in a dialogue. Throughout that dialogue she is revealed as a person whose perception grows until she responds in faith and becomes the good news bearer to her community, but only after she struggles to a correct understanding and response to Jesus' identity. Gail O'Day has remarked that the ambivalence of her final words, "Can this be the Christ?," in 4:29 has the narrative function of returning the reader to Jesus' self-revelation to decide for her/himself the appropriate response (1986:76). O'Day illustrates how the text engages the reader into participating in the revelatory experience of the narrative, leading us to encounter Jesus there, principally through the use of irony (1986:89-90). What she fails to note is how the anonymity of the woman facilitates this process. The reader's participation in her revelatory experience is aided because she is not a particular character whose name sets her apart as distinct from the reader but a woman (as you may be) who is scorned by her community (as we may sometimes be) because of her own life choices (choices we all must make).

From Samaria the narrative returns the reader with Jesus to Cana where an anonymous official believes the word Jesus spoke and goes his way in faith, a faith vindicated on the journey. His faith is in response not to a word of healing but to the life-giving word of Jesus. He stands as a "representative figure" in the text, inviting the reader also to respond to Jesus' life-giving word, regardless of position or standing (Collins: 40). The reader is reminded of Jesus' first sign by the geographical location of this second sign, Cana. Whereas at the wedding an anonymous mother was challenged to reconfigure her understanding of her son, here an anonymous father is asked to reconfigure his understanding of Jesus' identity as one whose power over disease is unencumbered by geographical distance.

The narrative movement takes us next to Jerusalem where Jesus encounters an unnamed lame man by a pool. In response to Jesus' command, the man's faith is evinced and his healing demonstrated. The reader's ability to bridge the identity gap between the reader's own identity and that of the man at the pool is facilitated by his namelessness and conditional upon her/his ability to enter the man's life condition. Perhaps most readers are not so physically incapacitated, but there is the common experience of having the answer to our need almost within grasp but lacking anyone to help us reach it, while others shove us aside and arrive there first. Furthermore, this anonymous lame man himself functions as the one to put us into the pool of understanding by drawing us into his own narrative and the narrative of the man born blind with its strikingly parallel structure (Martyn: 89-90).

Sandwiched between the disputes concerning Jesus' origins and the origins of his Jewish opponents is the textually troublesome incident of the adulterous woman. The textual evidence for its non-Johannine origin is universally accepted by textual critics. It is absent from the important early Greek manuscripts, as well as the Old Syriac and Coptic. Its early attestation is limited to a few Western texts. There are also notable stylistic and vocabulary differences from the Fourth Gospel. Yet, tantalizingly, this pericope has not been discarded from the Fourth Gospel, but rather relegated to "footnote" status. The assessment that this is probably an ancient independent piece of Jesus tradition has prevented its being ignored. Its inclusion within the Johannine narrative at the location following 7:52 is often explained with reference to its demonstration of Jesus' statement "I judge no one" in 8:15.

In spite of this pericope's textual difficulties it fits the narrative pattern of anonymous characters given significant textual space and a challenge to respond in faith to Jesus' word. This narrative is dense with indeterminacy. The woman's anonymity is paralleled by the concealment of Jesus' writing. In the context of this woman's narrative, was Jesus writing the narrative of her accusers? Could it have been the next chapter in the woman's own narrative? The indeterminacy of the woman's identity solicits the reader's entry into her narrative; the indeterminacy of Jesus' writing invites the reader to permit Jesus to write her/his own narrative as s/he responds in faith to his word. Unlike the preceding examples, this text breaks off without the reader knowing if the woman's faith response is forthcoming. This woman's narrative is interpolated between two disputes concerning origins. Jesus inverts this focus upon origins with his word to the woman to go forward in her life narrative, neither condemned nor controlled by her past.

The nameless blind man's narrative is extended and dramatic. He responds to Jesus' command to wash and is healed. His faith response continues after Jesus' departure and at substantial risk. The scene climaxes with the return of Jesus and the man's response of belief and worship. Again in this narrative the focus is on the issue of identity. The blind man's growing understanding of Jesus' identity is expressed through the naming progression: man called Jesus (v. 9), prophet (v. 17), man from God (v. 33), Lord (v. 38). What has also been recently observed is that the blind man, though anonymous, also undergoes a naming progression of sorts: beggar (v. 8), the man who had formerly been blind (v. 13), the blind man (v. 17), our son (v. 20), the man who had been blind (v. 24) (Staley, 1991:66). That this is a forward progression is not clear until the reader realizes that with the return of Jesus in v. 35 the man's former state is no longer mentioned since his blindness is fully conquered through his understanding of and response to Jesus' identity. As the restoration of his vision is completed he comes to know his own identity. The man whose first textual appearance is "as a colorless object of theological speculation" now is portrayed "as a character in his own right" (Resseguie: 300). This identity formation on the part of the anonymous, formerly sightless man encourages the reader's own identity re-formation through identification with this anonymous character. The reader's identification with this man's condition and progression is enabled by the man's anonymity, particularly for readers who themselves have been beggars of one sort or another, alienated from society, parents, or even their religious community.

The raising of Lazarus is a skillfully crafted narrative, but the prominent characters are all identified by name. What distinguishes them textually from the anonymous characters is their lack of a recorded faith response. Martha verbally expresses her belief but is challenged to no act of faith. A faith response is not asked of Mary, and Lazarus' response to Jesus' command is not the faith response of a human being but the reanimation of one who had lost his capacity to believe or respond.

As the first half of the gospel closes, the reader has been invited to identify with several anonymous characters whose identities are open and unfilled. These include a mother, one who is disenfranchised by both an accident of birth (gender and ethnicity) and her own life choices, two physically impaired persons (one an outcast from his religious community), an esteemed person of high status, and a violator of the law. All are challenged to a faith response and such a response is recorded for each except the adulterous woman. The reader's entry into the narrative, through filling the identity blank created by the character's anonymity with her/his own identity, is facilitated by her/his own parenting, social status, disenfranchisement, physical impairment, alienation from the religious community, and/or life choices.

The Anonymous Beloved Disciple

The appearance of the beloved disciple in the second half of the narrative has been preceded by these previous textual representations of anonymous characters that prepared the reader for identification with the final significant anonymous character, who is the paradigm of true discipleship. Thomas stands in contrast to the beloved disciple as a named character with a significant statement of belief, but Jesus' response to his delayed belief is a less than enthusiastic endorsement. Furthermore, as with Martha, no act of faith is required of him. The beloved disciple's faith response is evidenced by his taking Jesus' mother into his home, running to the tomb and entering, and—most significantly—bearing witness to the words and deeds of Jesus with his true testimony. He stands in contrast to Thomas, the named doubter, as the Samaritan woman does to Nicodemus.

Watty argues that the anonymity of the beloved disciple was for the sake of unity and continuity as this relatively late gospel was being shaped. As long as this disciple is not named, any disciple at any point in history may be the one whom Jesus loved (212). This theological and historical understanding of the anonymity of the beloved disciple needs to be supplemented. A literary analysis of the reader's experience helps clarify how the characterizations of these unnamed persons whose encounter with Jesus produced life-changing responses enables readers from any era, including our own, to make what Kurz describes as "their spontaneous identification with what happens in the narrative." This includes the reader's acceptance of and participation in the way of discipleship for which the beloved disciple serves as a paradigm (106).

Brendan Byrne understands the purpose of the Fourth Gospel to be to provide access to subsequent generations within the Christian community to the events of Jesus' life, death, and resurrection. The Johannine narrative assures them that "they can have an encounter with Jesus every bit as valid and indeed more fruitful" than even his own contemporaries. This is accomplished through the agency of the beloved disciple, whom he describes as "the point of insertion for the later generations" into the narrative world inhabited by Jesus in the Fourth Gospel (93). The beloved disciple's anonymity enables reader identification with him and entry into his narrative world. His identity has greater indeterminacy than the preceding anonymous characters. Nothing is revealed of his familial relationships, social standing, occupation, physical condition, or his past. The only aspect of his story that is initially revealed is that he was the recipient of Jesus' love. This greater indeterminacy facilitates the reader's filling the identity gaps in the beloved disciple's narrative with her/his own identity, entering and accepting the paradigm of discipleship that the beloved disciple presents.

The process by which a reader enters this narrative through identification with the beloved disciple is illustrated in the Jungian archetypal interpretation of the beloved disciple by Schuyler Brown. Of anonymity he states: "that which is without a name, or unknown, suggests the unconscious, whereas differential relations between characters suggest the complementary between the conscious ego and the unconscious psyche" (372). Reader identification with the character of the beloved disciple "can lead the psyche, through enemy lines, into the camp of the 'other.'" Through a process Jung called individuation, the reader in her/his psyche experiences "the other in myself," and the reverse is also true. This experience of the risen Jesus is available to any reader. The need to see the risen Lord personally is viewed in this gospel as evidence of a deficient faith. Through the anonymous beloved disciple the reader is led into a faith response that does not require the first-hand experience of seeing. It is necessary that the reader also recognize what she/he brings to the text and its interpretation. When individuation occurs, the reader makes identification with the beloved disciple, and the beloved disciple's representation of the reader's ego leads the reader into the narrative world. For the reader, the beloved disciple is not only "the disciple par excellence, but he is also the interpreter par excellence" (Brown: 376), guiding the reader in her/his faith response to the words and deeds of Jesus in the Fourth Gospel text.

Conclusion

The stated purpose of the Fourth Gospel narrative is that the reader might correctly respond to the issue of Jesus' identity through a life-altering identification with the Logos whose identity is intertwined with the identity of God. The textual strategies for confronting the reader with this identity issue include a series of textual encounters between Jesus and a varied spectrum of characters. Those characters whose responses most closely model the paradigm of discipleship the narrative demands of the reader are those whose names are unrevealed. The indeterminacy created by this anonymity engages the reader and entices her/him into identification with the character to experience the identity dilemma presented by the character's textual confrontation with Jesus. By entering into the narrative the reader may experience a re-formation of her/his own self-identity and become a part of the narrative of Jesus the Fourth Gospel presents. From the perspective of the Fourth Gospel, that narrative does not end with the Fourth Gospel text itself, nor with the "conclusion" of 20:30-31, nor even with the cessation of words at 21:25. Through the reader's encounter with Jesus in this narrative, facilitated by the anonymity of many of its characters, each reader is invited to allow Jesus to re-write her/his own life narrative.

Works Consulted

Alcorn, Marshall W., Jr. and Mark Bracher
    1985   "Literature, Psychoanalysis, and the Re-Formation of the Self: A New Direction for Reader-Response Theory." *Publications of the Modern Language Association of America* 100:342-54.

Alter, Robert
    1981   *The Art of Biblical Narrative*. New York: Basic.

Bal, Mieke
    1985   *Narratology: Introduction to the Theory of Narrative*. Trans. Christine van Boheemen. Toronto: University of Toronto Press.

Berlin, Adele
    1983   *Poetics and Interpretation of Biblical Narrative*. Bible and Literature Series 9. Sheffield: Almond.

Brown, Schuyler
    1990   "The Beloved Disciple: A Jungian View." Pp. 366-78 in *The Conversation Continues: Studies in Paul & John*. Ed. Robert T. Fortna and Beverly R. Gaventa. Nashville: Abingdon.

Byrne, Brendan
    1985   "The Faith of the Beloved Disciple and the Community in John 20." *JSNT* 23:83-97.

Campbell-Sposito, Mary
    1988   "Onomastics as a Defamiliarizing Device in Raymond Queneau's Novels." *French Review* 5:724-33.

Chatman, Seymour
    1978   *Story and Discourse: Narrative Structure in Fiction and Film*. Ithaca: Cornell University Press.

Collins, Raymond F.
    1976   "Representative Figures in the Fourth Gospel." *The Downside Review* 94:26-46, 118-32.

Culpepper, R. Alan
    1983   *Anatomy of the Fourth Gospel: A Study in Literary Design*. Foundations and Facets. New Testament. Philadelphia: Fortress.

Darr, John A
    1992   *On Character Building: The Reader and the Rhetoric of Characterization in Luke-Acts*. Literary Currents in Biblical Interpretation. Louisville: Westminster/John Knox.

Davies, Margaret
    1992   *Rhetoric and Reference in the Fourth Gospel*. JSNTSup 69. Sheffield: JSOT.

Docherty, Thomas
1983   Reading (Absent) Character: Towards A Theory of Characterization in Fiction. Oxford: Clarendon.

Fokkema, Aleid
1991   Postmodern Characters: A Study of Characterization in British and American Postmodern Fiction. Postmodern Studies 4. Amsterdam/Atlanta: Rodopi.

Forster, E. M.
1927   Aspects of the Novel. New York: Harcourt, Brace and World.

Fowler, Robert M.
1991   Let the Reader Understand: Reader-Response and the Gospel of Mark. Minneapolis: Fortress.

Funk, Robert W.
1988   The Poetics of Biblical Narrative. Foundations and Facets. Sonoma, CA: Polebridge.

Greimas, A. -J.
1966   Sémantique structurale: récherche de méthode. Paris: Larousse.

Hochman, Baruch
1985   Character in Literature. Ithaca: Cornell University Press.

Holland, Norman
1980   "Unity Identity Text Self." Pp. 118-33 in Reader-Response Criticism: From Formalism to Post-Structuralism. Ed. Jane P. Thompkins. Baltimore: John Hopkins University Press.

Iser, Wolfgang
1974   The Implied Reader: Patterns of Communication in Prose Fiction from Bunyan to Beckett. Baltimore: John Hopkins University Press.
1978   The Act of Reading: A Theory of Aesthetic Response. Baltimore: John Hopkins University Press.

Jose, Paul E.
1989   "The Role of Gender and Gender Role Similarity in Reader's Identification with Story Characters." Sex Roles 21:697-713.

Jose, Paul E. and William F. Brewer
1984   "Development of Story Liking: Character Identification, Suspense and Resolution." Developmental Psychology 20:911-24.

Kurz, William S.
1989   "The Beloved Disciple and the Implied Readers." BTB 19:100-07.

Martyn, J. Louis
1979   History and Theology in the Fourth Gospel. Rev. ed. Nashville: Abingdon.

Moore, Stephen D.
1989   Literary Criticism and the Gospels: The Theoretical Challenge. New Haven: Yale University Press.

O'Day, Gail R.
- 1986   *Revelation in the Fourth Gospel: Narrative Mode and Theological Claim.* Philadelphia: Fortress.
- 1992   "John 7:53-8:11: A Study in Misreading." *JBL* 111:631-40.

Pamment, Margaret
- 1983   "The Fourth Gospel's Beloved Disciple." *ExpTim* 94:363-7.

Pazdan, Mary Margaret
- 1987   "Nicodemus and the Samaritan Woman: Contrasting Models of Discipleship." *BTB* 17:145-48.

Pelling, Christopher, ed.
- 1990   *Characterization and Individuality in Greek Literature.* Oxford: Clarendon.

Queneau, Raymond
- 1952   *Le Dimanche de la vie.* Paris: Gallimard.

Resseguie, James L.
- 1982   "John 9: A Literary Critical Analysis." Pp. 295-303 in *Literary Interpretation of Biblical Narratives.* Vol. II. Ed. Kenneth R. R. Gros Louis. Nashville: Abingdon.

Scholes, Robert and Robert Kellogg
- 1966   *The Nature of Narrative.* Oxford: Oxford University Press.

Segovia, Fernando F.
- 1991   "The Journey(s) of the Word of God: A Reading of the Plot of the Fourth Gospel." *Semeia* 53:23-54.

Staley, Jeffrey Lloyd
- 1988   *The Print's First Kiss: A Rhetorical Investigation of the Implied Reader in the Fourth Gospel.* SBLDS 82. Atlanta: Scholars.
- 1991   "Stumbling in the Dark, Reaching for the Light: Reading Character in John 5 and 9." *Semeia* 53:55-80.

Sternberg, Meir
- 1985   *The Poetics of Biblical Narrative: Ideological Literature and the Drama of Reading.* Bloomington: Indiana University Press.

Watty, William W.
- 1979   "The Significance of Anonymity in the Fourth Gospel." *ExpTim* 90:209-13.

THE CHARACTER(IZATION) OF GOD IN 2 SAMUEL 7:1-17

Kenneth M. Craig, Jr.
Chowan College

ABSTRACT

Characterization is achieved in 2 Samuel 7 through a preponderance of dialogue, and virtually every phrase sheds light on God's character. Subtle yet significant artistic measures are isolated to show how God is portrayed. By paying attention to the contours of speech one gains insight into characterization in this passage, which is neither "dreary prose" nor "a mire of unintelligible verbiage" (Pfeiffer: 372). Shlomith Rimmon-Kenan's description of the narrator's "direct definition" and "indirect presentation" is transferred in this discussion to the characters themselves. Dialogue often sheds light on both the speaker and addressee, and a number of words are isolated to demonstrate that speech serves distinct rhetorical purposes. Free indirect discourse signals combined points of view in vv. 5a, 8a, and 11b. At precisely these three points in the oracle, two speech events are combined: that of the reporter and that of the reportee. Vv. 1-17 blend (and at times blur) several points of view while presenting God as a causal agent who transforms David's desire to build a temple. The human impulse to build a shrine is modified through speech as David learns that he will not build a בית ("house" or "temple") for God; God will build a בית ("dynasty") for him. Direct speech thus provides a dramatic means for conveying God's psychological and ideological points of view.

"The [Bible's] protagonists are characterized not only by direct means, but also, and in fact primarily, by what they say and do."
—Shimon Bar-Efrat

INTRODUCTION

Second Samuel 7 portrays David suffering from a guilty conscience because he is settled in his palace in Jerusalem while the ark of God resides in a tent. Just after David implies that now is the time to build a temple for the Lord, he receives the commendation of the prophet. Immediately thereafter, however, Nathan receives word from the Lord that David's thoughts are incompatible with God's. Most of the discussion about this chapter has focused on what has been perceived to be its complex literary history, and the author (or editor, if the argument about an elaborate literary tradition is accepted) has not fared well (Bussche, Kruse,

Noth, Pfeiffer, Simon, Tsevat [1963, 1965]). According to Robert Pfeiffer, for example, the author is responsible for "the muddle" and the "dreary prose of II Sam. 7." The author "sinks into a mire of unintelligible verbiage," and "his style is consistently wretched" (372). Now that the days of undervaluing the Bible's art have passed, a new perspective based on the integrity of the text of 2 Samuel 7 is possible.

From a thematic standpoint, the chapter stands out for at least two reasons: generally, it belongs to the category of divine revelations concerning temple building that was common in the ancient Near East,[1] and, more specifically, it highlights the Davidic dynasty. Rhetorically speaking, the chapter has another claim to notice: the narrator, in self-imposed silence throughout most of the chapter (vv. 2b, 3b, 5-16, 18b-29), departs from the biblical norm. After a brief description of action and conversation (vv. 1-4) and a short transitional passage (vv. 17-18a), all of the remaining verses are given over to the direct speech of the Lord (vv. 5-16) and David (vv. 18b-29).

The Bible does, of course, allow its characters to speak, but more often the narrator of biblical prose provides commentary to help the reader find his or her way through the stories. But in this chapter we hear from the narrator only in six verses, and at times only in portions of these (vv.1-4, 17-18). The surrounding chapters, 6 and 8, are instructive because they are made up almost entirely of the narrator's words.

In an effort to show that 2 Samuel 7 is *not* "unintelligible verbiage" and that the author's style is something other than "consistently wretched," we may pose one question: How is God portrayed? In chap. 7, where virtually every phrase sheds light on God's character, the question arises: If the preponderance of dialogue represents a departure from the norm in the deuteronomistic history, how does it affect the characterization of God? One should bear in mind that the characterization of God represents a special case. The portrayal of God is unique because most aspects typically associated with character—appearance, social status, place of residence, etc.—have no bearing on God at all (Sternberg, 1985:323). Certain information-seeking questions that human characters sometimes ask one another (Judg 12:5; 18:3; 19:17; 1 Sam 28:14; 30:13; 2 Sam 1:13) are not addressed to God.

In principle, any element in chap. 7 may indicate character. When assuming a less pronounced role in telling the story, the narrator allows characters to advance the plot by means of their spoken words, and this shift in point of view requires us to attend to the contours of speech. But even when withdrawn, the narrator is never completely absent. The

---

[1] Readers interested in temple building in the ancient Near East may wish to consult Hurowitz's excellent comparative and phenomenological study.

narrator frames the characters' speech by introducing the speakers and often nuancing their words: "the *king* said to *the prophet* Nathan" (v. 2); "*in accordance with all these words and with all this vision,* Nathan spoke to David" (v. 17); "then *King* David *went in and sat before the Lord,* and said" (v. 18a).

Shlomith Rimmon-Kenan's analysis of character provides a starting point for analysis. She asserts that the biblical narrator provides two basic types of character identicators. Borrowing from Joseph Ewen (1971 and 1980:47-48), she labels these as "direct definition" and "indirect presentation." The first type names the trait by an adjective (e.g. "she was good-hearted") or an abstract noun ("his goodness knew no bounds"). The second type, on the other hand, allows the reader to infer the quality of certain traits without mentioning them explicitly (Rimmon-Kenan: 59-60). She concludes, "such naming of a character's qualities counts as direct characterization only if it proceeds from the most authoritative voice in the text [that is, an authoritative narrator]" (60). As helpful as Rimmon-Kenan's understanding of character identicators is, the implications of her analysis extend beyond the narrator. In a chapter such as 2 Samuel 7 where the dramatis personae assume much of the responsibility for characterization, we see that such direct and indirect methods of portrayal also extend to the characters themselves. For example, David supplies "direct definitions" of God's character when he prays and says, "You have wrought all this greatness . . . Therefore you are great" (vv. 21-22). And after repeating God's name (or the Lord's name) twenty-five times in the span of only twelve verses, David says toward the end of the prayer, "O Lord God you are God" (v. 28). This frequent reference in the narrative to the Lord's name and position affects the reader's understanding of both the speaker and the addressee.

Certain portions of the chapter may also be described in terms of "indirect presentation." The Lord's first words to Nathan, "Go and tell my servant David" (v. 4), suggest a particular type of relationship between God and David before God delivers the oracle. This type of portrayal may also be observed in the very first verse of the chapter where we learn that the rest that David now enjoys is the result of the Lord's actions against the king's enemies. And finally, God's uniqueness is also suggested on both the temporal and spatial planes by God's own words in v. 6: "I have not lived in a house since the day I brought up the people of Israel from Egypt to this day, but I have been moving about in a tent and a tabernacle."[2] Obviously this distinction of direct and indirect portrayal helps to

---

[2] Other examples can be found, such as in v. 8b. This and other translations throughout this paper (with minor revisions) are those of the *New Revised Standard Version.*

show how characterization is achieved, yet more is at work here. Because of the preponderance of dialogue, we might focus on the characters' speeches themselves. After all, a narrator reluctant to offer direct and explicit comments about characters may still put words in their mouths that shed light on either (or both) the speaker and addressee. As Shimon Bar-Efrat notes:

> Traits of both the speaker and the interlocutor are expressed through speech, or to be more precise, all speech reflects and exposes the speaker, while it sometimes also brings to light qualities of the person being addressed (or reveals the speaker's opinion of that person). What people say witnesses not only to their thoughts, feelings etc., but is often slanted to accord with the character, mood, interests and status of their interlocutor (64-65).

An analysis of the portrayal of God is bound to yield complexities and nuances far beyond what can be explored here, but a more careful look at the dialogue may reveal how God's character is drawn while concurrently suggesting *how* earlier commentators missed the mark.

Nathan's Role: The Tables Turned

The characterization of God begins in the opening verse as the narrator conveys two pieces of information: a) the king is settled in his house; b) the Lord had given David rest from all his enemies. While the two images are linked by a simple conjunction (ו) that is typically translated as "and" (the king is settled *and* the Lord had given him rest), the issue at stake is more involved, because both author and audience share in a game of reading between the lines. By linking these particular two ideas the author invites the following interpretation of the *vav* conjunction: the king is settled in his house *but only because* the Lord had given him rest from all his enemies around him.

This reference to David's security and rest reverses the true chronological sequence: The Lord gives David rest; then the king is able to settle in his house. Such manipulation of temporal ordering is one of the hallmarks of biblical narrative,[3] and by reversing the sequence the author calls attention to the cause-effect relationship. With respect to the overarching story of David's rise to power in the deuteronomistic history, the statement that the Lord had given David rest also appears to be out of its chronological place. The Chronicler duplicates virtually all of the elements of the plot from the opening scene of 2 Samuel 7 (cf. 1 Chr 17:1-3), but omits the reference to the Lord giving David rest, perhaps because 2 Samuel 8's catalogue of David's wars makes it clear that David is not at

---

[3] Cf. the discussion in Craig, chap. 4.

this time enjoying rest from his enemies. Thus, information conveyed in the initial verse of chapter 7 appears to be chronologically out of place on two counts, and this rearranging serves a distinct rhetorical purpose: the initial statement sets the stage for the characterization of God in charge (or at least able to look after David) that will be approached from multiple angles throughout the chapter.

The opening verse also functions at another level. It contains key words (כל, ישב, בית) that may be interpreted in the light of former events and that gain in rhetorical strength throughout the chapter. The report of David's living in security stands in sharp contrast to the time when he and his troops "wandered wherever they could go" in 1 Sam 23:13 (cf. God's words in 7:6-7). David's first quoted speech about his "dwelling" (ישב) in a "house" (בית) in v. 2 is reminiscent of the narrator's first words in v. 1 (a form of ישב or בית is used by both David and the narrator), but David adds an important word: he now lives in a house *of cedars* (ארזים). A house of cedar would have been a well-constructed and impressive building fit for any king or queen. Tents, on the other hand, could be blown away or suffer the ravages of nature, and they were inhabited by nomads, members of a lower stratum of society. This repetition with variation on the word בית is but one clue among many that reveals the author as an artist. The word will be repeated a number of times in the chapter, and it will often carry a new shade of meaning. Characterization is achieved through this type of repetition. The contrast between a secure king and God's ark residing in a transportable tent is striking. Now that God has given David rest from his enemies, what could be more natural than acknowledging the favor?

In a chapter where key words (כל, ישב, בית) are often repeated, the reader may be struck by one word that is absent in v. 2. In conversation with Nathan, David alludes to his desire to build a house (i.e. temple) for the Lord, but conveys his thought without uttering the key word בית (temple).[4] Just as the narrator conveys two pieces of information in v. 1 (David's rest/God's responsibility for), David now conveys two facts in his speech to Nathan in v. 2: the king lives in a cedar house; the ark of God resides in a tent. This second sequence (v. 2) is not causal, as in v. 1, but contrastive. It is the comparison between David in a house and the ark in a tent that invites Nathan (and the audience) to infer David's desire. David's wish may be self-evident, yet he does not say the word בית when referring to the ark of God. Nathan also avoids the word in his prompt response to the king to do all that he has in mind. Thus this key term (בית,

---

[4] David does use the word בית to refer to his house, but avoids it when referring to his thoughts about a temple. When translating from the Hebrew, the single word is conveyed by multiple English words ("house," "temple," "palace," "dynasty").

with the nuance of "temple") is not mentioned in this opening scene, but it will often appear in the subsequent recorded speech.[5] Such changes at the linguistic level lay the groundwork for the subsequent changes at the thematic level as David's desire is recast by God.

The implications of this phenomenon, which we might describe as a reversal situation[6] (the key word בית is avoided [vv. 1-3], but then often repeated [vv. 5-16]), may be observed in a more pronounced and significant way by focusing on the prophet Nathan. Why does Nathan even appear in this context? Why doesn't David voice his thoughts directly to God (as he had on separate occasions as recently as 2:1 and 5:19)? And what are we to make of the prophet's poor advice in v. 3? The series of events in the opening scene may cause us to conjecture that the prophet's appearance serves some kind of rhetorical purpose, but what is it? Nathan appears in David's court on three separate occasions (here, in 2 Samuel 12, and in 1 Kings 1), and we may find provisional answers to these questions by looking for clues when Nathan appears at the court.

David seeks the advice of the prophet in 2 Samuel 7, and this situation is rare. Robert Polzin has called attention to the different postures that Saul and David take with respect to prophets. On the one hand, Saul actively seeks a prophet when inquiring of God (cf. 1 Sam 9:9-10; 28:6,15). David, on the other hand, is more reluctant to take the initiative (184). Thus in 2 Sam 12:1-15 Nathan appears, but unsummoned, to confront the king just after David lies with Bathsheba. Nathan appears on the scene having been "sent by the Lord" (2 Sam 12:1), and David is obviously unsuspecting, as his harsh words about himself reveal ("As the Lord lives, the man who has done this deserves to die" [v. 5b]). On this occasion, the court prophet avoids the language of the court. The narrator describes Nathan's entrance in a neutral tone: "[Nathan] came to [David], and said to him" (12:1); "Nathan said to David" (vv. 7,13); "then Nathan went to his house" (v. 15). Nowhere in the parable of the poor man's ewe lamb does Nathan adopt any of the titles or language of the court, as he will elsewhere.

In 1 Kgs 1:22-27 the prophet appears once again as an uninvited guest, but this time his speech is marked by a different tone; he addresses the king with words that follow the rules of court decorum. The narrator tells us that Nathan bows before the king with his face to the ground (v. 23), and then addresses the king with the words, "My Lord the king" (v. 24). The prophet subsequently refers to David's "servant Solomon" (v. 26) and then refers to David as "my Lord the king" (v. 27). Nathan also refers to himself as one of the king's "servants" (v. 27) and then again to David as

---

[5] Vv. 5, 6, 7. Cf. also vv. 1, 2, 11, 13, 16, 18, 19, 25, 26, 27, 29.

[6] The technical term is peripety.

"my Lord the king" (v. 27). In these two passages the correspondence between style and content reinforces the impact of the speeches.

It is in 2 Samuel 7 that David makes the unusual move by initiating conversation with Nathan, and it is the one time that Nathan's words mislead *us*. The prophet's instruction, "Go, do all that you have in mind; for the Lord is with you" (v. 3), is hardly surprising. As recently as 5:10, the narrator had reported that "the Lord . . . was with [David]," and previous actions against the Philistines (5:17-25) would also appear to support Nathan's commendation. Yet in this rare instance, the prophet misspeaks. Even though Nathan appears only for a short while—virtually all of the description and quoted speech is given over to David and the Lord in this chapter—his role in this scene is crucial in terms of the characterization of God. His presence and short speech create a reversal situation. This mis-direction that David (and we) experience results from what seems to be a reasonable desire on David's part and the prophet's encouraging words. That very night (v. 4) the word of the Lord comes to Nathan. We learn with Nathan that the prophet has given David bad advice, which God will correct subsequently in an extensive fashion. Having hardly recovered from God's quick attempt that night to correct God's own prophet, the reader will learn next how David's wish is transformed in the specific words of the extended oracle (vv. 5-16). The human initiative is negated, and our expectations are quashed as early as v. 5. Even the prophet emerges as a fallible spokesperson in this context. Immediately, and in an extended fashion, God is portrayed as re-directing the course of human desires.

Thus the reader is set up in the opening scene by means of David's initiative and the prophet's blessing. God responds, beginning in v. 5, with decisive words that alter the humans' situation. The prophet's complete submission to God—it is worth noting that Nathan's response to the oracle also characterizes God—is expressed subsequently in v. 17, where we learn precisely how the Lord's speech is conveyed to David: "in accordance with all these words and with all this vision" (ככל הדברים האלה וככל החזיון הזה). V. 17 complements v. 4 with a visual image (חזיון), and by the time of the report of Nathan's execution of the Lord's command (v. 17), the word כל ("all") is familiar: "all [David's] enemies" (v. 1); "go, do all" (v. 3); "I have cut off all your enemies" (v. 9); "I will give you rest from all your enemies" (v. 11). The doubling of ככל in v. 17, however, emphasizes the point that Nathan passes on God's words to David verbatim. Thus God is characterized before God speaks (vv. 1-4), in the extended oracle itself (vv. 5-16), and by the narrator's report of God's words revealed to David via Nathan (v. 17).

God's Questions and the Oracle

As mentioned above, the narrator frequently reports action in the Hebrew Bible (as we observed in 2 Samuel 6 and 8), but in 2 Samuel 7 the narrator's role is much reduced. The narrator does report that the "king was settled" (v. 1); that "the word of the Lord came to Nathan" (v. 4); that "in accordance with all these words . . . Nathan spoke" (v. 17); and that "David went in and sat before the Lord" (v. 18). But virtually all of the characterization in this chapter is accomplished by the speaking characters themselves. When God delivers the first major speech in the oracle of vv. 5-16, language and syntax continue to play an important role in characterization. The Lord's first words to Nathan, "Go and tell" (לך ואמרת) in v. 5, are reminiscent of the prophet's instructions to David reported outside the oracle itself in v. 3: "go, do" (לך עשה). Nathan gives David a green flag: "Go, do all that you have in mind." The Lord, on the other hand, re-directs Nathan (who later re-directs David) with the words "Go and tell . . . 'Are you the one to build me a house to live in?'" Such a shift in tone affects characterization. Nathan's initial words to David, "Go, do all," help the reader establish a first impression; however, the Lord's first words to Nathan quickly dispel the view that David is the one in charge here: it is the Lord who offers a great surprise through the spoken word and in so doing quickly makes clear the Lord's desire to control the action. The similarity in speech—Nathan's first word is the same as the Lord's—is not a coincidence. Neither is the difference reflected in the change of the second imperative (from "do" to "tell"), which anticipates the characterization that will be accomplished from this point forward by the speech of characters ("tell") rather than the narrator's report of action ("do").

Clues other than the large units of quoted direct speech suggest that the spoken word plays an important role in this chapter. For example, the Lord's words in vv. 5-16 are actually reported as the Lord's speech. That is, the narrator could have indicated initially that Nathan received words and a vision from the Lord, that Nathan approached David, and then that Nathan shared the Lord's words with the king *and with us simultaneously*. When Nathan approaches the king on a separate occasion (2 Samuel 12), the account of the Lord's speech is recorded through Nathan's voice: "Nathan said to David, 'You are the man! Thus says the Lord, the God of Israel: I anointed you king over Israel, and I rescued you from the hand of Saul . . . '" (v. 7). And Nathan continues, "Thus says the Lord: I will raise up trouble against you from within your own house . . . " (v. 11). God is characterized by means of direct speech, but Nathan's speech—not

God's—characterizes God in 2 Samuel 12. With respect to the Nathan passages,[7] the Lord's first-degree speech appears only in 2 Samuel 7.

Speech itself is also highlighted in 2 Samuel 7 by means of embedded markers. First, God alludes to God's own previous speech: "[in the past,] Did I ever speak a word with any of the tribal leaders of Israel . . . saying, 'Why have you not built me a house of cedar?'" (v. 7). Second, David, in his response to the oracle, quotes God: "For you, O Lord of hosts, the God of Israel, have made this revelation to your servant, saying, 'I will build you a house'" (v. 27). Third, God's extended speech in 2 Sam 7:5-16 falls into three parts. The three segments of the oracle (vv. 5-7; 8-11a; 11b-16) are marked off in slightly different fashions (in vv. 5a, 8a, 11b), but in each case an embedded speech pattern allows the addressee and the audience to re-focus attention on the material within the three layers of the oracle itself. The specific rhetorical function of each layer will be considered below, but first the introductions to these narrative blocks may be isolated:

1. Go and tell my servant David: Thus says the Lord: [First layer of the oracle]
(v. 5a) לך ואמרת אל עבדי אל דוד כה אמר יהוה...

2. Now therefore thus you shall say to my servant David: Thus says the Lord of hosts: [Second layer of the oracle]
(v. 8a) ועתה כה תאמר לעבדי לדוד כה אמר יהוה צבאות...

3. Moreover the Lord declares to you that the Lord will make you a house: [Third layer of the oracle]
(v. 11b) והגיד לך יהוה כי בית יעשה לך יהוה...

At each of these points of the oracle, the author introduces what appears to be the narrator's, as opposed to God's, words. Such a blending (and blurring) of points of view has been recognized as a literary technique of the modern era, and various descriptors have been used in labelling the combined voices. "Free indirect discourse" is perhaps the most popular, but the blurring of the narrator's commentary with the speech of a character is also designated as *"style indirect libre," "erlebte*

---

[7] In the third and only other passage where Nathan appears before the king (1 Kings 1), the prophet does not invoke the Lord's name. He advises Bathsheba that she should "go in at once to King David and say to him, 'Did you not, my lord the king, swear to your servant, saying: Your son Solomon shall succeed me as king, and he shall sit on my throne? Why then is Adonijah king?'" (v. 13). Bathsheba follows Nathan's advice but changes his words. *She* invokes the Lord's name. Bathsheba approaches David and says, "My lord, you swore to your servant by the Lord your God, saying: Your son Solomon shall succeed me as king, and he shall sit on my throne. But now suddenly Adonijah has become king, though you, my lord the king, do not know it. . . " (vv. 17-18). In similar fashion, David responds saying, "As the Lord lives, who has saved my life from every adversity, as I swore to you by the Lord, the God of Israel, . . . " (vv. 29-30).

Rede," "represented speech," "narrated monologue," and "combined speech."[8] T. Kalepsky, one of the first German critics to treat the subject, coined the term "veiled discourse" (*verschleirte Rede*) in 1913 to highlight the somewhat elusive phenomenon (Sternberg, 1982:70). Only in recent times have scholars working in the area of biblical studies recognized that free indirect discourse is part of the Bible's artistic repertoire. Doubling as archaeologists, these literary critics appear to have unearthed something as old as the Bible itself (Berlin: 66-70; Savran: 30,47,49; Sternberg, 1985:52-54; Weiss: 456-75).

If a report of direct speech is one of the most dramatic means of conveying characters' psychological and ideological points of view, the momentary blending of perspectives accentuates the spoken word. It is the combined viewpoints that allow us to sense the drama of Nathan's nocturnal encounter with God, and, ironically, the blending of points of view proves to be a fine rhetorical tool for conveying the author's view of God's place in Israel's history. At precisely these three points in the oracle (vv. 5a, 8a, 11b), two speech events are combined: that of the reporter (i.e. narrator) and that of the reportee (in this case God). I propose to call these places where another point of view enters the narrative *combined viewpoint markers.*

The first layer of the oracle (vv. 5-7). The first portion of the oracle is introduced with a double phrase. The conventional declaration, "thus says the Lord," is here preceded by the imperatives "go and tell my servant David." God's initial words to Nathan reinforce the type of relationship that exists between God and David: David is God's servant. An association had of course already been suggested by the narrator, who described David's security as the result of the Lord's gift of rest from the enemies (v. 1). In the much broader context of the deuteronomistic history, the word עבדי ("my servant") is especially forceful because it is so seldom conferred by God (Fokkelman: 214). God applies the title only to Moses (Josh 1:2, 7; 2 Kgs 21:8) and David (2 Sam 3:18; 7:5, 8; 1 Kgs 11:13, 32, 34, 36, 38; 14:8; 2 Kgs 19:34; 20:6) in the deuteronomistic history. By inviting a comparison with Moses, the author calls attention to the importance of God's speech even before the oracle is delivered. Like Moses, David plays a vital role in Israel's history; yet both leaders stand in a subordinate relationship to the Lord.

The Lord and David invoke several questions in 2 Samuel 7. Both use rhetorical questions to introduce their speeches. The important rhetorical function of questions in this chapter is emphasized when we recall that one central thought is on David's mind: may I build a temple for the

---

[8] See McHale's excellent survey of scholarship on this topic. He considers, among other things, descriptions and typologies.

Lord? Yet this thought is not expressed as an interrogative. The question David has on his mind is expressed as a declarative suggestion: A is the case; therefore B should follow. This discrepancy between thought (Should I build?) vs. speech (I should build) is revealing. David wishes to build, and by avoiding the interrogative in speech he is able to suggest that his desire *should* be realized. The important rhetorical function that questions play in 2 Samuel 7 is also evident when we observe that the Chronicler, who follows the text of 2 Samuel 7 closely, changes the initial rhetorical question that the Lord speaks to Nathan from "Are you the one to build me a house to live in?" (v. 5) to the statement, "You shall not build me a house to live in" (1 Chr 17:4).

The first layer of the oracle contains two questions that the Lord addresses to Nathan, which Nathan in turn addresses to David (v. 17). These questions serve a foundational role in the characterization of God.

> (a) Are (ה) you the one to build me a house to live in? (v. 5).
>
> (b) Wherever I have moved about among all the people of Israel, did (ה) I ever speak a word with any of the tribal leaders of Israel, whom I commanded to shepherd my people Israel, saying, "Why (לָמָּה) have you not built me a house of cedar?" (v. 7).

The characterization of God is achieved in part through these rhetorical questions because the asking itself suggests divine indignation (GKC: §150d). All of the questions that God, an omniscient, asks are rhetorical rather than information-seeking. Indeed, God has a monopoly on thoughts and performative utterances. Characterization is achieved not only through these rhetorical questions, but also by their answers. By definition, answers to rhetorical questions are implied, but here the Lord actually supplies an answer to make the point: "[No,] I have not lived in a house since the day I brought up the people of Israel from Egypt" (v. 6). God appears to reject dwelling in a temple, but the refusal is provisional as suggested by the emphatic pronouns in the Hebrew, which may be rendered: "Do *you* want to build a house for *me*?" God's denial concerns the person of David and not the temple itself as the emphatic position of the pronoun הַאַתָּה ("Do you?") makes clear. More of the answer to the question is found in the second layer of the oracle ("He shall build a house for my name," v. 13a), and emphasis is made in v. 13 where the emphatic הוּא יִבְנֶה ("he shall build") parallels the forceful denial of v. 5. By answering the rhetorical question, God emerges early as the one in charge; the choice of the builder is God's to make.

The two questions (a) and (b) form a frame in this first layer of the oracle, and they both contain key words: "you" (sing. and pl.), "build," and בַּיִת ("house"/"temple"). In the second rhetorical question of the frame, the singular "you" of v. 5 merges into the leaders of Israel ("you," pl.), who thus far have never built a dwelling place for the Lord (v. 7). David, the individual, fades from view and is replaced by a collective human partner, the Israelites. An important word, "build," that we conjecture David considers but does not utter in conversation with Nathan, also appears in both questions. What has been alluded to previously (v. 2) is now made clear, and it is God who leaves no doubt when expressing an opinion on David's plan about building. Just as God now takes the initiative in speaking, God will also take the initiative in building. God contrasts the past with the present by means of the word בית (vv. 5-6): "A house for me to live in" (בית לשבתי) in v. 5 is paralleled by the negative, "I have never lived in a house" (כי לא ישבתי בבית) in v. 6. God has not commanded the construction of the temple to any of Israel's past leaders, nor to David himself.

These two questions call the reader's attention to the material inside the frame: to history, the period between the exodus and the monarchy. The focus of God's interest in the welfare of the nation becomes obvious as Israel is mentioned as many as four times in vv. 6-7: "I have not lived in a house since the day I brought up the people of Israel from Egypt . . . Wherever I have moved about among all the people of Israel, did I ever speak a word with any of the tribal leaders of Israel, whom I commanded to shepherd my people Israel?" (v. 6). A contrast is suggested between David's residing (ישב) in a house of v. 1 and now God's "moving about" (מתהלך) in a tent and a tabernacle in v. 6. The contrast continues in v. 7 as God refers to "moving about" (התהלכתי) among the Israelites. God's existence is really not analogous to that of the well-intentioned David. The king suggested through analogy (v. 2) that God should have what David has, but God rejects the same sort of living quarters as the king. This opposition between the human and divine realms will be carried further in the second layer of the oracle, and the contrast will reach its highest expression in the final layer. In each layer of the oracle one finds an expression of the ideologically significant view that the Lord is not bound to one place but can choose a dwelling anywhere. By means of repetition throughout God's speech, a central concept is emphasized: God's ways contrast with the habits and customs of mortals.

The second layer of the oracle (vv. 8-11a). The second layer of the oracle highlights one family and establishes David as the founder of a dynasty. Throughout this layer God emphasizes leadership by means of chosen individuals (David, the judges). While the divine promise to David has already been mentioned (by David himself in 2 Sam 6:21), the view now emerges in a broader sense. The intimate relationship that God has had with the people, emphasized in the first layer, is concentrated in the blessing of an individual in vv. 8-9. God led the Israelites up from Egypt (v. 6) and then delegated authority to the judges to "shepherd" the people of Israel (v. 7). Now the delegation of authority is transferred to the shepherd David who is "to be prince over [God's] people Israel" (v. 8).

At the beginning of the second layer of the oracle proper, one finds the independent pronoun "I" (אני), which in the Hebrew is unnecessary since the pronominal suffix is attached to the verbal form לקחתיך ("I took you"). This emphasis highlights God's initiative, while the single word לקחתיך suggests an "I-You" relationship: David ("You") is presented as the beneficiary of the Lord's ("I") action. לקחתיך also reinforces the reference to "my servant" that stands at the beginning of the oracle (v. 5). In addition, the phrase "I have been with you" (ואהיה עמך) in v. 9 is reminiscent of the prophet's words to David, "the Lord is with you" (יהוה עמך) in v. 3.

We noted earlier that the narrator does not describe a great deal of action in 2 Samuel 7. However, action is revealed in the words of the characters throughout much of the chapter. This phenomenon of characterization through speech is particularly evident in the second layer of the oracle. Shlomith Rimmon-Kenan discusses the relationship between action and characterization, and concludes that "a trait may be implied both by one-time (or non-routine) actions [or] . . . by contrast, habitual actions [that] tend to reveal the character's unchanging or static aspect" (61). The Lord describes such "habitual actions" and thus reveals an "unchanging or static aspect" of character in this layer of the oracle. The specific guidance and care that David knows firsthand is recounted: "I took you . . . I have been with you" (vv. 8-9). It is the previous experience of God's care both for David and the people Israel that now provides a vision and foundation of hope for the future: "I will make for you a great name . . . I will appoint a place for my people Israel" (vv. 9-10). At the end of v. 10 the Lord appeals "to the very beginning" (בראשונה), a temporal designation that may cause the reader to think of the bondage in Egypt alluded to in the first layer of the oracle (v. 6). Again, the positive acts of God, appointing and planting (v. 10), are given meaning based on the past. This image of Israel, "planted" and secure—like David who is "settled" (ישב) in his house (v. 1)—calls attention to the author's attempt to highlight a difference between God and humans.

In this second layer of the oracle, the portrayal of God is also accomplished by God's words about the people of Israel. In vv. 9c-11b Israel becomes the direct object of God's concern. Promise of "a house" includes "a great name" for David in v. 9 as well as a place for the people of Israel "that they may dwell in their own place, and be disturbed no more" (v. 10). In the introduction (vv. 1-4), no attention was given to the people.

Our thoughts were drawn instead to the aspirations and advice of David and Nathan. In each of the layers of the oracle, on the other hand, God highlights the people of Israel (vv. 6-7, 8, 10-11, 12, 16). God's initiative will ensure that the kingdom provides security and justice for all Israel (v. 10). The "dynasty" (בית) is not an end in itself; it ensures God's proper, just rule of the people.

The third layer of the oracle (vv. 11b-16). We meet once again a combined viewpoint marker embedded within the Lord's own speech that signals a new layer of the oracle. This third speech marker (v. 11b) serves as a type of headline or announcement, which the third layer proper of the oracle (vv. 12-16) develops. The marker is followed by a series of "I" statements that punctuate the final part of the oracle: "I will raise up . . . I will establish his kingdom . . . I will establish the throne . . . I will be a father to him . . . I will punish him . . . I will not take my steadfast love . . . as I took it from Saul, whom I put away" (vv. 12-15). The author emphasizes in this passage that God is the causal agent.

The first combined viewpoint markers (vv. 5a, 8a) each contained two clauses, and once again this third layer of the oracle opens with two parts: "Moreover the Lord declares to you / that the Lord will make you a house." The first two markers each contained an introductory clause that called attention to speech: "go and tell" (אמרת) in v. 5a; "thus you shall say" (תאמר) in v. 8a. Both markers also incorporated a subsequent clause, the traditional prophetic formula, that reinforced the impulse of speech: "Thus says (אמר) the Lord" (vv. 5a, 8a). The third marker (v. 11b) is the first to open with a verbal form, in this case הגיד ("declare"), that accentuates the speech phenomenon. Again, unlike the first two markers, the second clause of v. 11b does not contain the expected "thus says the Lord" formula (found in vv. 5a and 8a). Instead, David learns (v. 17) that the Lord will make him a בית ("dynasty"). God's character is now drawn in this third layer by means of a new theme organized around a familiar word. In effect, David discovers that he will not build a בית ("house") for God; God will build a בית ("dynasty") for him. The Lord's initiative involves a pun on two meanings of the Hebrew word: the former requires building materials (a dwelling); the second requires people (a dynasty). David considers building a בית ("house") for the Lord in v. 2, and now that the Lord vows to build a בית ("dynasty") for David (vv. 11, 16), we are confronted with the main point of attack on David's plan to build a temple: if God requires a בית it will follow God's own plan. The human impulse to build a shrine is transposed to a new key through speech, as David is promised a new kind of בית. It is not a building that matters when it comes to the exercise of God's plan, but a human line that will serve as a conduit of divine care (vv. 12, 15-16).

The Lord does reveal that David's offspring will be allowed to build an edifice, but the building will not be a place of dwelling (ישב)—at least not in the same sense that the king "dwells" (ישב) in his house (v. 1). This בית will eventually be built, God announces, "for my name," and by the person God chooses (v. 13). In the rhetorically charged opening question, the Lord had asked David if he is the one to build the Lord a house to dwell in (v. 5). The change from בית לשבתי ("house to dwell in") in v. 5 to בית לשמי ("house for my name") in v. 13—the initial לש and final י sounds are similar—calls attention to God's uniqueness. This aspect of God's character is reinforced in this final portion of the speech when God indicates that nomadic life presents no real problem. In fact, God can do without the permanent security of residence that David now enjoys (v. 1). The contrast between God and David was suggested in the previous layer of the oracle and applied also to the people of Israel: "I will appoint a place for my people Israel and will plant them, so that they may live in their own place" (v. 10). The circuitous manner by which David expresses himself at the beginning of this story—David's thought is "May I build?" while his spoken words are "I am living in a house of cedar, but the ark of God stays in a tent"—now gains its true rhetorical strength: a nomadic existence (the ark in a tent) presents no problem for God at this moment in history.

Key words are repeated, once again, in the concluding portion of the oracle. God promises that David's בית ("dynasty") and kingdom "shall be made secure forever" (עד עולם) and that his "throne shall be established forever" (עד עולם; v. 16). The temporal phrase is duplicated in the short narrative space of a single verse, and it is the final word of God's speech. The author has attempted throughout to portray God as the one in charge of history: the rest that David now enjoys is the direct result of God's action (v. 1); the Lord speaks to Nathan that very night (v. 4) after David expresses his thoughts to Nathan; God refers to events both past and projected throughout the oracle (vv. 6-15); and, at the end, God emphasizes that David's בית ("dynasty"), kingdom, and throne will be established עד עולם ("forever"). Vv. 15b and 16a end with the same word, לפניך ("from before you"). Again the author uses events of the past to imply that God's words have implications that transcend the present moment. David is reminded that "Saul was previously put away from before you" (לפניך; v. 15b) and is then told: "Your house and your kingdom shall be made sure forever before you" (לפניך; v. 16a).

In retrospect, we discover that God never tells Nathan why David is not allowed to construct the temple. A specific reason will be given in 1 Chr 22:8. According to the Chronicler, it is not David who, with blood-stained hands from many wars, is allowed to build the temple, but the one whose name Šĕlōmōh (שלמה, "Solomon") is a reminder of šālôm (שלום, "peace") who is granted permission to build. Even David in his prayer recorded in vv. 18b-29 does not allude to any reason why he is denied the opportunity to build God's בית ("house"). This lack of specificity also characterizes God. David is not allowed to build solely because of God's desire expressed in the context of 2 Samuel 7. The main issue is that the initiative for building the temple and the choice of that builder shall come from God and not from the individual king. Thus 2 Samuel 7 blends four points of view (the narrator's, Nathan's, God's, and David's) to present the author's view of God transforming human initiative.

WORKS CONSULTED

Bar-Efrat, Shimon
    1989   *Narrative Art in the Bible.* Sheffield: Almond.

Berlin, Adele
    1983   *Poetics and Interpretation of Biblical Narrative.* Sheffield: Almond.

Bussche, Henri
    1948   "Le texte de la prophétie de Nathan sur la dynastie davidique." *ETL* 24:354-94.

Craig, Kenneth
    1993   *A Poetics of Jonah: Art in the Service of Ideology.* Columbia: University of South Carolina Press.

Ewen, Joseph
    1971   "The Theory of Character in Narrative Fiction" (Hebrew). *Hasifrut* 3:1-30 (English abstract, pp. i-ii).
    1980   *Character in Narrative* (Hebrew). Tel Aviv: Sifriyat Po'alim.

Fokkelman, J. P.
    1990   *Narrative Art and Poetry in the Books of Samuel: A Full Interpretation Based on Stylistic and Structural Analyses* (vol. 3). Assen/Maastricht: Van Gorcum.

Gesenius-Kautzsch-Cowley (GKC)
    1982   *Gesenius' Hebrew Grammar.* Ed. E. Kautzsch. Trans. A. E. Cowley. Oxford: Clarendon.

Hertzberg, Hans
    1976   *I & II Samuel: A Commentary.* OTL. Philadelphia: Westminster.

Hurowitz, Victor
  1992   *I Have Built You an Exalted House: Temple Building in the Bible in Light of Mesopotamian and Northwest Semitic Writings.* JSOTSup 115; JSOT/ASOR Monograph Series 5. Sheffield: Sheffield Academic.

Kruse, Heinz
  1985   "David's Covenant." *VT* 35:139-64.

Malamat, Abraham
  1966   "Prophetic Revelations in New Documents from Mari and the Bible." VTSup 15:207-27.
  1980   "A Mari Prophecy and Nathan's Dynastic Oracle." Pp. 68-82 in *Prophecy: Essays Presented to Georg Fohrer on His Sixty-fifth Birthday.* Ed. J. A. Emerton. New York: Walter de Gruyter.

McHale, Brian
  1978   "Free Indirect Discourse: A Survey of Recent Accounts." *Poetics and the Theory of Literature: A Journal for Descriptive Poetics and Theory of Literature* 3:249-87.

Noth, Martin
  1966   "David and Israel in II Samuel VII." Pp. 250-59 in *The Laws in the Pentateuch and Other Studies.* London: SCM.

Ota, Michiko
  1974   "A Note on 2 Sam 7." Pp. 403-7 in *A Light Unto My Path: OT Studies in Honor of J. M. Myers.* Ed. H. N. Bream et al. Gettysburg Theological Studies 4. Philadelphia: Temple University Press.

Pfeiffer, Robert
  1941   *Introduction to the Old Testament.* New York: Harper & Brothers.

Polzin, Robert
  1989   *Samuel and the Deuteronomist: A Literary Study of the Deuteronomic History (1 Samuel).* New York: Harper & Row.

von Rad, Gerhard
  1962   *Old Testament Theology* (vol. 1). Trans. D. M. G. Stalker. New York: Harper & Row.

Rimmon-Kenan, Shlomith
  1983   *Narrative Fiction: Contemporary Poetics.* London and New York: Methuen.

Savran, George
  1988   *Telling and Retelling: Quotation in Biblical Narrative.* Bloomington: Indiana University Press.

Simon, Marcel
  1952   "La prophétie de Nathan et le Temple: Remarques sur II Sam. 7." *RHPR* 32:41-58.

Sternberg, Meir
  1982   "Point of View and the Indirections of Direct Speech." *Language and Style* 15:67-117.

1985   *The Poetics of Biblical Narrative: Ideological Literature and the Drama of Reading*. Bloomington: Indiana University Press.

Tsevat, Matitiahu
1963   "What was David Promised in II Sam. 7:11b-16?" *HUCA* 34:71-82.
1965   "The House of David in Nathan's Prophecy." *Bib* 46:353-56.

Weiss, Meir
1963   "Einiges über die Bauformen des Erzählens in der Bibel." *VT* 13:456-75.

"GOD'S VOICE YOU HAVE NEVER HEARD, GOD'S FORM YOU HAVE NEVER SEEN": THE CHARACTERIZATION OF GOD IN THE GOSPEL OF JOHN[*]

Marianne Meye Thompson
Fuller Theological Seminary

ABSTRACT

The purpose of this essay is to apply some of the insights that have been gained from studies of characterization in biblical narrative to the characterization of God in the Fourth Gospel. These studies have suggested that we must not underestimate the degree of sophistication with which characters are portrayed in ancient narrative. They are not always static functionaries, types, or representative figures, but are often portrayed as developing throughout the course of the narrative. The emphasis on the reader's construction of character through the sequential reading of the narrative fits well with this view. Robert Alter's scale of characterization is used to analyze the presentation of God in the Fourth Gospel. Although many of the textual indicators of (human) character are present for God in the Gospel, others are missing. Both the presence and absence of various indicators contributes to the characterization of God.

Almost twenty years ago, in a programmatic essay entitled "The Neglected Factor in New Testament Theology," Nils A. Dahl asserted that New Testament scholars had "neglected detailed and comprehensive investigation of statements about God" (154). While studies of ecclesiology, eschatology, and especially christology are abundant, there are fewer investigations that take God as their focus. Dahl was speaking quite broadly of the field of New Testament scholarship. Ten years later, in a study with a different method and narrower focus, R. Alan Culpepper reiterated Dahl's point with respect to the Gospel of John, noting that "insufficient attention has been given to the theo-logy of the gospel per se" (113). Since the publication of Dahl's essay, a number of studies have begun to fill the gap to which Dahl called attention (see Barrett, on John; Donahue, on Mark; Beker, on Paul; and Wright, the first of a projected five-volume work on "Christian Origins and the Question of God"). And

---

[*] This essay was written during a sabbatical funded in part by the Evangelical Scholarship Initiative of the Pew Charitable Trusts, whose support I am happy to acknowledge.

since Culpepper's seminal literary study, there have been monographs and articles treating both the Bible as a whole and the Gospels, including the Fourth Gospel, in literary perspective. Among the literary studies of the Fourth Gospel some have included accounts of Johannine characterization (see du Rand; Staley; Stibbe; Davies). But none has focused on the characterization of God, although Culpepper includes a brief and suggestive sketch of the characterization of God in the Gospel of John. Perhaps the curious silence of scholars on the characterization of God is not accidental. As Culpepper notes, "It is difficult to describe the characterization of God in the gospel because God never appears and the only words He speaks are 'and I have glorified it, and I will glorify it again' (12:28)" (113). As we read in the gospel itself, "His voice you have never heard, his form you have never seen" (5:37, RSV, here and below). Is it even possible to speak of the characterization of God in the Fourth Gospel?

I believe that it is possible, and in this essay I hope to note some of the basic issues in considering "character" in narrative; to suggest how the general discussion of character affects characterization of God; and to offer a preliminary sketch of the characterization of God in the Fourth Gospel—a triplex purpose that also provides the outline for the paper. We begin, then, with an overview of the question of definition and portrayal of "character" in biblical narrative as a way of introducing the particular difficulties that arise in discussing the characterization of God.

Characterizing Characters

In the past, most definitions of "character" and "characterization" offered by literary theorists and the biblical scholars who have adopted their methods have been derived from analysis of works of fiction. An influential approach to characterization has been E. M. Forster's typology of "round" and "flat" characters (Culpepper:103-4; Bar-Efrat:90-92). Although some critics have used it profitably as a heuristic tool for analyzing character, others have offered various criticisms of the usefulness of Forster's categories in reading biblical (i.e., Hebrew Bible) or gospel narratives (Berlin: 23-24; Staley: 56-57; Stibbe: 25). Accordingly, studies of biblical narrative have tried to offer a course correction by exploring the distinctive features of biblical narrative and of characterization in it.

At least three features of characterization in recent discussions of biblical narrative are worth highlighting. First, some scholars have taken exception not so much to the actual designations "round" and "flat" as to the apparently reigning assumption that biblical characters are generally "flat" or "static," that they are generally "types," lacking development, individuality, or depth of personality (Alter: 117; Bar-Efrat: 90-92; Berlin: 23-24, 37-38; Sternberg: 326). By contrast to other forms of ancient narrative, biblical characters do not illustrate an ethical ideal or virtue, although they may be held up as models for certain exemplary behaviors. As often as not, however, they are presented "warts and all." It is inadequate to speak of biblical characters exclusively in terms of the role of the character (e.g. hero, villain, victim) or of the type of character (round, flat). Adele Berlin, for example, suggests a typology of characterization that speaks not of "kinds of characters" but of "degrees of characterization" (32).[1] Some characters may indeed be little more than plot functionaries or types, but others are full-fledged characters, about whom we know more than is necessary for the plot.

A second and closely related movement is the emphasis in studies of biblical narrative on the *development* of the character. In a suggestive essay (now four decades old) Erich Auerbach argued that characters in Hebrew narrative are distinguished from those in the Homeric writings because they are "much more fully developed," by which he meant they are presented as developing or having developed, in contrast to the characters of the *Iliad* and *Odyssey* who, while "splendidly described in many well-ordered words," nevertheless "have no development" (14). This insight was echoed by Scholes and Kellogg when they wrote, "The heroes of the Old Testament were in a process of becoming, whereas the heroes of Greek narrative were in a state of being" (1966:169; quoted in Culpepper: 103).[2] Or, in Berlin's categories, there are full-fledged characters, not just agents and types, in biblical narrative.

Third, the recognition that biblical narrative employs dynamic modes of characterization renders "hermeneutically insignificant" the debate over whether it is plot or character that has primacy (Darr: 39). Narrative criticism of the gospels has, to a large extent, concentrated its attention on plot. But literary theorists today accord more significance to characterization, as both theoretical discussion and treatments of the gospel demonstrate (Moore: 15, 39; Darr: 39; Bar-Efrat: 77).

In keeping with such insights, literary critics of biblical narrative prefer to speak of character not as though it were a fixed commodity simply

---

[1] She identifies these as the agent (function of the plot or part of the setting), the type (stereotyped traits), and the character (about whom we know more than is necessary for the plot). Compare also the schema of characterization (protagonists or central characters; intermediate characters, including ficelles or typical characters; and background characters) offered by Culpepper:103-4.

[2] Alter (115) attributes the mode of biblical characterization to the biblical view of humankind: although human beings are created in God's likeness, that likeness is never "an accomplished ethical fact." Rather the human person is "abandoned to his own unfathomable freedom." Hence, biblical narrative necessarily portrays human beings as agents who choose and who rise or fall because of their choices.

to be unearthed from the raw materials of the text, but rather as the result of the reading of the text. Rather than mining the text for the specific virtues and traits possessed by a particular character, they mine the text for its rhetorical and literary strategies in presenting characters. Thus the emphasis falls not so much on *what* a character is (e.g. honest, virtuous, brave, pious, etc.), but on *how* that character is constructed by the reader (i.e. through actions, speech, description, etc.) and *how* these elements of characterization are progressively coordinated by the reader (Alter: 116-17; Moore: 15; Berlin: 38). John Darr weaves together the threads of this approach in the following statement:

> A pragmatic approach to characterization requires that we be especially sensitive to the narrative's sequence. The goal is not to arrive at a static conception of a character (for example, the author's mental image of that persona), but rather, to follow the reader's *successive* construction and assessment of that character while reading the text. Like all narrative elements, *character is cumulative* (42).

(Similar definitions can be found in McKnight: 263, 285; Burnett: 125; Martin: 118-19.)

This definition of character and emphasis on the process of reading has two results: (1) It emphasizes the *moment-by-moment* or *sequential reading* of the narrative, since readers meet a character successively, gradually, through various episodes of the plot. For some, but not all, literary critics this reader is conjectured to be the "first-time reader," who knows a character only through the reading of the text. (2) "Characters" are strictly *literary phenomena*, either "bound" to the texts in which they appear or, even more precisely, the effect of the process of reading the text. The character is not "in" the text or even "in" the formal elements of the text but is constructed as the reader reads the text.

Although not all critics adopt the conjectured "first-time" reader as a useful construct in reading a text, some do.[3] This hypothetical, untutored reader comes to the text for the first time and reads it quite naturally from beginning to end, guided only or primarily by the formal elements of the text (rather than by factors deemed extrinsic to the text) in constructing character. The first-time reader is a construct of the critic, as the critic readily acknowledges. But we may still ask whether the construct of the "first-time reader" does justice either to the way readers actually read or to the gospels themselves.

---

[3] There is a discussion, with examples, of the various understandings of "the reader," including "the first-time reader," in Moore:17-24, 72, 78, 111-12. It should be noted that Darr himself, although he emphasizes a sequential reading of the text, does not work with the construct of the first-time reader. Moreover, he tends to give interpretive priority to the extratextual repertoire of the original reader.

"Actual readers" of the gospels may well have access to the characters in the narrative in other ways, whether through oral or written tradition, and these other "narratives" surely influence the way they read. The construct of the "first-time reader" too quickly brushes aside the "extratextual repertoire" that a reader brings to the text. Stephen Moore comments, "The tradition-attuned hearers/readers that the gospel texts presuppose surely know more than the reader-oriented exegetes . . . give them credit for. If so, then the virgin reader is an anachronistic construct for gospel research" (95). Literary criticism that pays significant attention to the historical, social, and religious context of the reader is better suited to critical readings of the Gospels, for it takes the original audience seriously (Darr: 25). Here, of course, it should be kept in mind that the original and contemporary readers of the Gospels bring different "extratextual repertoires" to the text, and it is no easy matter to say what is in the reader's experience.

One may further question whether the strictly sequential or moment-by-moment reading of the text does justice to a gospel. Adele Reinhartz contends that it does not, since a gospel is not like a mystery novel, which loses its real power after the first reading. Rather, a gospel is intended to be read—and reread. Reinhartz is not referring to the didactic or theological value of the gospel but rather to its rhetoric: "Almost in every case the reader is given information at the end of the gospel which prompts a reevaluation of the entire gospel." Thus both a sequential reading (in the order of the text) and a holistic reading (the gospel taken as a whole) are important in "building character" (12). The more that we assume that the reader of the gospel is a "re-reader," then the less the emphasis falls on a sequential reading, for the reader always rereads with the whole of the text in view.[4]

To what extent, then, is the character a "literary phenomenon"? "Should characters be treated like autonomous individuals or as strictly literary phenomena? Are the figures we come to know in a narrative world persons or words? Do they transcend the text or are they entirely constrained by it?" (Darr: 46; cf. Bar-Efrat: 48). Darr concludes, "Although our ways of knowing real people invariably inform constructions of literary character, the narrative context itself remains the primary limiting and shaping framework. As Forster put it, characters are 'bound in a hundred ways to their literary context'" (46; cf. McKnight: 263). Shimon Bar-Efrat (48) notes that even in discussing ostensibly historical personages, "we

---

[4] See the approach of Robert Tannehill, who writes that his reading of Luke-Acts "represents part of what might be said after a second, third, or fourth time. It is not confined to what is happening when reading for the first time, with much of the text still unknown" (6).

know them *only* as they are presented in the narratives, and it is to this alone that we can refer" (emphasis added; Martin: 116-18). And as Berlin summarizes, "The reader is shown only what the author wishes to show. Never can the reader step behind the story to know a character other than in the way the narrative presents him" (43).

These views exhibit a movement away from both a representational or imitative view of character, in which characters are understood to mimic or correspond to people "in real life," and historical-critical approaches whose primary task is to reconstruct the historical individual or facts about him or her behind or through literary characterization. Instead, literary theories of character stress the rhetorical, literary, and narrative elements of the text and the ways in which readers read in order to give due credit to the actual form of the text and its power to engage the reader.

Yet as valuable as such correctives are, it is difficult in practice to stay within the bounds of such a theoretical construct. The ways in which literary critics of biblical narrative discuss characters suggest that it is not so easy to speak of characterization along strictly literary lines. The language that is used to describe characterization often belongs more to the realm of psychology or human development than it does to literary theory. Consider the language of "development." Can a "character" develop? *Characterization* can be developed, or a character can *be portrayed* as developing, but "development" belongs to persons. Thus when Bar-Efrat (90) writes "How great is the difference between the young Jacob who steals the blessing intended for Esau his brother, and the Jacob, who, after twenty years of suffering in exile, begs his brother to accept his 'blessing,'" we have an application of terms of human development to a literary figure. More precisely, there is a difference *in the ways in which Jacob is characterized*, and so one has the impression of "development" in the character. But the impression of "development" is the effect of reading the story.

Or, again, take the following statement: "Since one's inner nature is embodied in external behaviour a narrator can present the characters in action rather than spelling out their traits. In biblical narrative deeds do in fact serve as the foremost means of characterization, and we know biblical characters primarily through the way they act in varying situations" (Bar-Efrat: 77). To speak of the "inner nature" of a character does suggest a preconceived persona whom the author commits to writing, as it were, rather than character as the cumulative effect of the reader's reading the text. Even when the critic accentuates the formal methods of characterization and reading, it is difficult to avoid language that smacks much more of the realm of psychology or personality theory. Berlin writes, "The purpose of character description in the Bible is not to enable the reader to visualize the character, but to enable him to situate the character in terms of his place in society, his own particular situation, and his outstanding traits—in other words, to tell *what kind of a person he is*" (36; emphasis added). Robert Alter (116-17) offers a way of analyzing characterization that begins with information conveyed about the "motives, attitudes, the moral nature of characters." He continues up the scale to strategies in characterization that leave less room for inference: "With the report of inward speech," Alter writes, "we enter the realm of relative certainty about character: there is certainty, in any case, about the character's conscious intentions, though we may still feel free to question the motive beyond the intention."

The language of person, personality, inner or moral nature, intention, motives, and attitudes suggests how greatly our ways of knowing real people inform constructions of literary character, and how much we value development, the importance of motive and intention, and "inward being." One is tempted to say that the premium placed on these items in characterization strikes one as more Western and modern than ancient. But the point is that even those critics with formalist sensitivities cannot escape description of characters in terms that sound much more like a psychological analysis than a literary appraisal.

Not that this is necessarily inappropriate. For as Darr puts it, although characters are not "real people" they are still "persons" (47). But precisely for this reason, a reading that supposes that characters are "bound" to their texts will give us only a partial description of the way that the reader actually reads the text, since readers will bring to their reading all the conceptions that have to do with the ways we know real people, including emotional and imaginative responses. The character is always greater than the sum of his or her literary parts.[5] As Wallace Martin comments,

---

[5] There is a fascinating example of characterization in a review of a book about Shylock of Shakespeare's *The Merchant of Venice* that appeared recently in *The Atlantic* (June, 1993). The author of the review, John Simon, in comparing Iago (of *Othello*) and Shylock writes: "Iago preoccupies our minds because his malignity seems to be, if not exactly motiveless, vastly disproportionate to any offense incurred. Shylock, on the other hand, is now thought to have many plausible reasons for acting as he does. . . . With Iago, the problem is to find the motivation; with Shylock, to disentangle the true cause from an embarrassment of riches" (p. 128). John Gross, the author of the book *Shylock: A Legend and Its Legacy* (New York: Simon & Schuster, 1992), labels Shylock "a big character . . . someone who bursts the bounds of the play in which he appears" (cited by Simon, p. 133). In a recent interview the Chilean novelist Isabel Allende commented that her uncle "convinced her that the characters in his books escaped their pages and roamed the house at night" (*Los Angeles Times*, Monday, May 31, 1993). Note also Dorothy Sayer's puckish description of her "meeting" with Lord Peter Wimsey. "I do not, as a matter of fact, remember inventing Lord Peter at all. My impression is that I was thinking about writing a detective story, and that he walked in, complete with spats, and applied . . . for the job of hero. . . . At the first interview

"The ultimate reference of fact and fiction is our experience, and it is entirely consistent with experience to say that I understand Huck Finn more or less well than I understand my next door neighbor. Our sense that fictional characters are uncannily similar to people is therefore not something to be dismissed or ridiculed but a crucial feature of narration that requires explanation" (120).

It is impossible and unnecessary, then, to escape the view that characters are representational, in one respect or another, of "real people." Nevertheless, we can be profitably directed by the formalist cautions that the text itself is the primary shaping framework for understanding character. After all, we are usually interested in a character in a particular text, since most characters are to be found within a particular narrative. If we want to know about the character of Nicodemus or Peter in the Gospel of John we obviously have to read the Gospel of John. But when the character in question appears in more than one narrative (for example, a hero who reappears in a series of novels), it is harder to limit oneself to the framework of a single narrative in "building character," since "all narratives which are known to the reader are significant in the production of meaning for that reader" (McKnight: 276).

And who is this "reader"? In the end, every reader is a mirror of the person who construes the reader (Darr: 170). So perhaps the reader is not merely a critic's construct, but the critic. I am the reader. Not all readers bring to the text what I bring to it. But we are all reading the same "text," if by text we mean the actual words on the page. Thus I do not suppose that the reader brings "all the meaning" to the text nor that all the meaning is in the text. Rather, meaning is produced by the interaction of the reader and the text, both of which are shaped by their cultural location. And the text itself is the result of an author's intention to communicate. Insofar as that intention is "embodied" or "objectified" in the text we may speak of the author's intention.[6] A full-blown description of the characterization of God in any gospel would require a full-length study of all those factors noted above (author, text, reader, and cultural location). This essay

---

Wimsey informed me that he had a rather attractive mother. Later on, I gathered more details about his personal tastes and habits. I also discovered that he was two years older than myself" (quoted in *Dorothy L. Sayers*, by James Brabazon [New York: Avon Books, 1981], p. 120). Of course in this last statement Sayers is indulging in her own fantasies a bit, but one still wonders whether what the authors of fiction think about their characters differs rather markedly from what critics tell us they are.

[6] The phrases "embodied" and "objectified intention" are from Sternberg (9), by which he means "the author's intention to communicate using certain linguistic and structural tools to produce desired effects on the addressee." As Moore (12) notes, it is a small step to take from speaking of a text that produces specifiable effects to speaking of the author who intended such effects. An example of a study that successfully coordinates historical and literary criticism is Stibbe's *John as Storyteller*.

is simply a preliminary sketch of some of the factors one might consider in discussing the character of God. But before turning to the narrative itself, I would like to suggest why and how the characterization of God differs from that of other characters.

Characterizing God

There are at least three distinct challenges posed by consideration of the characterization of God (discussed by Sternberg, 322-41, who in his fine study emphasizes the differences in the portrayal of God and other characters). First, if it is difficult to apply the stricture that a reader can never "step behind the story to know a character other than the way the narrative presents him" (Berlin: 43), it is especially difficult in narratives in which God figures as a character, for two reasons. One is that few readers come to a narrative in which God figures without preconceptions of what "god" signifies or who "God" is. And inevitably these preconceptions will be brought to bear in reading the text. Berlin's healthy caution about "stepping behind" the story needs to be tempered in speaking of God because not only are there many other written narratives about God, but knowledge of God is not understood to be limited to what texts have to say. One might argue that Nicodemus or the Samaritan woman or Lazarus or Mary are accessible to us only through the narrative itself. But those readers reading biblical narrative, or for that matter any narrative in which God figures, may well believe that there is "access" to God through prayer, meditation, philosophical and theological speculation. As they read the narrative they bring to bear knowledge they understand themselves to have gained in other ways. In fact it is hard to imagine readers agreeing with the statement that they "cannot step behind the story to know a character other than the way the narrative presents him."

Second, it is difficult to speak of the characterization of God because many of those things that generally combine in producing a character, such as appearance, speech and words, actions (particularly those explicable by a cause-and-effect frame within the temporal world), origin, parentage, descent, and geographical and social location, are unavailable in speaking of the biblical God (a point made by Sternberg: 323). Indeed, the very absence of these is already part of the characterization of God in biblical (including gospel) narrative, and yet to the extent that characterization depends on these, their absence obviously creates difficulties.

Third, as noted above, recent literary studies have suggested that biblical characters are individuals, not types; that, consequently, human character as portrayed in the Bible tends to variability; and that "development" is a chief feature of biblical characterization. But, as Meir

Sternberg comments, the character of God tends to "constancy" (324). This is not a theological point about the immutability of God in narrative guise. Rather, Sternberg's point is that the same characteristics tend to be ascribed to God in different narratives across broad periods of time (325). On the whole, writers use few angular strokes in painting God's portrait. Although we can speak of the particular features emphasized in one narrative or another, there is likely to be as much continuity between these documents as there is contrast or difference.

Sternberg also comments that the constancy in God's character tends to make God "more transparent" relative to the human cast of characters (324). One or two scenes tell us more about God than a few scenes would tell us about a human character. This is related to a further point: that biblical narrative seldom employs the correction of first impressions in order to illuminate the character of God. What is said about God, when the comment is not insincere or understood to be false via signals in the text (spoken by a false prophet, for example), is understood as reliable and authoritative. God's portrait is seldom redrawn.

Indeed, it is hard to imagine a biblical narrative that does not portray God in accordance with one of the most basic convictions about God, namely, the reliability or faithfulness of God. If human beings change and develop, God does not. Perhaps there is a difficulty here with the multiple meanings of "character." For when we speak of "the character of God" usually we mean something closer to the very nature or essence of God. We are trying to answer the question "What is God like?" or "Who is God?" But for the purpose of this paper we are trying to consider God as a literary figure, and in that sense a "character," within the Fourth Gospel. One might believe in the unchangeable nature or "character" of God and still argue for an active construal of "character" through the process of reading. As Sternberg notes, even the most static characters are revealed by a dynamic process (346). But given the ideological conviction of God's reliability or constancy that many of the Bible's readers bring to the reading process, the question of the characterization of God is not so much whether the character "lives" beyond the page, but whether in fact the narrator can make God "live" for the reader.

Paradoxically, while God—of all the characters in a gospel—is the least circumscribed for the reader by the text itself (since many other avenues to knowing God and narratives about God exist for the reader), the reader's conception of God is also the most textually bound. For precisely because there is so much to be said and known and thought about God, and because the narrative chooses to say some things but not all, the narrative's directives assume greater significance in building the character of God. The reader is always held in tension between the objective constraints of the text and the constraints of the knowledge, imagination, cultural location, religious convictions, and spirituality by which her or his reading of God is informed.

On the one hand, the formalist critic does justice to the guiding role of the text in the construal of character, particularly of the character of God. On the other hand, the critic who tends to speak of character as imitative of "real people" is faced with an entirely different sort of problem in the characterization of God, at least in terms of biblical narrative, for God is not a "real person." Ancient Greek authors, for example, accounted for the movements of their gods, and moved them across the stage of the narrative in ways substantially similar to their descriptions of human beings. Biblical authors, on the other hand, generally cannot or do not account for God's movements nor, often, for God's intentions or motives (Auerbach: 3, 7-9; Crites: 40; Sternberg: 323-25). God is often described as much by contrast to human beings as by analogy with them. Still, as Stephen Crites notes, "Even if it is a god or an angel who appears as a character in a story he can appear only in the form of a person. To be drawn into a story is to be personified, someone who can be addressed, who remembers and responds, who is underway in action" (26). In theological terms, this is the problem of anthropomorphism (see Caird: 172-182, who ably links the theological and literary problems).

It is important, then, to conceive of our task specifically as "the characterization of God in the Gospel of John," and by "characterization" to imagine primarily a literary exercise that must be addressed by a literary critical method (Darr: 12). But since the theory for assessing and constructing character in narrative takes as its norm human characters who, in some respect or another, are like "real people," one wonders whether the best we ever do is to offer a characterization of God in terms that we usually use to characterize human beings. So what conclusions do we draw when many of the textual indicators of character that we have for human characters are simply lacking for God? If God is not dramatized as speaking or active in the narrative, does the reader think of God as distant and aloof? Or does the reader respond with a knowing nod: of course God does not appear on the scene of human history in quite that way. Ambiguity is inevitable in portraying God as a human character. Even to recognize this factor, however, contributes substantially to the characterization of God in the Fourth Gospel, to which we now turn in more detail.

CHARACTERIZING GOD IN THE GOSPEL OF JOHN

To examine the characterization of God in the Gospel of John, I would like to use Robert Alter's scale of characterization. In increasing order of explicitness, the scale is as follows: the actions of a character; his/her appearance, gestures, posture, or costume; comments by another character; direct speech by the character; inward speech, whether summarized or quoted; and finally statements by the narrator (116-17; Berlin: 37-38, 46; Darr: 44-45). This scale of characterization moves from the portrayal of a character from the outside, from the viewpoint of others, to the representation of the same character from the inside, from the character's own point of view. As we move from actions and appearance to speech and thought, we move from the way the world views a character to the way the character views the world. To what extent the reader will be allowed to view the world from God's perspective remains to be seen.

It has already been suggested that certain indicators of the character of God are missing from biblical narrative. Edgar McKnight goes so far as to say that God does not figure in the NT as a character in the stories. Although implied, God is neither named nor present as a character in his own right (304-305). Yet even though God never appears in the narrative, God is a character in the Gospel, for his actions are implied and necessary to the narrative. In Thomas Docherty's phrase, God may be called a "kinetic character," that is, one who is able to be absent to the text, whose motivation extends beyond what is necessary for the accomplishment of the plot, and who moves in other spheres than the one we are engaged in reading (cited in Martin: 224). Indeed, this is part of the characterization of God in the Gospel. For as Jesus reproves his audience: "God's form you have never seen; God's voice you have never heard." Their lack of knowledge virtually parallels the absence of God from the narrative. According to the Gospel, their only access to God is through Jesus, the incarnate Word of God, who speaks so that God is heard, and in whom they see the Father. God is known primarily through the agency of Jesus. And the reader encounters God in the pages of the Gospel only as mediated by the character of Jesus.

However, it is important to remember that the Gospel does not confuse or conflate Father and Son. As Culpepper notes,

> God is characterized not by what He says or does but by what Jesus, His fully authorized emissary, says about Him. Even to describe the situation in these terms, however, is to risk distortion. It might be better, therefore, to say that God is characterized by Jesus and that having understood the gospel's characterization of Jesus one has grasped its characterization of God (113).

Note that the point is not so much that Jesus tells us *about* God, so that we have an instance of one character describing another, but rather, it is the words and deeds of Jesus that serve as a characterization of God.

If God's words and actions are missing from John, another striking missing textual indicator in John is the name of God. Darr follows

Docherty in labeling a name a "gap" that prompts the reader to fill "with significance the empty space in the name as it occurs in the fictional world" (45; on the significance of naming, see Burnett: 125; Berlin: 59.). But "God" is not a name. In fact the Johannine God has no name. Even though the Gospel several times says that God has given his name to Jesus, we are never told what that name is.[7] God's name is to be found, apparently, only through Jesus. But while God may be nameless, "God" is not void of meaning for the reader. We might say that whereas the denotative meaning of "god" allows the reader entry into the narrative, the connotative meaning is provided largely by the associations of the term "god" with Jesus and other human beings (Caird: 45). In particular, terms of familial relationship are important in John, as they often are in biblical narrative (Berlin: 59). The most significant designation of God is "Father." Clearly the characterization of God in the Fourth Gospel will entail discovering who this "Father" is, and of whom he is "father." We turn therefore to an examination of the indicators of the characterization of God in the Fourth Gospel.

The Actions of God

The actions attributed to God in the Gospel are either implied or assumed, or else understood indirectly through the actions of Jesus. The actions that are "assumed" actually fall under the category of comments by another character (usually Jesus) or comments by the narrator. For example, the statements "all things were made through [the Word]" (1: 3) and "the law was given through Moses; grace and truth came through Jesus Christ" (1:17) are statements by the narrator that imply God's actions. The narrator also implies that God sent John (1:6) and that God begets (or gives birth to) the children of God (1:12-13); and states explicitly that God loved the world (3:16); and gave or sent the Son (3:16,34); gives the Spirit (3:34); and loves the Son, and gave all things into his hand (3:35). The narrator also speaks of the wrath of God that rests on unbelievers (3:36).

Otherwise, the actions of God are made known to the reader by the words of Jesus. One finds the following statements: The Father seeks true worshippers (4:23); works (5:17, 19-20); loves the son (5:20; 10:17; 15:9;

---

[7] The oldest known prohibition against uttering the name of God (the Tetragrammaton) when reading the Jewish Scriptures is apparently found in 1QS 6:27-7:2. Josephus (*Ant.* 2.12.4 §276) refers to "the name that we are forbidden to speak"; cf. *J.W.* 5.10.3 §438, "the hair-raising name." As Hengel notes, the Jews made a virtue out of necessity by arguing that not only was one forbidden to speak the name of God, but that the true God was "nameless" (I.266). In 4 Bar 5:35, God's name cannot be known. Cf. Apuleius, *On the Teaching of Plato* 1.5: "God is unnameable."

17:23, 26); shows the Son what he is doing (5:20); raises the dead and gives life (5:21); gives authority to the Son to have life (5:26) and execute judgment (5:27); gives his works to the Son (5:36); sent the Son (5:37, 38; 6:29, 39, 57; 8:16, 18, 26; 11:42); testifies to Jesus (5:37; 8:18); set his seal on the Son of man (6:27); gives true bread from heaven (6:32); gives "all" to the Son (6:37; 13:3; 17:2, 7); "draws" people to him and teaches them (6:44-45, 65); judges (8:16); instructs Jesus (8:28); is with Jesus (8:29); seeks Jesus' glory (8:50, 54); knows the Son (10:15); consecrated the Son (10:36); hears the Son (11:41); honors those who serve Jesus (12:26); glorifies his name (12:28); will come and "make his home" with believers (14:23); will send the Holy Spirit (14:26); prunes the vine (15:2); loves the disciples (16:27; 17:23); glorifies Jesus (17:1, 24); "keeps" what has been given to the Son (17:11, 15); sanctifies believers in the truth (17:17).

Although God's activity is rather fully described, nowhere are God's actions dramatized so that the reader may draw his or her own inferences from them. There is more "telling" about the actions of God than there is "showing" what God does. As a result, the character of God remains only indirectly accessible to the reader, and accessible only through the words of Jesus or, less often, the narrator. However, most of the statements about God are sentences with active verbs, rather than predications of virtues ("God is good") or essence ("God is omnipotent"). Although some of the verbs refer to past action and some to future, many refer to present action, and almost all the verbs have Jesus as the object (loves, knows, sends, gives) or agent of the action, or the believer as the object (keeps, sanctifies, loves).

But the actions and words of Jesus are in some sense also a characterization of God. Following Sternberg's lead that, because of the constancy of God, God can be rather fully characterized by a shorter narrative or shorter units of narrative than is the case with human beings, I would like to look at a few episodes in the Gospel to see what characterization of God emerges.

In the story of the changing of the water to wine (2:1-11), for example, God is not mentioned. But because this story follows directly upon the promise of the opened heavens (1:51), a metaphor for divine revelation, the episode may be read as an instance of such revelation. Jesus' act "revealed his glory" (2:11). And it is a "full" glory (1:14, 16), for the provision of wine far surpasses the need. As one writer notes, "What is striking in this story is the utterly gratuitous nature of this deed. . . . It is precisely this gratuitous generosity that is the glory revealed in this sign" (Whitacre: 109). It is possible that the reader is reminded that the coming age of deliverance would be an age of abundant physical and spiritual blessings, including the abundance of both the harvest and the revelation of the glory of the Lord (e.g. Isa 66:11).

There is similar extravagant provision in the feeding of 5000, where twelve baskets of bread are left over. The opening lines of chapter 6 are reminiscent of the story of the wedding feast in chapter 2. There are crowds gathered, and there is a lack. Jesus prays; then distributes the loaves to the people. Through his action, the need is met. In fact the need is more than met. Twelve baskets of bread are left over, an extravagant provision indeed, which comes in answer to Jesus' own prayer. The narrative and discourse of chapter 6 call to mind themes of the first Passover and the Exodus from Egypt, where manna was given in response to Moses' intercession on behalf of the people, so that they might not starve in the wilderness. The same God who sustained the children of Israel now provides "true bread from heaven" (6:32), the bread that brings life. And the generous provision may well call to mind the promise of the return of manna from on high in the messianic age (on Exodus motifs behind chapter 6, see Gärtner and Borgen; on the return of the treasury of manna in the end times, see Gärtner: 14-20; Brown: 1:265; and Guilding: 61-68).

The narrative of the healing of the man at the pool of Bethesda begins with a conversation between Jesus and the man. Like many Johannine dialogues, the conversation moves by question and counter-question. When asked by Jesus, "Do you want to be healed?" the man nevertheless seems to find plausible reasons why he cannot be healed (Staley: 59). Jesus overcomes his objection, gives the command to walk, and then vanishes, which leads to the questioning of the man, "Who did it?" The question is double-edged: the man must find out who Jesus is, but for the reader there is the deeper possibility that God did it (5:17, 20-21, 25-26). Even so, one could not put a name to God, as one could to Jesus. To name the one who did it, one would have to say "Jesus"—which implies, nevertheless, that God did it.[8]

It matters "who did it" because it was done on the Sabbath day. "The Jews" are interested in the one who gave the command for the man to carry his bed and so violate the Sabbath; the reader and the man as a character in the story are apparently more interested in affairs from the healed man's point of view. Those who know Jesus as the one who gave the command to break the Sabbath law know God as the giver of Sabbath law; those who know Jesus as healer know God as healing and life-

---

[8] Stibbe (111) suggests that in John 18-19, Jesus is known as Judge, King, and "elusive God." Although Stibbe does not develop the latter suggestion very much, one wonders whether the "elusive God" best characterizes Jesus or the Father.

giving.⁹ Typical of John, this action will be explained in a long monologue by Jesus, who explains that as his Father continues to work, so too the Son must continue to work (5:17)—even on the Sabbath. For "as the Father has life in himself, so he has granted the Son also to have life in himself" (5:26). As this statement (and other historical sources) attest, the prerogative of bestowing life was understood to be God's.¹⁰ The discourse of chapter 5 also speaks of Jesus' power to judge, which is simply another way of speaking of his power to grant eternal life (5:22, 27-29, 30), as the following statement makes clear: "he who hears my word and believes him who sent me, has eternal life; he does not come into judgment, but has passed from death to life" (5:24).

At the outset of chapter 8, Jesus tells the crowds, "I am the light of the world. Those who follow me shall not walk in darkness, but will have the light of life" (v. 12). The Pharisees object to Jesus' claims (8:13). He tells "them" (unclear referent) that they will die in their sin (8:21) and that they "cannot follow him." Both of these statements stand opposed to statements in the first chapter: Jesus is the "Lamb of God who takes away the sin of the world," and his invitation to would-be disciples is "follow me." Jesus speaks of "truth" that will "set them free" (8:26, 32, 34, 40, 45), but they deny that he speaks the truth and that they are in bondage. They claim God as father, but Jesus retorts, "If God were your father, you would love me, for I proceeded and came forth from God; I came not of my own accord, but he sent me" (8:42). They are doing the work of their father (vv. 41, 44), which is to ignore the words of God (v. 47); they "do

---

⁹ In the short episode of the healing of the official's son (4:46-54) there is again an objection raised to Jesus' action, but this time it comes from Jesus himself. But if Jesus raises the objection, he also overcomes it, and promises (or foresees?) healing. Moreover, this brief episode is marked by the repetition of the phrase "your son will live" (4:50, 51, 53). Although God is not mentioned, it is suggestive that the short narrative in 4:46-53 features a father and his son and, by its very brevity and repetition of the phrase, "your son will live," emphasizes the father/son relationship and the promise of life. Is the reader led to ponder the relationship of father and son?

¹⁰ The debate and monologue in chapter 5 may reflect similar discussions of the "two powers of God" (sometimes the two "attributes" or "measures" of God), usually deemed to be the power of mercy and the power of justice. See Segal:39, 159, 170-217. Wolfson (II.135) calls attention to the fact that there are a variety of schemas by which Philo tries to enumerate the powers of God, sometimes counting four (creative, regal, propitious, and legislative), sometimes two (i.e. merciful and authoritative, *Cherub.* 9 §§27-28; *Sacr.* 15 §59; or beneficent and kingly, *Abr.* 25 §§124-125; *Quaes. in Exod.* 2.68). Philo assigns the creative power (identified with goodness) to the term *theos*, and the royal or authoritative power to *kyrios*. In the end it is the peculiar property of God to act with goodness as well as authority, with graciousness as well as punishment. The Rabbis similarly discussed "the two powers of God" as the powers of justice and mercy, but assigned mercy to God as *kyrios* (Yahweh) and justice to *theos* (Elohim). There is a stimulating discussion of these passages and their parallels in Philo in Neyrey:25-29.

not listen." But Jesus claims to do the work of his father, the work of God, a truth-telling work that sets people free.

These words reiterate earlier statements in the Gospel: as the Son of God, Jesus brings light, life, truth. But the actions that embody these statements are not healings and feedings of abundant proportions but judgments that exclude those who do not believe—excluding them not just from Jesus' own community but, by implication, from the fellowship of the children of God. If God is characterized by what Jesus says and does, then at this point God is known as one who judges.

Implicit in the story of the healing of the blind man in chapter 9 is a debate about what constitutes "God's work." Jesus tells his disciples that the man was born blind "so that God's power might be displayed in curing him." As one scholar writes, "The disciples' question, and the viewpoint behind it, are rejected altogether. They see suffering as an occasion for moralizing about the victim. Jesus sees it as an occasion for doing the works of God, that is, for relieving the suffering.... The 'work of God,' it turns out, is not punishing sinners with suffering but overcoming the suffering.... Simply, the world *is* blind, and it is God's work to heal it" (Rensberger: 44). As in chapter 5 with the healing of the lame man, Jesus gives the command ("Rise, take up your bed and walk"; "Go, wash in the pool of Siloam")—and then disappears, leaving the rest of the characters who ask, as they did in chapter 5, "Who did it?" The Pharisees assert the priority of the Sabbath law, and hence conclude that God could not have done it; but Jesus asserts the primacy of God's healing work. The blind man, now healed, has been enlightened: he understands that God has done this deed through Jesus (9:30-33).

Through Jesus' actions in these episodes, God is characterized as generously and even indiscriminately gracious, healing, life-giving, judging, liberating, illuminating, revealing.[11] Every one of these characteristics is manifested actively and concretely, that is, through Jesus' actions or words directed to a specific person. Strictly speaking these are the actions of Jesus, not God, although insofar as the characterization of God is achieved through the characterization of Jesus, then God is an active and present God (against Culpepper: 113-14: "If Jesus is 'aloof' or 'distant,' God is necessarily more so"; see also his comment that statements such as "God is light" and "God is spirit" "further emphasize His

---

[11] Indeed these very activities characterize the work of Jesus as the work of God. The ability to help by way of healings, offerings of safety and protection, acts of deliverance and revelations (oracles or prophecies) was deemed characteristic of deity in the Graeco-Roman world. For example, Philo (*Mut.* 12 §128) notes that one distinguishing trait of one who is "god" is "to procure the good gift for others" and writes, "Beneficence is the peculiar prerogative of a god" (*Mut.* 12 §129). See the discussions in Grant:54-61 and Ferguson:158-65.

distance or otherness"). At least it is open to the reader to decide: Is God present, active, working, liberating, healing? Why, then, does God never act, work, free, or heal? Or does he?[12]

Appearance

Physical appearance as applicable to God is altogether ruled out in biblical narrative, although there are divine manifestations in the forms of visions (Isaiah's throne vision, for example) or theophanies (Moses' burning bush) or angelic visitants (as to Abraham). But none of these is found in the Fourth Gospel. The Gospel in fact contains explicit denials about "seeing God." "No one has ever seen God," (1:18; 6:46); "God's form you have never seen" (5:37); and Philip's request, "Show us the Father" (14:8), all point in the same direction. But they point not so much in an ontological direction as towards the "invisibility" or the "spirituality" of God, for it is implied that God can be seen.[13] Indeed, the Son has "seen" him (1:18; 6:46). In John, God is not so much invisible as unrecognized (Stibbe: 132-33). But the vision of God desired by human beings is not available apart from perception of Jesus. "Show us the Father, and we shall be satisfied," says Philip, to which Jesus answers in effect, "You have had the vision in your midst all this time" (14:8-9; cf.

---

[12] An obvious parallel is the book of Esther, which, as is well known, does not mention "God." Does the narrative imply the presence or absence of God? Similarly, 1 and 2 Maccabees tell essentially the same story, but whereas in 2 Maccabees God is frequently mentioned and said to act on behalf of the Jews, and there are angelic beings and miraculous deliverances, 1 Maccabees tells the story in a straightforward manner with few references to divine intervention and supernatural beings. Does the narrative of 1 Maccabees necessarily convey to the reader less of the sense of God as a character in the story?

[13] According to Exod 24:10, Moses and others "saw the God of Israel." But according to Exod 33:20, God says to Moses, "You cannot see my face, for no one shall see me and live." The rabbis reconciled these two traditions by noting that Moses and others saw the glory of the Lord (Segal, 40, 168; compare John 12:42). In retelling the story of the giving of the Law at Sinai, Pseudo-Philo glosses Exod 20:19f ("And they said to Moses, 'You speak to us, but do not let God speak to us lest perhaps we die'") with the following statement, "For behold today we know that God speaks to a man face to face and that man may live" (*Bib. Ant.* 11:14), thus contrasting what might happen to them if they were to see God with what would happen to Moses (cf. *Bib. Ant.* 42:10). According to Philo, Moses saw God (*Mos.* 1.28 §158). Gen 17:1 ("The Lord was seen of Abraham") is explained by Philo not as an appearance of "the Existent One," but as "the manifestation of one of the Potencies which attend him" (*Mut.* 3 §§15-17). John is close to Philo (and Pseudo-Philo) in limiting the vision of God to a mediator (in John, of course, to the Son only). The literature of the Johannine circles echoes the tradition that one can see God (1 John 3:2; Rev 4-5). In other traditions (Jewish, Christian, and philosophic), God is invisible and hence cannot be seen (*T. Abr.* 16:3, 4; Josephus, *Ag. Ap.* 2.22 §§190-91; *Sib. Or.* 3:11, 17; 4:12; 1 Tim 6:16).

6:36; 1:51). This is the surprise twist, which causes the reader to reread the story from the beginning: where is God to be seen?

Comments by Other Characters

There are not many direct comments about God by characters in the story, except for those by Jesus and the narrator. In fact there is almost a complete lack of explicit description of God in the Gospel. Once (6:57) we have the epithet "the living Father," reflecting the common biblical phrase "the living God."[14] There are also few predications about God, mostly on the lips of Jesus or the narrator. These include: God is true (3:33, narrator); God is spirit (4:24, Jesus); and "one alone is God" (5:44, Jesus). Against their cultural setting, none of these statements is particularly unusual.

But the lack of epithet, adjective, and other kinds of descriptive statements about God stands in contrast both to the other gospels and to the OT and Jewish narratives. In those sources, "God" appears most often with a genitive referring to a person (God of Abraham; God of Abraham, Isaac, and Jacob; God of our fathers; God of Israel, and so on),[15] or often with a descriptive adjective preceding it (Most High God),[16] or even in the form of a circumlocution (Power, Heaven). Descriptive phrases such as

---

[14] For examples of the phrase "living God," see Deut 5:26; Josh 3:10; 1 Sam 17:26, 36; 2 Kgs 19:4; Ps 84:2; Isa 37:4, 17; Jer 10:10; Dan 6:20, 26; Hos 1:10; Bel 5, 24; Add Esth 16:16; Matt 16:16; 26:63; Acts 14:15; 2 Cor 3:3; 6:16; 1 Thess 1:9; Heb 3:12; 9:14; 10:31; 12:22; Rev 7:2; *Jub.* 1:25.

[15] For various forms of "the God of our Fathers" see *T. Sim.* 2:8; 4 Macc 12:18; "the Lord, the God of Joseph" (*Jos.As.* 3:4; 6:7; 21:4); "Lord God of my father Israel" (*Jos. As.* 8:9); "O Lord God and King, God of Abraham" (Add Esth 13:15; 14:1, 18); "The Lord Almighty, God of Israel" (Bar 3:1, 4); "Lord God of my ancestor Simeon" (Jdt 9:2); "God of my ancestor, God of Israel's heritage" (Jdt 9:12); "Lord God of Shem" (*Jub.* 8:18). There are almost countless variations identifying God with either an individual (usually a patriarch), several individuals together, or the nation of Israel as a whole.

[16] We can give only a sampling of the variety of epithets and designations for God. "Most High" appears often and in various forms. Some examples include: the Most High, *T. Levi* 3:10; 4:2; 5:7; Holy Most High, *T. Levi* 5:1; God Most High *T. Jud.* 24:4. In *T. Abr.* chs. 16-17 there are a host of epithets: Master of creation, immortal king, unseen Father, unseen God, Most High, immortal God, living God, my heavenly God. "King of the gods and Master of all dominion" and "All-seeing God and Savior" are found in the Greek additions to Esther (Add Esth 14:12; 15:2). Jud 9:12 has a long string of designations for God: "God of my father, God of the heritage of Israel, Lord of heaven and earth, Creator of the waters, King of all your creation." Wis 9:1 has a petition to "God of my ancestors and Lord of mercy." In the *Sibylline Oracles*, Book 3, we have: Great God, 3.91, 97, 162, 194, etc.; God the great king, 3.499; the immortal one, 3.101; immortal God, 3.276, 283, 300; immortal begetter of all men, 3.604 (contrast 3:278); God the great immortal king, 3.617; heavenly God, 3.174, 286; the Most High, 3.519, 574, 580; Most High God, 3.719. The OT, apocryphal, and pseudepigraphical books are, on the whole, far richer in epithets for God than most of the New Testament is.

"God of gods," "Most High God," or "the Lord God of Israel," are used to identify which God is being addressed or spoken of. When the world claims "many lords and gods" (1 Cor 8:5) even those who believe in one God search for appropriate language to identify that God. By contrast, the Gospel of John consistently uses the simple "God," or "the Father," or the characteristic "the Father who sent me," and so approaches the identification of God indirectly.

One instance of this indirect characterization is that there are far more genitive phrases in the form " . . . of God" than there are "God of . . . . " For example, rather than "the God of Abraham" or "the God of Israel," we have the following genitive phrases: son of God, lamb of God, gift of God, bread of God, holy one of God, work of God, kingdom of God, glory of God, and so on (see Culpepper: 113-14). Notice that most of these genitive phrases serve to characterize Jesus or something that Jesus mediates, brings, or gives. The narrative continues this way, speaking of Jesus in terms of his relationship to God, without defining who "God" is. But by shifting the emphasis from descriptive phrases and statements about God to statements that begin with things or human beings (especially Jesus) and show their relationship to God, the character of God is made known primarily through other characters or things in the story.

The most common designation of God is "Father." God is first identified as the Father of the Son by the narrator (1:14, 18; 3:35; 5:18), but most of the references to God as Father are in direct speech, and specifically in the words of Jesus. There are three places in the Gospel where the use of Father appears most often: first, in the discourses of Jesus in the central section of the Gospel (chapters 5-6, 10); second, in Jesus' acrimonious debate with the Jews (chapter 8), and third in the farewell discourse (chapters 14-16).[17] It is Jesus who speaks of God as Father most often (2:16; 4:21, 23; 5:17, 19, 20, 21, 22, 23, 26, 36, 37, 43, 45, etc.), in self-revelation, debates with the Jews, and instruction of his disciples. It is Jesus' prerogative to identify God as his Father. The "Jews" challenge him on just this score ("he called God his own Father") and make the counter-claim that God is in fact *their* father, a claim that Jesus asserts to be falsified by their actions, just as his claim to have God as father is verified by his actions.

The term "father," in historical context, connotes two ideas primarily. First, "father" refers to the one who is viewed as the source of life of a family, and so connotes kinship and descent. Second, "father" suggests

---

[17] My counts are roughly as follows: there are no references to God as father in chapters 7, 9, 19, and 21; in chapters 1-4, 11-13, 17, 18, and 20 there are 27 altogether; and for the remaining chapters, the numbers are as follows: chapter 5, 15x; chapter 6, 12x; chapter 8, 18x; chapter 10, 13x; chapter 14, 23x; chapter 15, 10x; chapter 16; 13x. Most of these are found on the lips of Jesus.

providence or care, inasmuch as the father has the obligation to care for his children.[18] Although the idea of kinship or relationship is important, the idea of "intimacy," frequently associated with "father," is less significant. When the Johannine Jesus calls God "Father," he speaks of God in terms of family kinship and relationship, and he draws believers into that relationship. Hence the description "my father and your father, my God and your God" (20:17) is almost synonymous parallelism, and the terms "Father" and "God" are nearly interchangeable in the Gospel (e.g. 8:41; see Sir 23:1, 4; *T. Abr.* 20:13; 3 Macc 5:8; 1 Cor 8:6; cf., Krentz: 81-86). In the debates in chapter 8, Jesus is shown as denying that his audience either knows God (8:54-55) or has God as Father (8:41-47). Although Father is not an unknown epithet for God in the ancient world, nevertheless, God can be characterized as the Father only of Jesus and his followers (this may reflect the view that God is Father of the righteous, as in *Jub.* 1:25; Wis 2:13-20).

Direct Speech

There is one instance of the direct speech of God in the Fourth Gospel and many instances in which God's speaking is implied or assumed but not reported in direct or indirect discourse. Given the frequency of direct discourse in biblical narrative (Alter: 117; Berlin: 64-65; Sternberg: 346-84), this omission is marked (even though in the Gospel of John only Jesus, the Samaritan woman, the blind man, and the Jews are characterized through the frequent use of direct discourse; see Staley: 71). Examples of God's implied speech are the many instances in which Jesus asserts that God has spoken to him so that he in turn speaks the words of God to others. Jesus hears the words of God; but does the reader? Again the reader is called

---

[18] For the use of Father with respect to protection and care see Tob 13:4; Wis 11:10; Sir 23:1, 4; 51:10; 3 Macc 6:3, 8; 7:6; *Jub.* 1:25, 28. For Father with the sense of progenitor or source of life, see Jer 31:9; 3 Macc 2:21; Philo *Opif.* 2. §7, §10; *Cher.* 14 §49, "Father of all things for he begat them"; *Mut.* 4 §29; *De. fug.* 20 §109. The stylized designation of Zeus as "Father of gods and of human beings" (see Homer, *Iliad*, 15, 47) refers to Zeus as both the source of life and the power of providence over it. Josephus (*Ag. Ap.* 2 §§239-42) criticizes the Greek conceptions of Zeus because "the father of gods is in reality a tyrant and a despot," who cannot even save his own offspring; in *Ant.* 12.11.2 §22 Josephus states that the correct view of God is based on the etymology of the name as meaning one who "gives life." In the NT, compare 1 Cor 8:6, "One God, the Father, from whom are all things and unto whom we exist"; Eph 2:18; 3:14-19; 4:6, "One God, father of the universe"; 5:20; 6:23. See also Schlatter:14-16, and the instructive study by Mary Rose D'Angelo (621), who asserts that in early Jewish literature God is addressed or referred to as "Father" (1) when called upon as the refuge of the afflicted and persecuted, especially those persecuted by unbelievers; (2) in connection with petitions for assurance of forgiveness; (3) when acknowledged as the power and providence that govern the world. She gives examples of these usages, and many more could be added.

upon to pay special attention to the narrative itself in order to discover what the words of God are. They turn out to be, primarily, witness to the Son. God's own words testify to the Son. But this testimony is missed by Jesus' opponents in the narrative: they have never heard God's voice, because God's word does not dwell within them. Through their inattention they have missed the voice of God, because they have disregarded the words of Jesus. Once again, access to God (here, God's voice or speaking) comes only through the mediating agency of Jesus. There are no words of God, only words of Jesus.

There is, however, one example of direct speech, in John 12:28. In response to Jesus' prayer "Father, glorify thy name," a voice from heaven comes, saying, "I have glorified it, and I will glorify it again." The voice is understood by Jesus—and presumably by the reader, who can at least read the words as written. But it is not understood by the crowds who think that "it had thundered" (12:29). The one time in the Gospel where there is direct communication by God, there is puzzlement and failure to understand. One could perhaps justly designate this scene as the climax of the story. In a gospel where so much depends on speaking and seeing, God is never heard or seen directly—until this episode. And then, in the speaking, there is not the illuminating flash of light but the crashing confusion of thunder. Jesus warns them, "You have the light a little longer." Indeed, Jesus will be in their midst for an indefinite time. But all his teaching will now be directed to his disciples; the voice has thundered and now falls silent. The words of God are "more of a drawn shutter than an open window" (Alter: 117).

Inward Speech

This category in Alter's system is missing in John since we are never given access to the mind or thoughts of God, except insofar as we have it through the words of Jesus or the narrator.

Comments by the Narrator

Finally, we come to comments by the narrator. In the final analysis, of course, all the categories noted above also fall under "comments by the narrator," for the entire narrative is presented through the narrator's point of view, and the biblical narrator is consistently an omniscient and reliable narrator (Alter: 117; Bar-Efrat: 13-45; Berlin: 43; Culpepper: 26-34; Staley: 57; Sternberg: 63-70). The omniscient narrator of the Gospel could allow access into God's thoughts, but there is an understandable reticence to do so. The narrator gives limited insight into the thoughts, intentions, and motives of God. There is a sense in which God is "unknown" even to the narrator, almost as if the words of Jesus come *to* him as well as *from* him. The narrator both hides and reveals "the mind of God." On the one hand, God's thoughts remain hidden and unknown, since they are never expressly stated. But, on the other hand, there are certain explicit statements from the narrator that allow us to see the world from the divine perspective, more so than in the other Gospels. The narrator intrudes more frequently. Moreover, inasmuch as Jesus is the one who speaks only what he has heard and does only what he has seen, the reader may infer that God's "thoughts" (intentions, motives) are known through Jesus. Thus there is (indirect) access to the mind of God.

There are few explicit statements about God. The opening of the Gospel, for example, reads not "In the beginning, *God* . . ." but "In the beginning was the Word, and the Word was with God." The assertion about the Word is explicit (the Word was in the beginning); the correlative (God was in the beginning) is implicit. John is "a man sent from God" (not "God sent a man named John"). Those who believe become "children of God." Even the assertion "no one has ever seen God" is not the narrator's appraisal of the character or nature of God but a statement about human beings (none of whom, despite possible contrary claims, has actually seen God). And it then becomes an assertion about the Son's revelatory function: "the only Son, who is in the bosom of the Father, has made God known." The prologue of the Gospel, which is something of an opening character sketch of both the Word and God, presents God as Creator and, accordingly, the giver of life and light, a source of abundant graciousness and truth, and as the Father of Jesus and of those who believe in Jesus. At the outset of the Gospel God is characterized, albeit indirectly, in terms that point to originating and life-giving actions. God created the world through Jesus and so gave it life; God continues to give life to those who follow the illuminating light brought in Jesus. The abundance of God's provision is underscored as well: the Son is "full of grace and truth" and from "his fullness have we all received, grace upon grace" (1:16).

Later, the narrator explicitly tells the reader: "God so loved the world that he gave his only Son, that everyone who believes in him might not perish but have eternal life" (3:16). This is probably as close as we come, albeit in the narrator's own words, to getting at the thoughts or motives of God. God loved the world. This is the world from God's point of view, rather than God viewed from the point of view of the world. The narrator again intrudes at the end of chapter 3, with affirmations of God's truthfulness (3:33), God's generous gift of the Spirit (3:34), and the gift of life in Jesus. But whereas the Spirit of God rests on Jesus (1:33), the wrath of God rests on the one who does not believe in Jesus (3:36). At the top or most explicit end of the scale, then, we have a statement that God is turned toward the world with life-giving actions, and that these actions are manifested through the gift of the Son and the Spirit. But for those who do not see God's activity in these actions, there is wrath or judgment. Faith is a matter of discernment. The invitation to read is a call to read with discernment: "Jesus did many other signs in the presence of his disciples that are not written in this book. But *these are written* that you may believe that Jesus is the Christ, the Son of God, and that believing you may have life in his name" (20:30-31).[19] To read the narrative with discernment is to read it with an eye towards the activity of God manifested through the character Jesus.

Summary: The Johannine God

At the risk of being pedantic, I would like to draw together the threads of the previous discussion. Of greatest importance in characterizing God are the actions and comments of Jesus and the comments of the narrator. The indicators that are, at first glance, less important are the appearance of God, the comments of characters other than Jesus, and the direct or interior speech of God. However, the fact that these indicators are conspicuous by their absence already tells us something about the characterization of God in the Fourth Gospel. God is always portrayed indirectly. God's appearance is never described, not even in a vision such as Revelation 4-5 (where we actually have the impression that God makes, rather than a description of God). But of course it is significant that God cannot be seen except in Jesus. The comments of other characters add little, if anything, to the characterization of God, but they serve as foils so that most of the characterization of God occurs through what the narrator says and through what Jesus says and does. Direct quotations from God are almost completely missing, and we have no interior speech or monologue. The reader knows God through the characterization of Jesus and the telling of the story.

But the story functions not so much by giving information about God, although much about God is assumed or implied in the text, as by drawing the reader into the narrative so that the reader will understand God from the point of view of the narrator and Jesus, the principal character. Thus the primary purpose of the Gospel is not "informational" but

---

[19] O'Day:47 stresses the inseparability of form and content in answering the question, "How is God made known in the Fourth Gospel?" She asserts that "The locus of revelation is thus seen to lie in the biblical text and in the world created by the words of that text." See Stibbe's concluding statement, "The next step from a book such as this must surely be to ask the following question: 'If John's story is revelatory, then how much of that sense of disclosure is due to John's exploitation of the narrative form?'" (199). Our answer to Stibbe's question is: "quite a lot."

"formational." The reader is often told that what Jesus does is "the work of God" or reveals the "glory of God." But the reader is never actually shown "God." The reader is told that God grants life, gives true manna from heaven, and raises the dead, but the reader only reads of these things in reading of the actions of Jesus. Essentially, here is a story in search of a conversion—a conversion, that is, in the way it is read. It wants to be read not by an observer of Jesus, but through the eyes of Jesus. It wants the reader to move up the scale of characterization, from the outward manifestations of character (actions, appearance) to the inward manifestations (thoughts, motives, intentions), seeing the world from the point of view of God. To see it that way would be to see that God loves the world, that God sent Jesus to speak truth to it, and that in hearing this truth there is life.

For, above all, God is characterized as *the God who is known through Jesus*. The narrative repeatedly makes this point by avoiding dramatization of the appearances, direct acts, or speech of God. Jesus says, "You will see the heavens opened" (1:51). But there is no grand finale, no climactic revelation, no vision or word that dispels all the darkness. Both Jesus and the narrator state, "No one has ever seen God." But if God makes no appearances, how is anyone to "see God" at all? Jesus reproves his audience, "You have never heard God's voice." But if God but seldom speaks, how are they to hear? And the situation seems much the same for the reader. There is no dramatic depiction of the opening of the heavens, no vision of God, no theophany, and only one instance of God's speaking. What seems to characterize the plight of Jesus' audience applies to the reader as well: "God's voice you have never heard; God's form you have never seen." Or have you?

WORKS CONSULTED

Alter, Robert
    1981   *The Art of Biblical Narrative*. New York: Basic.

Auerbach, Erich
    1953   *Mimesis: The Representation of Reality in Western Literature*. Princeton: Princeton University Press.

Bar-Efrat, Shimon
    1989   *Narrative Art in the Bible*. Bible and Literature Series 17. Sheffield: Almond.

Barrett, C. K.
 1976 "Christocentric or Theocentric? Observations on the Theological Method of the Fourth Gospel." Pp. 361-84 in *La notion biblique de Dieu*. BETL 41. Ed. J. Coppens. Leuven: University Press.

Beker, J. Christiaan
 1990 *The Triumph of God: The Essence of Paul's Thought*. Minneapolis: Fortress.

Berlin, Adele
 1983 *Poetics and Interpretation of Biblical Narrative*. Bible and Literature Series 9. Sheffield: Almond.

Borgen, Peder
 1965 *Bread From Heaven: An Exegetical Study in the Concept of Manna in the Gospel of John and the Writings of Philo*. NovTSup 10. Leiden: E. J. Brill.

Brown, Raymond E.
 1966 *The Gospel According to John*. Vol. 1. Garden City: Doubleday.

Burnett, Fred W.
 1991 "The Undecidability of the Proper Name 'Jesus' in Matthew." *Semeia* 54:123-44.

Caird, G. B.
 1980 *The Language and Imagery of the Bible*. Philadelphia: Westminster.

Crites, Stephen W.
 1975 "Angels We Have Heard." Pp. 23-63 in *Religion as Story*. Ed. James B. Wiggins. New York: Harper & Row.

Culpepper, R. Alan
 1983 *Anatomy of the Fourth Gospel: A Study in Literary Design*. Philadelphia: Fortress.

Dahl, Nils A.
 1991 "The Neglected Factor in New Testament Theology." Pp. 153-63 in *Jesus the Christ: The Historical Origins of Christological Doctrine*. Ed. Donald H. Juel. Philadelphia: Fortress. Originally published in *Reflections* 75:5-8.

D'Angelo, Mary Rose
 1992 "'Abba' and 'Father': Imperial Theology and the Jesus Traditions." *JBL* 111:611-30.

Darr, John A.
 1992 *On Character Building: The Reader and the Rhetoric of Characterization in Luke-Acts*. Literary Currents in Biblical Interpretation. Louisville: Westminster/John Knox.

Davies, Margaret
 1992 *Rhetoric and Reference in the Fourth Gospel*. JSNTSup 69. Sheffield: JSOT.

Donahue, John R.
 1982 "The Neglected Factor in Markan Studies." *JBL* 101:563-94.

du Rand, J.
  1985   "The Characterization of Jesus as Depicted in the Narrative of the Fourth Gospel." *Neot* 19:18-36.

Ferguson, Everett
  1987   *Backgrounds of Early Christianity*. Grand Rapids: Eerdmans.

Gärtner, Bertil
  1959   *John 6 and the Jewish Passover*. ConBNT 17. Lund: C.W.K. Gleerup.

Forster, E. M.
  1972   *Aspects of the Novel*. New York: Harcourt, Brace & World.

Grant, Robert M.
  1986   *Gods and the One God*. Library of Early Christianity. Philadelphia: Westminster.

Guilding, Aileen
  1968   *The Fourth Gospel and Jewish Worship: A Study of the Relation of St. John's Gospel to the Ancient Lectionary System*. Oxford: Oxford University Press.

Hengel, Martin
  1974   *Judaism and Hellenism*. Trans. John Bowden. Philadelphia: Fortress.

Krentz, Edgar M.
  1989   "God in the New Testament." Pp. 75-90 in *Our Naming of God*. Ed. Carl E. Braaten. Minneapolis: Fortress.

Martin, Wallace
  1986   *Recent Theories of Narrative*. Ithaca: Cornell University Press.

Mastin, B. A.
  1975   "A Neglected Feature of the Christology of the Fourth Gospel." *NTS* 22:32-51.

McKnight, Edgar
  1978   *Meaning in Texts: The Historical Shaping of a Narrative Hermeneutics*. Philadelphia: Fortress.

Moore, Stephen D.
  1989   *Literary Criticism and the Gospels: The Theoretical Challenge*. New Haven: Yale University Press.

Neyrey, Jerome H., S.J.
  1988   *An Ideology of Revolt: John's Christology in Social-Science Perspective*. Philadelphia: Fortress.

O'Day, Gail R.
  1986   *Revelation in the Fourth Gospel*. Philadelphia: Fortress.

Reinhartz, Adele
  1992   *The Word in the World: The Cosmological Tale in the Fourth Gospel*. SBLMS 45. Atlanta: Scholars.

Rensberger, David
    1988   *Johannine Faith and Liberating Community*. Philadelphia: Westminster.

Schlatter, Adolf
    1910   *Wie Sprach Josephus von Gott?* Beiträge zur Förderung christlicher Theologie. Gütersloh: Verlag C. Bertelsmann.

Scholes, Robert and Robert Kellogg
    1966   *The Nature of Narrative*. New York: Oxford University Press.

Segal, Alan F.
    1977   *Two Powers in Heaven: Early Rabbinic Reports About Christianity and Gnosticism*. SJLA 29. Leiden: E. J. Brill.

Staley, Jeffrey
    1991   "Stumbling in the Dark, Reaching for the Light: Reading Character in John 5 and 9." *Semeia* 53:54-80.

Sternberg, Meir
    1985   *The Poetics of Biblical Narrative: Ideological Literature and the Drama of Reading*. Bloomington: Indiana University Press.

Stibbe, Mark W. G.
    1992   *John as Storyteller: Narrative Criticism and the Fourth Gospel*. SNTSMS 73. Cambridge: Cambridge University Press.

Tannehill, Robert C.
    1986   *The Narrative Unity of Luke-Acts: A Literary Interpretation*. Vol. I, *The Gospel According to Luke*. Philadelphia: Fortress.

Whitacre, Rodney A.
    1982   *Johannine Polemic: The Role of Tradition and Theology*. SBLDS 67. Chico: Scholars.

Wolfson, H. A.
    1947   *Philo: Foundations of Religious Philosophy in Judaism, Christianity, and Islam*. 2 vols. Cambridge: Harvard University Press.

Wright, N. T.
    1992   *The New Testament and the People of God*. Vol. 1. Christian Origins and the Question of God. Minneapolis: Fortress.

DIVINE AND ANONYMOUS CHARACTERIZATION IN BIBLICAL NARRATIVE

Robert Polzin
Carleton University

Within the formal-functional poetics that provides the context for the studies of Reinhartz, Craig, Berg, and Thompson, hard questions about characterization abound. When, however, we set out to discuss the characterization of those in biblical narrative who have no name, or whose name is, by tradition, unspeakable, we cannot avoid increasing the complexity of such questions. So I hope the following remarks reflect my conviction that the degree of difficulty of the issues that these four authors tackle is enormous. In any case, each paper contains valuable insights that help us see these problems in a new light.

Adele Reinhartz's paper on anonymity and character in 1-2 Samuel is full of insight in its treatment of individual passages and anonymous characters. Nevertheless, her concluding exegetical treatment of the women of Endor, Tekoa, and Abel, precisely because it is successful in, as she admits, challenging the typification of anonymity that forms the preceding two sections of her paper, tends to highlight the difficulties inherent in her theoretical discussion and system of classification of anonymous characters or character groups in 1-2 Samuel.

Reinhartz's remarks on her trio of anonymous women emphasize the paradox that these nameless ones embody within the story: how can such anonymous characters achieve the degree of individuality that Reinhartz successfully suggests they possess? Does not this reading-effect run counter to the commonsensical notion that anonymity tends to typify rather than individuate, stereotype rather than characterize? In truth, the wise woman of Tekoa and her two companions are three "unique, unusual, even atypical individuals." All one has to do is compare what the anonymous Tekoite does in 2 Samuel 14 to what a properly named individual, Michal, accomplishes in 2 Samuel 6 to see that Reinhartz's exegetical insight is important for our understanding of the art of ancient Israelite narrative: whether named or not, some characters achieve a kind of narrative identity and individuality that complements whatever roles they also play in moving the plot along, in helping to characterize the named individuals they accompany in the story, or even in embodying the narrator's point of view.

Even when she is engaged in the theoretical and systematizing sections of her study, Reinhartz sprinkles her analysis with exegetical illustrations that provoke our interest. For example, I was struck by her suggestion that Saul's unnamed servant in 1 Samuel 9 and his unnamed armorbearer of 1 Samuel 31 form an anonymous personal *inclusio* bracketing the beginning and end of Saul's story.

Taken together, then, the central and incidental anonymous characters discussed in this paper do suggest that the topic of anonymity in mimetic narrative deserves the kind of study that Reinhartz here proposes. This is an important contribution of Reinhartz's paper. Nevertheless, the limitations of Reinhartz's paper at both the theoretical and conceptual levels detract from the exegetical pleasure of her text. Her theoretical discussion of the functions of proper names and anonymity in the first part of her paper and her conceptual system of classification (of anonymous characters and character groups) in the second part are less successful in achieving their stated goals.

Reinhartz's treatment of anonymity and mimesis operates on the assumption that the functions of both proper names and anonymity in mimetic literature parallel their functions in everyday life. Citing Searle and Chatman, Reinhartz suggests that proper names in everyday life point to rather than describe, just as they do in mimetic literature. Proper names are simply pegs upon which we hang our descriptions of people in literature as in life. But then Reinhartz moves from Searle's contention that proper names in real life "enable us to refer publicly to objects without being forced to raise issues and come to agreement on what descriptive characteristics exactly constitute the identity of the object"—that is, point to people without having to characterize them—to her own conclusion that the use of proper names in mimetic literature goes hand in hand with full characterization, whereas anonymity tends toward characters that are merely types or agents. Whereas modern philosophy of language (or at least a representative branch of it) emphasizes that proper names are empty signs that can have whatever reference or semantic content the linguistic, literary, or real life context suggests, and that they are most often independent of the many conflicting descriptions or characterizations that numerous users will understand by the proper name they employ, Reinhartz unaccountably associates the use of proper names with full-fledged characterization and the use of anonymity with its absence.

Then, when Reinhartz introduces into her discussion Natanson's phenomenology of anonymity in everyday life, her discussion moves to, as it were, a phenomenal misreading of Searle-ly proper names. For Natanson, anonymity tends to stereotype, whereas those who have or know a proper name recognize "the fullness of one's individuality." So, Reinhartz concludes, "there is a direct relationship between our ignorance of another's proper name and our tendency to perceive that person soley or primarily as an agent performing a typified role." Concerning the function of proper names in everyday life, however, it is clear that Natanson's view is the polar opposite of Searle's: Natanson sees naming as the heart of full characterization and individuation, Searle as the necessary condition of life whereby we constantly point to people whom we couldn't possibly characterize or whom different people can fully characterize in any number of conflicting ways. "John Smith" can simply be a stereotypically common name, or an anonymously repeated name in a phonebook, or a name used with great knowledge and affection by someone's mother, or with bitter thoughts by a victimized wife. So when Reinhartz combines the insights of Searle with those of Natanson, she introduces into her discussion a theoretical confusion it can ill afford. The Searle and Natanson models are mutually contradictory concerning the central functions of naming and anonymity in life and in literature.

The whole question of the relationship of proper names and anonymity to full-fledged characterization versus typification or mere plot development is better treated, I would suggest, by the adaptable principle Sternberg discusses in more than one place, wherein a single form (say, properly named or anonymous characters) can function in many different ways, and a single function (say, typification or plot movement) can be achieved by a number of different forms (1982:148-54; 1985: 437-38). In terms of our present topic, "Bathsheba" may act like an agent in 2 Samuel 11 but comes across with much more definition in 1 Kings 1-2. Similarly, the anonymous woman of 2 Samuel 14 and the Amalekite lad of 2 Samuel 1 may achieve some measure of individuality, whereas other nameless individuals never rise above their stereotypical fates.

The second part of Reinhartz's paper contains a system of classification of anonymous characters or character groups. Reinhartz wants this system to "illustrate the role of anonymity in the construction of character and plot development," but this section is handicapped by the theoretical problems I have just discussed and by other difficulties at the conceptual level. For one thing, I doubt that the idea of *group* characterization can avoid being unwieldy as an analytic tool even within Reinhartz's own model. If, as Reinhartz maintains, the mimetic function of a proper name is to unify a character or to differentiate one character from another so as to achieve some measure of personal, individual recognition, then the very idea of a character *group*, whether named or not, seems to me to preclude in principle the kind of "individuation" she maintains is possible concerning some character groups that have proper names.

Yet Reinhartz's instincts—if not her system of classification—are on target, as her comments on Phinehas's wife in 1 Samuel 4 illustrate. This anonymous woman does succeed in depicting not just the misfortunes of the family of Eli but even those of Israel: "The glory is gone from Israel" (1 Sam 4:22) names the woman's son but at the same time addresses the nation into which he is born. What Reinhartz's system of classification does not so clearly recognize, then, is that in 1-2 Samuel full-fledged characterization of individuals is *social* or *communal* in a double sense: first, the recognition of how a proper-named individual fits into her social group is a necessary feature of that individuation that goes beyond stereotyping or mere plot movement; and second, the Books of Samuel continually flesh out their most important characters as particularized illustrations of the fate of Israel itself, the most frequently named "character group" within the text—and perhaps the primary focus of the story. Thus the characterization of Hannah and her son in 1 Samuel 1-7 also serves as a profound depiction of monarchic Israel, just as the complex characterization of David in 1 Samuel 16 – 1 Kings 2 serves as a wonderfully detailed description both of his house and of his tribe and nation.

I would suggest, therefore, that there is not the clearcut distinction between individual and group, nor the degree of correlation between anonymity/proper-namedness and typification/full-fledged characterization that Reinhartz proposes. Rather, full-fledged, proper-named individuals can serve to connote an un-named group everywhere present beneath the surface of the story; named characters like Michal in 2 Samuel 6 or unnamed individuals like the woman of Abel in 2 Samuel 20 can each be a momentary but powerful personification of an impersonal or anonymous narrator/author; and both the named and the anonymous can here typify, there individualize.

The ultimate paradox in 1-2 Samuel's schema of characterization may lie in its ability to use the names of prominent individuals like Samuel, Saul, or David as pegs upon which to hang wonderfully complex and subtle characterizations, but at the same time to use such characterizations as typical pegs upon which to hang the fate of a nation: the proper name can stand for an unnamed unity, and the individual for a typical, even social, entity.

Beck's study on anonymity in John fares better than Reinhartz's treatment of the same feature in Samuel for two reasons. Whereas John's Gospel foregrounds anonymity in the persons of the beloved disciple and the faithful, unnamed ones who precede him, Samuel, like Hebrew narrative in general, gives much less functional prominence to anonymous characters. Reinhartz succeeds in showing that the anonymity of certain characters in Samuel plays a greater hermeneutic role than readers have heretofore realized, but the fact remains that anonymous characterization is a major feature of John's Gospel, a minor one in Samuel. Second, Beck confines his remarks to anonymous individuals in John, whereas Reinhartz saddles herself with the task of discussing not just anonymous characters but even anonymous character groups. As I have suggested, the idea of group characters and their characterization does not fit in well with the models of characterization, anonymous or otherwise, that Reinhartz invokes in her study.

Both Beck and Reinhartz point to Docherty's book on characterization in fiction, quote his views on the function of naming, but fail to point out that he tackles the topic of character anonymity not so much focussed on mimetic literature as on postmodern fiction. When Beck and Reinhartz utilize his insights, therefore, are they claiming postmodernist tendencies in Samuel or John, or can they indicate that Docherty's thesis on anonymity and reader participation can apply equally well to mimetic literature?

Turning to Craig's study of the character of God in 2 Samuel 7, one must applaud his laudable goal of making sense of a chapter erroneously thought of as filled with "unintelligible verbiage." Craig's remark on the important compositional contrast between God's "first-degree speech" of 2 Samuel 7 and the divine second-degree speech in 2 Samuel 12 and his important content-analysis of the "three levels" of God's speech in vv. 1-16 are valuable contributions toward understanding this chapter. At the same time, despite Craig's attempt at recovering the literary art behind 2 Samuel 7, he makes two unfortunate moves: first, he employs characters' words as direct and indirect means of characterization without very much indicating how the text situates such words within the narrator's/author's manifold means of characterization; and, second, in the one case where he does try to indicate how precisely the narrator's words merge with a character's, his analysis of God's utterance in verses 1-16 seriously misunderstands its voice structure.

First, following Rimmon-Kenan's typology of characterization by direct definition and indirect presentation, Craig asserts, "In a chapter such as 2 Samuel 7 where the dramatis personae assume much of the responsibility for characterization, we see that such direct and indirect methods of portrayal also extend to the characters themselves." That is to say, what characters say, in 2 Samuel 7 as elsewhere, can characterize themselves and others either directly or indirectly. So far so good. But certainly not far enough. For once we grant that what a character says in the story can portray him or her in such and such a way, precisely in what way his or her own words portray a character is determined by all the direct and indirect means the author/narrator may employ to put characters and their words in proper, that is, authoritative, perspective. Craig's assertion, then, that "virtually all of the characterization in this chapter is accomplished by the speaking characters themselves," is accurate in the sense that characters do much of the talking in the chapter, but not very helpful in the sense that Craig's analysis does little to answer this question: beyond analyzing the content of the characters' speech (here Craig does a very good job indeed), how precisely does the author/narrator use these characters' words to characterize them?

Take Craig's conclusion that God's words in the chapter clearly portray him as one who is in charge. God's utterance does make it abundantly clear, as Craig's analysis of its rhetoric shows, that God's building of a permanent house for David is timely, but that David's building of a permanent house for God is unnecessary. But if we want to know how God's self-characterization and the narrator's characterization of God each operates in this chapter, and how they interact, we ought to address the question most on the minds of those who have tried to connect up the portrayal of God in 2 Samuel 7 with the story that follows: what kind of God is this who first promises a permanent house for David, but then hangs a permanent sword over it? Is this deity characterized as really omniscient or simply capricious and short-sighted? Or is the narrative characterization of God really deficient here, contrary to Craig's assumptions of its artfulness? And is it accurate to state, as Craig does in the end, that Chronicles at least attempts to answer the question, "Why is it timely for Solomon not David to build God a temple?" whereas the Deuteronomic History (apparently) does not address the problem?

All of these questions simply underline the effects of Craig's not going far enough with his analysis of the character's speech in 2 Samuel 7. Certainly the way God, as the supreme authority figure in the narrative, describes things in 2 Samuel 7 contributes something to what Bakhtin would call the ultimate conceptual authority of the text. Nevertheless, a necessary part of the characterization of God here involves saying something about how what is in this chapter coheres with what precedes and what follows. For example, how does what God says in 2 Samuel 7 cohere with what he will say in 2 Samuel 12?

Second, whereas Craig's assumption that analysis of the voice structure of God's words in verses 1-16 will help us hear not only the voice of God but also that of the narrator is correct, Craig's analysis is at times problematic. Most notable here is his introduction of "free indirect discourse" in a chapter where none exists. Recent articles, starting with Sternberg, whom Craig cites, up to Niehoff's more recent treatment of this phenomenon in biblical narrative, have done much to attune our ears to the many examples of "free indirect discourse" in the Bible and to alert us to the hermeneutic importance of this phenomenon. However, Craig's invocation of this compositional aspect of reported speech with respect to 2 Samuel 7 is simply incorrect and entirely mysterious to me. Verses 5a, 8a, and 11b have nothing at all to do with what scholars call "free indirect discourse," and Craig's adaptation of this phenomenon in what he calls "combined viewpoint markers" is mistaken. So Craig's central and solitary example showing how the narrator's speech permeates a character's speech in 2 Samuel 7 fails to do the job.

Thompson, like Craig, tackles the general problem of the characterization of God in biblical narrative, and her view is much more expansive than Craig's, not only because her narrative is an entire book rather than a single chapter, but also because she takes pains to preface her specific discussion with a series of reflections on scholarly attitudes toward characterization itself and how these influence matters when God is the one characterized. Such prefatory remarks take up half of her paper and exhibit a lively and engaging mind, one that recognizes many of the theoretical problems involved in trying to write about how God is characterized in John. I will leave it to those who know more about John than I do to offer substantive responses to the heart of Thompson's paper. Here are some remarks on important preliminaries of her study that may need clarification.

Too many of Thompson's reflections on theories of characterization are based upon treatments of general literary theory that are already biblicized, that is, processed by other scholars writing on the Bible. Alter, Berlin, Sternberg, or Moore figure centrally in her discussions and surely are worth citing for their important contributions to the subject. But I get the sense that Thompson's views on, say, reader response theory would be wider and perhaps clearer were she to reflect not only on what Darr, Moore, or Tannehill have written about the reader's role, but especially on how her, not their, reading of Iser or Jauss has influenced the second half of her study. Similarly, when she chooses to raise the question of how psychological analysis and literary appraisal influence one another in respect to readerly views of God in the Gospel of John, although she does cite Martin's citation of Docherty, and refreshingly quotes *The Atlantic* and the *Los Angeles Times* in a note, she ignores all the relevant sources that Beck, himself writing on the Gospel of John, finds worthy of note: Alcorn and Bracher on literature and psychoanalysis, Hochman on character in literature, Jose and Brewer on characterization in developmental psychology, or Holland on identity formation in the reading process. We also get other kinds of twice-told theory, Thompson quoting Culpepper quoting Scholes and Kellog, or Thompson quoting Darr and Martin who are quoting Docherty.

Thompson's bibliographic indirection is intriguing—and consequential. One nominal example of how matters may get skewed by such consultative indirection is the unfortunate way in which Thompson begins her discussion of the characterization of God in John: "But 'God' is not a name. In fact the Johannine God has no name." These statements are supposed to justify Thompson's basing her analysis of John on the proposition that "it is the words and deeds of Jesus that serve as a characterization of God." However, that God is characterized in John largely through Jesus's statements and actions therein may be defensible; that "God" is not a name—in John or outside it—is difficult to accept. When I say "He is a god," or "I just saw a god," I use "god" as a predicate not a name. But when the narrative voice in John says, "God so loved the world . . .," it uses the word "God" precisely as a name. And it does this many times in John.

It appears to me that Thompson could also be clearer about some basic issues of voice structure in narrative, issues that must directly affect the central topic of her paper. Her statement that Alter's category of inward speech, when applied in John to what God is supposed to have said to himself, is missing "except insofar as we have it *through the words of* Jesus or *the narrator* [emphasis mine]," is illustrative of this problem. *All* inward speech of characters, in John as in the rest of biblical narrative operating with an omniscient narrator, is reported through the words of the narrator. How could we get to a character's inward speech other than by the narrator telling us about it, or by a reliable character like Jesus telling us about it? Thompson's comment, then, seems to imply that there could be another way, in principle, to report inward speech in John, but what in the world could this way be?

I would suggest, finally, that 2 Samuel 7 is a wonderful example of how the central characterological problems investigated by Reinhartz, Craig, Beck, and Thompson—group vs. individual characterization, named vs. anonymous, divine vs. human—can all be represented and integrated in biblical narrative. The characterizations of David and God in 2 Samuel 7 are pegs upon which to hang an evaluative description of that "character group" the History calls the house of David, and the fate of *this* house serves to depict the fate of that social entity, if not characterized, at least named many times in 2 Samuel 7 (vv. 6, 7, 8, 10, 11, 23, 24) as "(God's) people Israel" (Polzin: 71-89).

WORKS CONSULTED

Niehoff, M.
    1992   "Do Biblical Characters Talk to Themselves? Narrative Modes of Representing Inner Speech in Early Biblical Fiction." *JBL* 111: 577-95.

Polzin, Robert
    1993   *David and the Deuteronomist: A Literary Study of the Deuteronomic History: Part Three: 2 Samuel.* Bloomington & Indianapolis: Indiana University Press.

Sternberg, Meir
    1982   "Proteus in Quotation-Land: Mimesis and the Forms of Reported Discourse." *Poetics Today* 3: 107-56.
    1985   *Poetics of Biblical Narrative: Ideological Literature and the Drama of Reading.* Bloomington: Indiana University Press.

READING READERS READING CHARACTERS[1]

Evelyn R. Thibeaux
Georgetown University

The four studies addressed by this response approach characterization in biblical literature through literary methods. As recent conversations show (see, for example, Culpepper and Segovia, and the papers by Parsons, Powell, Staley), biblical scholars using literary approaches are joining other literary scholars in the ongoing discussion of what it means to write and to read literature—and indeed, what literature itself *is* and *does*. We are now at a point where we can review the preliminary results of such efforts, while exploring the range of new possibilities and increasing our theoretical and critical sophistication (Stephen Moore's *Literary Criticism and the Gospels* accomplishes these tasks in an exemplary fashion for gospel studies).

I think it is important to introduce into these considerations two questions often asked by non-professional readers of the Bible when confronted by our scholarly commentaries: "So what?" and "What for?" In the present context, versions of these questions might be, "What is gained, and lost, or simply ignored, by applying a literary method of a particular sort to the books of Samuel or the Gospel of John?" And "What difference does it make to anyone, or to someone, or to certain people, if the characters in these texts are understood in a certain way?" My response to the studies of D. Beck, K. Craig, A. Reinhartz, and M. Thompson will engage these questions in the context of the above-mentioned discussions on the shifting contours of literary criticism.

The question concerning results may be raised first in relation to Craig's study of 2 Samuel 7. Using Rimmon-Kenan's narratological categories to describe characterization in terms of "direct definition" and "indirect presentation" allows Craig to tell how much we can know of God in such a short time—2 Sam 7:1-17—especially when these verses are examined in relation to other texts in Samuel, Kings, and Chronicles. His analysis leads to several related conclusions about *what* God is: the one whose ways are not human ways, the one who cares for Israel, and the one in charge of history. These qualities differ little (if at all) from fairly

---

[1] The title is inspired by John Darr's first chapter in *On Character Building*, "Reading Readers Reading Luke-Acts."

commonplace descriptions of God in scholarship on the Deuteronomistic writings, or on the Hebrew Scriptures in general, or even in what could be thought of as a "common sense" reading of the passage.

What, then, is gained from the kind of close reading Craig gives to the text? One thing is a better understanding of what Thompson calls the text's "rhetorical and literary strategies in presenting characters" (in this case, God)—that is, *"how* [a] character is constructed by the reader" and *"how* these elements of characterization are progressively coordinated by the reader." When Craig describes the text of 2 Samuel 7 as one that presents "the author's view of God transforming human initiative," he implies an ideal reader who, in following the process closely, is led to accept this view of God and will perhaps himself/herself be transformed in accordance with it.

Craig's critical approach, then, privileges the literary text as the locus and determinant of meaning, drawing from several types of formalist literary criticism: the structuralist narratology of Rimmon-Kenan; the kind of rhetorical criticism proposed by James Muilenburg in his programmatic essay "Form Criticism and Beyond"; and a kind of reader-response criticism whose "parents" are "mainstream . . . exegesis on the biblical side, and reader-in-the-text formalism on the nonbiblical side" (Moore:107).[2] Such an approach, focusing on the formal elements of the texts as objective indications of the author's viewpoint, extends the range of historical-critical scholarship while remaining well within its traditional goals. Craig's analysis reflects what Thomas Docherty (33) says of traditional texts read traditionally: "In a God-centred (and therefore stable) fictional universe, the informing [of the reader] comes from the *verbe* of God whose word is the universe."

Though few biblical scholars would dispute that the biblical texts are traditional in this sense, a significant number have begun to question whether our *reading* of them should or can be as straightforward as is Craig's. Some are concerned that formalist literary methods operate out of a modernist paradigm whose claims of objectivity, long standard in critical biblical scholarship, have been exposed as impossible and deceptive (or at least self-deceptive). This critique is pressed by what Docherty sees as "the necessity, in the twentieth century, for the acceptance of the relativistic, partial and limited point of view" (33) and a correlative view of texts and reading that can be labeled "postmodern": "In the act of reading

---

[2] "That," comments Moore, "is why reader-oriented exegeses can often read disappointingly like the familiar critical renditions of the given biblical passage, lightly reclothed in a reader vocabulary" (107). I hasten to acknowledge, again, that Craig's use of reader-response criticism is implicit: It is the flip side of his narratological descriptions of the text's strategies.

... the reader now has a voice, and a voice which can speak from a series of subjective first-personal positions which the text's descriptions of characters will constitute for that reader" (33). Yet as described by Docherty, that view is problematic for biblical scholars, since it assumes "acceptance of the relativistic and atheistic (and therefore unstable) postulation of a human-centered fictional universe, [in which] the informing is done by ... the human voice which informs or constitutes characters and readers ..." (33).

In the minds of most of us, then, there is something inherently dissonant in "postmodern" readings of the Bible, which take seriously the radical subjectivity and accompanying authority of the human person—both of characters in the narrative and of the reader. That cognitive dissonance may explain why, even when Craig introduces into his reading of 2 Samuel 7, the literary technique of "free indirect discourse" as an indication of multiple points of view in the text,[1] he ends up seeing only one point of view—God's—which is identical with the omniscient narrator's, and for which the human characters' viewpoints are mere foils. As Craig says, "All of the questions that God, an omniscient, asks are rhetorical rather than information-seeking. Indeed, God has a monopoly on thoughts and performative utterances."

This result—which is correct on its own terms—raises interesting questions about our choices in reading biblical texts. On the one hand, are there some texts that genuinely lend themselves to the possibility of seeing multiple points of view, that is, human as well as divine ones, as legitimate voices informing or constituting meaning—or exercising power? Are there even texts in which God's presence is implicit and God's viewpoint largely subsumed within those of human characters—for example, the Joseph novella in Genesis (Humphreys: 97)? Or again, would the inclusion of the rest of chapter 7, David's speech, in Craig's discussion have provided another point of view on the character of God as well as on what it means to be human in relation to God—or merely a gloss on the same view? On the other hand, are there not methodological approaches, literary or otherwise, that lend themselves to seeing, even in a text such as 2 Sam 7:1-17, a genuine plurality of viewpoints, a possibility for human subjectivity, for dialogue as well as monologue (Bakhtin comes to mind)?

---

[1] Here I note that in fact I disagree with Craig's designation of vv. 5a and 8a as free indirect discourse, since they seem to me to be clearly God's own words and to reflect God's own viewpoint. Verse 11b is a less clear case, since it is not God's imperative to Nathan (as are 5a and 8a). At the most, it could reflect Nathan's point of view (not directly the narrator's, as Craig asserts); but I see it as merely God's viewpoint of what Nathan would say in delivering God's message to David—just as are the phrases "Thus says the Lord" and "Thus says the Lord of hosts" in vv. 5 and 8.

Reinhartz's study of the books of Samuel offers interesting contrasts to Craig's, most of them directly related to her choice to do a "mimetic" reading of characters. Most obviously, she does not deal at all with God as a character, though this choice is presumably made also because she does not consider God to be anonymous (as does Thompson; see Thompson also on the problems inherent in speaking of God as we do of human characters). Whereas Craig's formalist approach makes his reading straightforward by remaining within the world of the text, Reinhartz's realist approach makes hers likewise straightforward in assuming a relatively unproblematic parallel between that world and the real world. This assumption allows her to introduce the insights of social science (the philosophical-sociological phenomenology of Natanson) and social history (such as Camp's study of the wise women of 2 Samuel), as well as aspects of narrative criticism, in such a way that the theory does not tread heavily upon the text.

Reinhartz's gain is that she can focus on the anonymous characters' contributions to a wonderful story—and not as mere agents of the plot but in their mostly ordinary, often poignant, sometimes surprisingly assertive *humanity*. One understands in Reinhartz's account, almost as one knows the sheer reality of everyday life, that grand dramas like that of God and Israel are in truth acted out by real people whose subjectivity is no less vital for their being anonymous. Her section on Eli's daughter-in-law and David and Bathsheba's first child is particularly effective in describing the relationship between textual anonymity and human tragedy. It throws into sharp relief her discussion of how the three wise women emerge out of anonymity—as significant role-takers, individual persons, and partners in dialogue—when considered in the context of their social world and not simply as literary blanks that one can fill with a series of traits.

Reinhartz describes her study of anonymity thus: "In forcing us to attend to what is absent from the text, it also alerts us to what is present." To my mind, she undervalues the significance of her way of reading anonymity when she names it—rather too formally—as "a literary convention which works together with others in the skilled creation of mimetic narrative." I would add that, as she herself seems to recognize, literary convention is intimately connected to culture; and, more broadly, the reading of texts cannot be severed from the reading of culture. The real value of her approach is that it moves in the direction of what Clifford Geertz calls "ethnography," in which particular social and symbolic behaviors—in texts as well as in cultures—are shown through careful observation and correlation to be part of larger "webs of significance" (see Garrett:5-7).

Thompson's article lays out the major theoretical "coordinates" for exploring biblical literary characters as a more complex phenomenon. She considers the author (as discernible in the features of the text) *and* the reader; both the reader-in-the-text as respondent to textual cues *and* the reader outside the text as "real" person; real readers as inclusive of the original readers *and* others who may also read (including the reader/critic who writes about the text); texts as somehow determinant of meaning *and* as indeterminate space for the creation of meaning; texts as worlds unto themselves *and* as bound in myriad ways to the social worlds in which they are written and read. Thompson seems also to recognize the importance, noted by Jane Tompkins, of conceiving a text not only as a sign to be interpreted (read for the meaning it occasions) *but also* as a "force acting on the world" (read for the impact it has upon action and behavior) (Tompkins, 1980b:203).[2]

Thompson begins to explore the implications of such a multi-faceted approach in her discussion of characterizing God. The issue I find most interesting is related to this statement: "Given the ideological conviction of God's reliability or constancy that many of the Bible's readers bring to the reading process, the question of the characterization of God is not so much whether the character 'lives' beyond the page, but whether in fact the narrator can make God 'live' for the reader." It is clear that, for countless numbers of readers through the ages, biblical narrators have done just that; I believe the real question is whether we reader-critics of the Bible can suggest ways of reading that allow readers of today to re-appropriate that vital experience. And the answer, it seems to me, depends on how seriously one takes Thompson's statement that "the reader is always held in tension between the objective constraints of the text and the constraints of the knowledge, imagination, cultural location, religious convictions, and spirituality by which her or his reading of God is informed."

---

[2] Darr (11-22) outlines an excellent proposal for a literary method that integrates these various elements. See especially his "Critical Premises" (17).

The importance of focusing upon the effects of texts has led some biblical scholars—most notably Wilhelm Wuellner and Elisabeth Schüssler Fiorenza—to urge that rhetoric be the foundation for an integrative approach to biblical texts. They speak, however, not of the "rhetoric restrained" that characterizes Muilenburg's method but of a practical criticism that "strives for a 'rhetoric revalued' (B. Vickers), rhetoric reinvented (T. Eagleton), in which texts are read and reread, interpreted and reinterpreted, 'as forms of *activity* inseparable from the wider social relations between writers and readers'" (Wuellner, 1987:453; quotation from Eagleton:205-6). Rhetorical criticism, in this view, is double-sided: It operates from a "conception of language as a meaning-making activity, an essential element in the social construction of reality" (Lunsford and Ede:48); and it sees language as *"the management of symbols in order to coordinate social action"* (Hauser:3, his emphasis). A rhetorical approach, thus, focuses squarely upon the relationships of power among the various participants in the reading of texts.

Perhaps Thompson's answer is that we may not be able to do everything that we know is important to do. In the end, she says, the critical task of describing God's characterization is "primarily a literary exercise that must be addressed by a literary critical method." Does this mean simply taking on the formalist's role of describing "the objective constraints of the text"—even though we know they are never simply objective? Does it mean not discussing certain things, like what may happen when less-than-ideal-readers—say, the many who do *not* think of God as reliable and constant—read the biblical texts? Does it mean taking a position in which we ourselves are "not dramatized as speaking or active" in our critical narratives, and then perhaps having others think of us as "distant and aloof"?

But Thompson's final section on characterizing God in John's Gospel instead answers simply that we cannot do everything all at once, or all together—and so she offers a "preliminary sketch" of the manifestations of God in the text. These manifestations are revealed through Alter's essentially formalist "scale of characterization"; yet Thompson uses the scale masterfully to explore their relationships and meanings (as, for example, in her elegant summary of God's qualities as seen in Jesus' actions). Particularly illuminating is the way she explores the perspectives in the text—Jesus' and God's—to suggest how the reader's perspective may be engaged in the *krisis* precipitated by John's Gospel: the decision about whether God is "present, active, working, liberating, healing" in Jesus. The great value of this reading of God (who is "not so much invisible as unrecognized") is that it opens a reader's eyes about as far as someone else can open them—and then invites her to see. But it leaves open the question whether the invitation is to see what everyone else, surely, sees, or to see for herself.

Beck's study of anonymity in John's Gospel sets out more resolutely along the path of a holistic reading. It also shows how daunting is the task of trying to create our own maps *en route*. Because Beck at least touches upon all of the "coordinates" described by Thompson, and because he draws from such a wide range of critics, what may seem like a fairly simple argument has a subtext, a multi-voiced dialogue, which I find not only fascinating but immensely instructive.

Beck's argument concerns several identities and identifications (the latter in two senses). In John's Gospel, the characters' task is to recognize and respond appropriately to Jesus' identity; in this life-changing response, they find their own identity. The reader, by virtue of certain characters' lack of identity (defined as anonymity), identifies with these characters and most importantly with the beloved disciple; this means that the reader is put into the position of having to recognize (identify) and respond to Jesus' identity, and is aided in doing so by the faith response of these anonymous characters. The ultimate result—and the purpose for the text—is the reader's identification with Jesus, and in this the re-creation of the reader's own identity.

To ground this argument, Beck turns primarily to two literary critics: Thomas Docherty on anonymity and Norman Holland on identity. His statements from and about Docherty's chapter on "Names," to which he confines himself for this study, generally reflect Docherty's views accurately. But it seems to me that the point of the chapter is stretched to fit Beck's purposes, and that the direction of Docherty's theory of characterization as a whole makes it problematic for Beck's argument.

The first of these critiques may be illustrated by Beck's statement that, according to Docherty, the functions of names in the reading process—to provide various kinds of centralizing focus—"can *only* be present when names are used consistently in a narrative" (emphasis mine). Docherty, in fact, says that this is "generally" true (74); but much of his chapter is spent in illustrating the inconsistent use of names and/or the use of anonymity in fiction, and he notes immediately preceding his summary of the function(s) of the name that this function "seems to persist in fact whether there are actual proper names or not" (73). My reason for quibbling with Beck on this point is that I think it parallels his reading of John's Gospel itself: generalizations, valid though they may be, leave too little room for exceptions and for particularities.

For example, Beck's conclusion that "those characters whose responses most closely model the paradigm of discipleship the narrative demands of the reader are those whose names are unrevealed" makes it necessary for him to link anonymity and a "faith response" as criteria for characters to model true discipleship in John. This means that he cannot see John the Baptist as such a model, even though John sacrifices his own identity in recognition of Jesus' and carries out the same all-important function as the beloved disciple in bearing witness to Jesus (John 1:7, 15, 19-23, 26-27, 29-34; 2:27-30[36?]). It means also that Martha, whose faith response (11:27) is at least as strong as any character's but the beloved disciple's, and Mary, who shows an active faith response in 12:1-8, are excluded from this inner circle, despite the narrator's (i.e. the beloved disciple's?) indication that they are beloved of Jesus (11:5). On the other hand, Beck sees the woman caught in adultery as paradigmatic even though she exhibits no faith response; and he sees Jesus' mother's request/command in 2:5 as a faith response after what he questionably describes as her being "challenged to reconfigure her understanding of her son."

Perhaps most intriguing is Beck's suggestion (common among Johannine scholars) that Nicodemus cannot model discipleship (much less its paradigmatic form) in the Johannine worldview. It is certainly not true (contra Beck) that Nicodemus does not dialogue with Jesus, nor that he vanishes from the text after evoking Jesus' monologue. Despite his initial lack of understanding—and faith—he indeed reappears in 7:50-52 to try to mediate between the Pharisees and Jesus and in 19:39-42 to bury Jesus. Even if, on these slim qualifications, Nicodemus "stands in the narrative as one whose potential for discipleship remains unfulfilled," is he unqualified as someone with whom a reader might identify on the road to faith (see Schneiders)—and that because he has a name?

What is lost, or at least suppressed, in Beck's major line of argument is the possibility of reading John's Gospel other than in the role of the ideal reader, whose responses are carefully orchestrated and wholly determined by the all-powerful implied author. The loss is significant because it belies Beck's considerable efforts to open up such possibilities—for example, his suggesting how real, individual readers can identify with the anonymous Johannine characters in the exigencies of their lives; and his recognizing the importance of readers' "social location" (his own and others') in shaping their reading experiences.

The kind of tension I see here is evident also in the juxtaposition of Docherty's theory of character and Holland's theory of reading. Beck notes that in Docherty's view character anonymity fosters a "decentralization of the self" for characters and for readers, resulting in reader empathy for the character rather than (mere) sympathy, and in the reader's "freedom of subjectivity" within a "community of subjectivity." Beck would probably agree with Docherty that if a character is entirely centered in a "core of self" to which everything can be referred, then "the possibility of authentic response . . . is precluded," and the character loses "life"; concomitantly, if a reader is radically involved in such a text, she or he will likewise "'die' as an effective subjectivity" (Docherty: 80). But Beck leaves unnoted Docherty's discussion of what might be called the "shadow side" of decentralization, or loss of self, that is used as a remedy for this kind of deadening "response*a*bility." There are two dangers: 1) character and/or reader face "a loss of the self in real existentialist terms"—that is, a loss of the respons*i*ble self (Docherty:81); and 2) "the reader is faced with an authorial procedure which, in permitting instantaneous and irresponsible changes of position, also encourages the belief in the possibility of complete and perhaps tyrannous intrusion of the reader's subjectivity upon an Other" (83). Docherty's overall theory, as I read it, is intended to argue that, despite such potential excesses of freedom and empathy, this way of reading is necessary if we are to overcome the devastating effects of the modernist paradigm engendered by Cartesian dualism: among other things, the excesses of authoritarianism and individualism.

The response of most biblical scholars to such postmodern ideas ranges from ambiguous to nervous to downright hostile. We are much more comfortable, I would guess, with a theory like Holland's, the nature of which, according to Jane Tompkins, seems to be determined by his "moral aims" (1980a:xix) and which still relies largely on the categories of the "modern" paradigm. For Holland, the prerequisite of reading/criticism is knowledge of the self—one's "identity theme"—which facilitates the goal of reading, the "mixing" or "merging" of self and other (reader and author) even while they maintain their own independent existence: sympathy, not empathy. As Beck points out, Holland's view of the self is so strong that he must be defended against charges that "the reader's pre-existing self identity . . . remains unaltered by the text"; the reader's identity *can* be re-created or re-formed in the reading process. But in contrast to Docherty's reader, who follows characters in adopting the various positions created by the text, Holland's reader exercises considerable power in shaping the material—including the characters—in the text.

Beck's account of what happens to characters in John's Gospel, and to readers in reading it, shows the ambiguity inherent in trying to negotiate the passage between modern and postmodern paradigms of reading. One might press him thus: Does the reader identify with a character by "filling" the identity gap left by the character's anonymity, or by "bridging" it? Is "filling" the same as empathy, and does it disregard, by overlooking or intruding upon, the character's Other-ness? Is "bridging" like sympathy, and does it require too little giving up of self in the encounter with one who is truly other-than-oneself (as would be someone with a name)? Does the reader fill the identity gap "with her/his own identity," or simply identify (with) the character's traits or circumstances that happen to be also her/his own (as Beck describes in several places)? To press further: is it the reader who re-creates her/his own identity in "mixing"/"merging" with the identity of Jesus recognized through reading the text? Or is it Jesus who re-writes her/his "life narrative" by subsuming it into his own?

Perhaps there is no one answer to these questions; there is no either/or. Beck's use of Schuyler Brown's Jungian interpretation of the beloved disciple illustrates once again how difficult it is to live with the ambiguity. Again I observe two underreadings by Beck. First, Brown says that "differential relations between characters suggest the complementarity between the conscious ego and the unconscious [part of the] psyche" (Brown:372). Brown seems to mean here relations between characters at least one of whom is *named*, since "that which is without a name, or unknown, suggests the unconscious"; he uses the example of the beloved disciple and Peter. Since the goal of reading, on a Jungian analysis, is to lead the reader's psyche to an integration of its conscious and unconscious parts (individuation), it would seem that the named characters in John's Gospel have some crucial role in the process—for example, that they may represent the reader's conscious ego, perhaps denying or defending itself against the fearsome demands of the unconscious.

This leads to the second issue: Who represents what? Does Beck see the anonymous beloved disciple representing the reader's unconscious, or her/his (conscious) ego? Brown says that indeed it could be either, since "insofar as the Beloved Disciple is the expression of a Christian ideal, he may represent the standpoint of the ego" (372). Brown's point is that in applying "a Jungian perspective to a narrative," the reader is allowed "to consider which of the related characters [the named or the unnamed] represents his or her ego standpoint and which the unacknowledged 'other'" (372). But Beck does not want to choose between the ideal reader and a real reader. Further, Beck's view of the beloved disciple's function—to lead the reader to the experience of the risen (living) Jesus, which is the equivalent of integrative individuation—should make Brown's "option" attractive. But his overarching argument about anonymous characters does not allow him to acknowledge this option consciously.

Perhaps that is why the process of Beck's argument seems something like the individuation process itself. According to Jung, the creation of the integrated self is fostered by the experience of dreaming, in which the shadow, the "unconscious elements in the dreamer's psyche that are unacceptable to his or her self-image or *persona*[,] . . . seeks to trip up the ego's conscious functioning by provoking indeliberate lapses, . . . which thwart the ego's purposes" (Brown: 372). Beck's ambitious venture in reading has demonstrated that "'the shadow is a tight passage, a narrow door, whose painful constriction no one is spared who goes down to the deep well'" (Brown: 372, quoting Jung: 21). But the encounter with the shadow is an essential task if we are to gain and regain the experience of the living text. And John's Gospel itself invites the encounter while thwarting any reader's moves to dissect it as if it were already dead.[1]

---

[1] See Wuellner, 1991:125 on the value of rhetorical criticism for "putting life back into the Lazarus story." He argues that "the rhetorical critic, with resources other than the familiar ones from traditional literary criticism, highlights the fact that, despite the discernible 'will for coherence and the striving for design' (the focus of traditional composition criticism and redaction criticism [as well as narrative critics]), the Johannine narrative has its own measure of 'anomalies, impossible combinations, and internal contradictions'" (quotations from Moore:53). Following Staley (1988), Wuellner

WORKS CONSULTED

Bakhtin, Mikhail M.
    1981   *The Dialogic Imagination.* Ed. M. Holquist. Slavic Series 1. Austin: University of Texas Press.

Brown, Schuyler
    1990   "The Beloved Disciple: A Jungian View." Pp. 366-78 in *The Conversation Continues: Studies in Paul and John.* Ed. Robert T. Fortna and Beverly R. Gaventa. Nashville: Abingdon.

Culpepper, R. Alan and Fernando F. Segovia, eds.
    1991   "The Fourth Gospel from a Literary Perspective." *Semeia* 53. Atlanta: Scholars.

Darr, John A.
    1992   *On Character Building: The Reader and the Rhetoric of Characterization in Luke-Acts.* Literary Currents in Biblical Interpretation. Louisville: Westminster/John Knox.

Docherty, Thomas
    1983   *Reading (Absent) Character: Towards A Theory of Characterization in Fiction.* Oxford: Clarendon.

Eagleton, Terry
    1983   *Literary Theory: An Introduction.* Minneapolis: University of Minnesota Press.

Garrett, Susan R.
    1989   *The Demise of the Devil: Magic and the Demonic in Luke's Writings.* Minneapolis: Fortress.

Hauser, Gerard
    1986   *Introduction to Rhetorical Theory.* New York: Harper & Row.

Humphreys, W. Lee
    1988   *Joseph and His Family: A Literary Study.* Columbia: University of South Carolina Press.

Jung, Carl G.
    1980   *The Archetypes and the Collective Unconscious.* Princeton: Princeton University Press.

Lunsford, Andrea A. and Lisa S. Ede
    1984   "On Distinctions between Classical and Modern Rhetoric." Pp. 37-49 in *Classical Rhetoric and Modern Discourse.* Ed. Robert J. Connors, Lisa S. Ede, and Andrea A. Lunsford. Carbondale, IL: Southern Illinois University Press.

---

calls these "ways of victimizing the implied reader in John"—and I am suggesting that they also victimize the real reader/critic of John who denies them even unintentionally.

Martin, Wallace
 1986 *Recent Theories of Narrative*. Ithaca: Cornell University Press.

Moore, Stephen D.
 1989 *Literary Criticism and the Gospels: The Theoretical Challenge*. New Haven: Yale University Press.

Muilenburg, James
 1969 "Form Criticism and Beyond." *JBL* 88:1-18.

Parsons, Mikeal C.
 1992 "What's 'Literary' about Literary Aspects of the Gospels and Acts?" Pp. 14-39 in *Society of Biblical Literature 1992 Seminar Papers*. Ed. Eugene H. Lovering, Jr. Atlanta: Scholars.

Powell, Mark
 1992 "What Is 'Literary' about Literary Aspects?" Pp. 40-48 in *Society of Biblical Literature 1992 Seminar Papers*. Ed. Eugene H. Lovering, Jr. Atlanta: Scholars.

Schneiders, Sandra M.
 1987 "Born Anew." *Theology Today* 44:189-96.

Schüssler Fiorenza, Elisabeth
 1988 "The Ethics of Biblical Interpretation: Decentering Biblical Scholarship." *JBL* 107:3-17.
 1989 "Biblical Interpretation and Critical Commitment." *Studia Theologica* 43:5-18.
 1991 *Revelation: Vision of a Just World*. Proclamation Commentaries. Minneapolis: Augsburg Fortress.

Staley, Jeffrey L.
 1988 *The Print's First Kiss: A Rhetorical Investigation of the Implied Reader in the Fourth Gospel*. SBLDS 82. Atlanta: Scholars.
 1992 "Reading with a Passion: John 18:1-19:42 and the Erosion of the Reader." Pp. 61-81 in *Society of Biblical Literature 1992 Seminar Papers*. Ed. Eugene H. Lovering, Jr. Atlanta: Scholars.

Tompkins, Jane P.
 1980a "An Introduction to Reader-Response Criticism." Pp. ix-xxvi in *Reader-Response Criticism: From Formalism to Post-Structuralism*. Ed. Jane P. Tompkins. Baltimore: Johns Hopkins University Press.
 1980b "The Reader in History: The Changing Shape of Literary Response." Pp. 201-32 in *Reader-Response Criticism: From Formalism to Post-Structuralism*. Ed. Jane P. Tompkins. Baltimore: Johns Hopkins University Press.

Vickers, Brian, ed.
 1982 *Rhetoric Revalued*. Medieval and Renaissance Texts and Studies 19. Binghamton, NY: Center for Medieval and Renaissance Studies.

Wuellner, Wilhelm
 1987 "Where is Rhetorical Criticism Taking Us?" *CBQ* 49:448-63.

1991 "Putting Life Back into the Lazarus Story and Its Reading: The Narrative Rhetoric of John 11 as the Narration of Faith." *Semeia* 53:113-32.

www.ingramcontent.com/pod-product-compliance
Lightning Source LLC
Chambersburg PA
CBHW021808220426
43662CB00006B/230